FARMERS, LANDLORDS AND LANDSCAPES

Farmers, Landlords and Landscapes

Rural Britain, 1720 to 1870

Susanna Wade Martins

WINDgather
PRESS

Farmers, Landlords and Landscapes
Rural Britain, 1720 to 1870

Published by: Windgather Press Ltd, 29 Bishop Road, Bollington, Macclesfield, Cheshire SK10 5NX, UK

Distributed by: Central Books Ltd, 99 Wallis Road, London E9 5LN

British Library Cataloguing-in-Publication Data
A catalogue record for this book is available from the British Library

ISBN 0 9538630 9 3

Designed, typeset and originated by Carnegie Publishing Ltd,
Chatsworth Road, Lancaster.
Printed and bound by Cambridge University Press.

Contents

List of Illustrations

Figures

Tables

Acknowledgements

This book is the culmination of thirty years spent ruminating on the meaning of the word 'improvement' in an agricultural context while both tramping the countryside looking at landscapes and buildings, and trawling documents and libraries. Over this time I have met farmers, land agents, archivists and librarians who have all helped and inspired me, making my researches a joy to pursue.

Lively discussion with friends and colleagues in the Historic Farm Buildings Group, Centre of East Anglian Studies at the University of East Anglia, English Heritage and the Royal Commission of Historic and Ancient Monuments of Scotland has stimulated the development of ideas and at the same time resulted in the rejection of some of my more far-fetched ones.

When the gestation period has been so long, it is impossible to mention all those who have helped and influenced my thinking. Much of the research included here is the fruit of collaborative work with Tom Williamson of the Centre of East Anglian Studies, Jeremy Lake of English Heritage and Geoffrey Stell, with firstly Graham Douglas amd then Miles Glendinning and Alison Darragh at the Royal Commission on the Ancient and Historical Monuments of Scotland. I am grateful to all of them and the happy hours we have spent on cold hillsides, in derelict farmsteads and warm pubs and common rooms together.

The many people and institutions who have allowed their material to be used as illustrations are acknowledged individually under the captions. I am particularly grateful to Phillip Judge for his work on the drawings. My thanks too to my publisher, Richard Purslow, for his enthusiastic help and patience on the production of this book.

For encouragement when the going was tough no-one could equal my long-suffering husband, Peter.

CHAPTER ONE

'The Age of Improvement' 1720–1870: The Philosophies Driving Farming Change

The phrase, 'age of improvement' has been used by various historians to cover different periods, but here it is has a very specific meaning, delimiting the one hundred and thirty years or so when agriculturalists used the word 'improvement' to describe their efforts to increase productivity to meet the needs of an ever increasing and urbanised population. Recent exhaustive work has chronicled the ways in which this was achieved through new farming practices and techniques,[1] all of which would have been the responsibility of the farmer to implement. Indeed the farmer is a crucial player in the story of 'improvement': yet very little is written about him other than as an economic being. His place in rural society and his role in farming and social change in the countryside has been largely ignored.

On the other side of the coin and still a topic of much controversy, is the role of the landlord. He was the provider of the infrastructure within which the new farming methods could be carried out. He provided the enclosed fields, farm roads and buildings. He worked, often in partnership with his tenant on the drainage, marling and liming of the land to produce the 'landscapes of improvement' with which we are familiar over much of arable Britain today. It is this inter-relationship – between the landlord, the farmer and his farm – and its manifestation in the farming landscape which will be explored in this book.

New farmers, new landscapes: the beginnings of change, *c.* 1600–*c.* 1720

The idea that it was almost a moral duty of the landowner and the farmer to improve land and increase production can be traced back to the late seventeenth century. As impoverished royalists returned from the intensively farmed Low Countries, they brought with them ideas that they hoped to implement on their estates. As early as the 1660s, Lord Winchelsea had plans for reclamation on his Yorkshire estates which involved the drainage and enclosure of his low lands. Farms were to be built and stocked with cattle, cart and riding horses. However, it seems that few of his suggested improvements were carried out.[2] Thirty years later, in the immediate aftermath of the last major famine to hit Scotland, in the 1690s, Lord Belhaven wrote 'The scarcities of the last few years, I must impute in part to our great neglect of Husbandrie ... so it ought to be an Incitement to all those whom God has blessed with Estates, to Double their Diligence in the Improvement of their Grounds' ... for 'Husbandrie enlarges a Countrie and makes it as if ye have conquered an other Countrie adjacent thereto. And I am sure that a conquest by the Spade and Plough is both more just and of longer continuance that what is got by Sword and Bow'.[3]

Indeed, the seventeenth century is seen by some as constituting an 'agricultural revolution'. Land hunger and population increase had stimulated change which saw the decisive break with medieval husbandry practices. As the feudal system finally collapsed and the monastic lands were sold from the 1530s, the independent, often land-owning, 'yeoman farmer' emerged. New crops and rotations were introduced. Kerridge sees as 'the backbone of the agricultural revolution' the conversion of permanent tillage and permanent grassland to cultivated arable alternating between temporary tillage – typically up to seven years of cereal crops followed by grass leys of six to twelve years. This system of up-and-down husbandry spread rapidly between 1590 and 1660 especially in mainly livestock areas such as the midland plain, where as much as three quarters of the land could be in grass at any one time.[4] In spite of the gradual rise in population from 1670, grain prices were falling, indicating that production was more than keeping up with demand. To keep profits up, farmers had to diversify, particularly into livestock. In the 1670s and 1780s the Norfolk landowner, William Wyndham at Felbrigg was building dairies, leasing out cows, improving neglected pastures, buying clover seed and perhaps most radically, experimenting with leases, or 'letting to halves' which shared the risk between landlord and tenant.[5]

Alongside the changes in farming methods on already cultivated land went the bringing of new areas into cultivation, such as parts of the Peak in Derbyshire and the wastes of Lancashire around Rossendale. A start was made on the drainage of the coastal marshes and most famously, the Fens of Cambridgeshire and Lincolnshire. Enclosure continued and, importantly, water meadows were constructed, which provided an early bite of grass, thus allowing more stock to be kept through the winter and so more manure to be produced.

FIGURE 1.
Water meadows at Britford, near Salisbury (Wiltshire). This elaborate scheme dates from the seventeenth century and is only one of a series to be found between Salisbury and Downton. Five major channels, fed from the river Avon, flow on the top of ridges which discharge water into smaller channels, also on ridges. From here water flows down the slopes into lower ditches which return the surplus to the river.

The idea of creating water meadows that could be irrigated at will through a system of hatches and channels dates back to the early seventeenth century in the Golden Valley, Herefordshire, from where it very quickly spread to Wiltshire (Figure 1) and the Earl of Pembroke's estates. Unlike changes in farming practice, such as those involved in up-and-down husbandry, these major projects were expensive and were unlikely to be undertaken by individual enterprise. The earliest reference to a fully developed system is to be found in the Manor Court books of Affpuddle over the years 1605–1610, when the manorial court appointed three men to oversee the watering of the meadows; the tenants were to pay for the work in proportion to their holdings of meadow land. It is probably no coincidence that this was a parish where the landlord,

Sir Edward Lawrence, was keenly interested in agricultural improvement. Until the late eighteenth century the practice was mainly confined to the south of England where chalkland systems could make good use of them. Several Dorset landowners were active in their creation, often sharing the costs with their tenants. In 1636 the Earl of Suffolk signed an agreement with 22 of his tenants 'in consideration the said Earle is pleased by way of watering ... to improve the Meadow called Winfrith Mead'.[6] Here we have some of the earliest examples of major landlord/tenant co-operation in land-improvement schemes.

As a result of what John Worlidge of Petersfield described in 1669 as 'one of the most universal and advantageous improvements in England within these few years', it was possible to provide grass in March and April, when the hay stocks were exhausted and some six weeks before natural growth had started for the sheep flocks which were an essential part of the chalkland farming system. It also increased the hay crop to sustain the flocks during the winter. The water meadows and the sheep flocks they supported were the 'pivot around which the downland farms revolved'.[7] Without the manure from the sheep the cash crops of wheat and barley could not be produced. Between 1629 and 1665, the creation of water meadows seems to have been at its height, with the extension and improvement of already existing schemes carrying on into the early eighteenth century.[8]

By the Civil War it would seem therefore that 'improvement' was under way in parts of England, particularly in the livestock areas of the midlands where up-and-down-husbandry aimed to increase yields of cereal and the grass acreage; and also in the southern sheep-grazing areas where sheep kept up the fertility of the arable and were also of great value in their own right. Only in the laying out of water meadows, however, was landlord capital likely to be required to any great extent. A change in farming practice was very much the concern of the farmer himself.

How much of a break to this general picture of progress was caused by the Civil War is difficult to gauge. The Fussells quote a Yorkshire source for the village of Darrington which states that life 'went on very much as usual, men planting and sowing, reaping and garnering in the accustomed way, while the primitive canonn flung their balls from Baghill across the valley into the grim walls built five hundred years before by the Normans under Ilbert de Lacy'.[9] The Royalist Lestrange family at Hunstanton were not so lucky. In 1644 the crop of wheat on the recently embanked Holme marsh was 'sequestered and reaped by some of the rebels of Holme by virtue of a presumed ordinance of parliament grounded upon a most false and clamorous petition'. Oats too suffered a similar fate.[10]

In spite of the exhortations (to the landowners) by men such as Lord Belhaven it is likely that most early improvements were the result of the work of a group whom we might call 'professional farmers': either large tenant farmers or owner-occupiers. Very few landlords were investing in farm improvement before the 1750s. Instead any surplus capital was used for increasing the acreage of their estates.[11] Allen argues that 'the big rise in output and much of the increase in labour productivity were accomplished by small-scale owner-occupier farmers in the yeoman's revolution of the seventeenth and early eighteenth centuries', and much of this achievement took place in the open fields.[12]

Certainly the agricultural literature of the period was written for this class of practical farmer. Improvements in farming practice were suggested in the text books, the most comprehensive of which was John Worlidge's *Agricultural Encyclopedia* of 1669. He promoted the digging of water meadows as well as the growing of new crops such as clover and turnips, which were already becoming established in parts of eastern England. It is to this post-restoration period that a distinctive phase of developments can be safely dated. We know that Sir Richard Weston was experimenting with the growing of sainfoin and clover as 'artificial' grasses to improve the hay crop as early as 1645 and that a few closes of turnips were being grown in Suffolk by the middle of the seventeenth century. Again, we see innovation being designed first and foremost to increase the volume and range of fodder crops and it is in the cattle rearing areas such as south Norfolk and north Suffolk that turnips were first grown in East Anglia in any quantity. Progress towards the regular growth of these crops within a rotation was slow with no more than 3 per cent of the cropped acreage of East Anglia being devoted to artificial grasses by 1750 and 8 per cent to turnips – hardly enough to suggest its widespread use in rotations, but rather a few fields for use as animal feed.[13]

With the beginning of new farming methods such as up-and-down husbandry, a new farming landscape developed, containing water meadows in the southern chalklands, and elsewhere more enclosed fields with new farm crops such as artificial grasses and turnips, promoted through an increasing farming literature. A new type of farmer was responsible for this new environment. Kerridge saw him as 'bursting with enterprise' and Thomas Fuller in the 1660s wrote, 'He improveth his land to a double value by good husbandry. Some grounds that wept with water or frowned with thorns, by draining the one and clearing the other, he makes both to laugh and sing with corn. By marl and limestones burnt he bettereth his ground and his industry worketh miracles by turning stones into bread.'[14]

This new commercial attitude, which was beginning to turn family farmers into capitalist tenants, coupled with the years of low prices put farmers in a strong position when negotiating rents with landlords. It was a brave owner who in hard times when tenants were scarce, 'resolved to run the hazard of getting a new Tennant'. A new tenant of William Wyndham's was no better than the last. He was 'not able' and finally failed, owing £555.[15] To survive, tenants had to be good businessmen as well as good farmers and this is indicated by a slow but perceptible improvement in farm account keeping by 1750, but it was only possible because of the opening up of national markets, which allowed regional specialities to develop.

Regionalism and provincialism in the home market were breaking down and a national market was emerging by the mid-eighteenth century. The hundred years after 1640 was one in which the export of grain was an important element and the growth of internal markets is illustrated by the proliferation of fine market halls in many English market towns. Gradually, Burghs of Barony began to be established as market centres across Scotland, with planned villages also providing a commercial focus from the early eighteenth century. Not until the 1720s, with the increase in London newspapers from which provincial journals took their information was there anything like a national price, but improved transport, both by road and coastal trade meant that such a situation was becoming more realistic. Private marketing increased as inn yards, parlours and shop doorways became the effective places of trade, together with the farm gate as wholesale and retail trades diverged. The droving routes too were becoming more established allowing lean cattle to be brought from Scotland, Ireland, and a lesser extent, Wales, for fattening on lowland farms. The growth of London's population by 70 per cent from 1640 to 1740 meant that its food demands were having to be met from an ever-expanding hinterland.[16]

There is no doubt, therefore that the adoption of new farm practices has a long history beginning at least as early as 1600. However, Allen and Kerridge's 'revolutions' were set in the mainly pastoral areas of the midland plain and the light chalk sheeplands of the south and even here the 'revolution' was unfinished. As late as 1772, Arthur Young could write of the south, 'I would not be understood to expect too much from the common farmers reading this, or indeed any book; I am sensible that not one farmer in five thousand reads at all. But the country abounds in gentleman farmers whose ideas are more enlarged and whose practice is founded less on prejudice.'[17] It is not until the eighteenth century that these new ideas move out from Young's 'gentry' of the south to the great open arable lands of the east.

What then did the farming landscape of the seventeenth century look like? The century saw a great increase in the number of maps drawn, indicating the interest of landowners in the extent of their often newly-purchased estates. All would have been drawn for a purpose, which would often have been to establish who exactly held land where and on what terms. This might well be a necessary pre-requisite to the re-allocation of lands as part of a programme of enclosure and 'improvement'. Land was often let on long leases at low rents which were supplemented by high entrance fines paid by the new tenant.[18] It was in the interest of the landlord to change this system and slowly, from the eighteenth century, we find leases becoming shorter (anything from two to 21 years), rents higher and entrance fines less important. All leases automatically came to an end when an enclosure act was passed, and so the re-negotiation of the tenancy arrangement often coincided with the reorganisation of the farming landscape and the consolidation of scattered holdings which usually took place at enclosure. Farm leases with husbandry clauses began to appear generally from the late seventeenth century, although a few survive from earlier. They provided the tenant with security and also made him a partner in the process of land improvement. As landed estates increased in size from the Restoration, the independent small 'yeoman' farmers declined in number and were replaced by the expanding tenants class many of whom lacked the security of a lease. The agent for an estate at Horsford, near Norwich, wrote to the absentee landlord in 1694, 'for as long as they are tenants-at-will (i.e. have no formal lease) there will be no care taken to improve the estate'.[19]

Estate reorganisation might well involve some degree of enclosure, although sometimes it only resulted in a rationalisation within open fields. It is in those areas where livestock production was important that we find most early

FIGURE 2. Hall Farm, South Burlingham (Norfolk). The wealth of the seventeenth-century yeoman-farmers on the fertile loams of the broadland edge is shown in their fine houses, often with elaborate façades.

enclosure, with not only many of the midland counties and the heavy claylands of East Anglia in individual fields by 1600, but also much of the south-west, including Somerset, described by Norden in 1607 as 'prosperous through enclosure'. However, the situation was immensely complicated with open fields surviving alongside early enclosures.[20] Estimates of the impact of enclosure vary, but it is likely that by 1600 nearly half of open-field England had been enclosed, with a further quarter disappearing in the next hundred years, making this the most crucial period in enclosure history when the country swung from being a mainly open to a mainly enclosed landscape.[21] Of course this takes no account of the huge areas of open common and heath which were to survive for another hundred years.

Hanoverian expansion

As the Hanoverian period opened therefore much of the landscape had already taking on the 'improved' qualities of enclosed fields and reclaimed fen that was to become for the eighteenth-century improvers, the mark of a civilised society. The farmers too were changing. Those who read and took advantage of the increasing opportunities for travel were learning from their neighbours and trying out new methods. Their increased prosperity is indicated by the number of fine seventeenth-century yeoman houses, sometimes with nearby barns, which survive across the country (Figure 2). Landowners, too who were hoping to have a share in the increasing profits of farming, were beginning to take a greater interest in the land and management of their estates and to invest in change. Many of the building blocks for the greater advances which were to come were in place.

1670 to 1750 were generally years of stagnation in agricultural prices and population grew slowly until the 1730s. This could be compensated for by exports, encouraged by the Corn Bounty Act of 1688 which helped cushion farmers from the full effects of over-production. The only way for farmers to keep up their incomes was by increasing output. This could be done through enlarging cultivated acreages and increasing yields. The best estimates available suggest that the acreage under cereals in England and Wales grew between 1690 and 1750 from 5.375 million acres to 5.732 million and in some cases we know that the initiative for this reclamation came from the landlord. The extent of the improved methods adopted by farmers in this period are evident: although the acreage under cereals rose by 7 per cent, output of cereal went up by 19 per cent,[22] supporting Allen's argument for a 'yeoman revolution' preceding the 'landlord revolution' of post-1750. The potential for increased output, and therefore increased farming income to the farmer, which land reclamation allowed for, was not lost on landlords who could see the opportunity for rent rises. The advocates of 'improvement' now found a receptive audience.

The philosophy of improvement

The Age of Enlightenment

While men such as Lord Belhaven had been promoting improvement as a social and patriotic duty from the 1690s, it was not until the 1720s that these ideas were taken up more generally. They fitted conveniently with the ideas of the Enlightenment and interest in classical civilisations, which were spreading amongst the aristocracy as relative peace in Europe made the 'Grand Tour' which included Italy, fashionable. Cultivation of land as described by Virgil in the *Georgics* was seen as a symbol of civilisation. He advocated a patriotic combination of beauty and utility, pleasure and profit: land and commerce with a strict, but benevolent, social hierarchy.[23] Human civilisation was synonymous with the conquest of nature. Neatness, symmetry and formal patterns, so typical of the early eighteenth-century landscape garden, represented the divide between 'culture' and 'nature'. Indeed many landlords saw little difference between the laying out of parks around their houses and the new farmland beyond. All were classed as 'improvements' and the language of the landscape gardener and modernising farmer were often juxtaposed in the same paragraph. These theories remained in vogue for much of the Hanoverian period. As late as 1809, J. C. Curwen wrote, 'I have yet to learn the principle which excludes the mixture of lawn and cultivation near a mansion ... I would ask such as are acquainted with Holkham [Norfolk], what can be more beautiful than the diversified scenery that there presents itself ... The effect of order and industry, combined with abundance, must be gratifying to every spectator.'[24] Even the down-to-earth farmer-radical and journalist, William Cobbett wrote, 'I have no idea of picturesque beauty separated from the fertility of the soil.'[25] Agricultural propagandists saw untilled soil as wasted resources where human labour could restore the beauty and order of Eden. John Houghton regarded Hampstead Heath as a 'barren wilderness in urgent need of cultivation'. Arthur Young wanted to bring the 'waste lands of the kingdom into cultivation and to cover them with turnips, corn and clover instead of lyng'.[26]

This link between beauty and utility is one that is frequently made and these ideas were not only supported by the agricultural writers, but also the fashionable *literati* of the time. In 1726, Jonathan Swift wrote in *Gulliver's Travels* that 'whoever can make two ears of corn or two blades of grass grow upon a spot of ground where only one grew before, would deserve better of mankind than the whole race of politicians put together'. Alexander Pope took up the theme in his *Epistle to Lord Burlington* when he criticized those who laid out extravagant gardens on potentially good farmland. He wrote in the 1740s,

> 'Tis use alone that sanctifies expense ...
> Whose ample lawns are not ashamed to feed
> The milky heifer and deserving stead.

By the 1770s, agriculture was receiving encouragement from the highest in Society.

George III saw it as 'that greatest of all manufactures' and 'beyond doubt the foundation of every other art, business and profession'.[27] 'I wish I were king', wrote Arthur Young in 1784, '[I would] order the necessary enclosures, buildings, and expenditures for the establishment of farms on tracts now waste. They (the faithful House of Commons) would be happy in promoting the royal pleasures that had for their end the cultivation, improvement and population of the kingdom; making deserts smile with cultivation – and peopling joyless wastes with the grateful hearts of men.'[28]

A regular contributor to Young's *Annals of Agriculture* was the Suffolk squire Thomas Ruggles. An enthusiastic tree planter, he admitted his plans were only suited to owner-occupiers who could look for long-term returns in the form of timber from mature trees: 'The farmer of a hired occupation, whose gains are his bread, cannot, unless assisted by his landlord, be supposed to attend to the landscape of his farm.'[29] However, in a series of letters, entitled 'picturesque farming', he frequently reiterated the phrase 'my leading principle is the preserving of a union between the profitable and the beautiful'.[30] This union is seen at its clearest where landscape features could be used for practical purposes. At West Lexham, Norfolk, the lake in front of the high status farmhouse fed the system of water meadows.[31] At the Home Farm, Culford (Suffolk) and also at Letheringsett (Norfolk) the ornamental lakes served as millponds for water-powered machinery in barns.

FIGURE 3 (*overleaf*). Plan of Darnaway Forest and Park (Moray). This plan was drawn for the Earl of Moray in 1760 and shows the potential of the area, both as a pleasure park (the possible sites for summer houses and seats are located) as well as for agriculture. The quality of soil is indicated. MORAY ESTATES

CONTENTS in Scots Measure
Total Darnway 3186.677
DOUNDUFF
The Corn Lands 75.055
The Woods and Braes amongst the cornfields 98.795
Sum= 824.669
Darnway and Dounduff 4010.746
PLAN
of the PARK and FOREST of DARNWAY
with the FORESTRY an Ancient Noble
SEAT and ESTATE of
The Right Honourable
JAMES EARL of MORAY
As also the WOODS
LANDS & MOSSES
of DOUNDUFF
Surveyd 1766
COLDHAME
Whitemire Burn
Peat Road
Newton Burn or Stripe
Border in the Hill with LETHEN
Border in the Moor
1246.334
BRADSHAW
New House
FORESTRY Green MOOR
Cunzickavel Burn
South Field
White Ditches
MOORS and MOSSES of DOUNDUFF
LANDS and
WOODS of DOUNDUFF
Hole Land
Long Fold
Gall Burn
CROFT FOWLER
Brae Moray Road
Road from Braemoray
SLUIEHILLS
DUNEARN HILL
Very Romantique Place
Dunearn Burn
The East Hills & Moor would naturally grow Wood
FINDORN River Rappid thro' a very Rock
Border in the MOORS & MOSSES with Kilbraths Lands

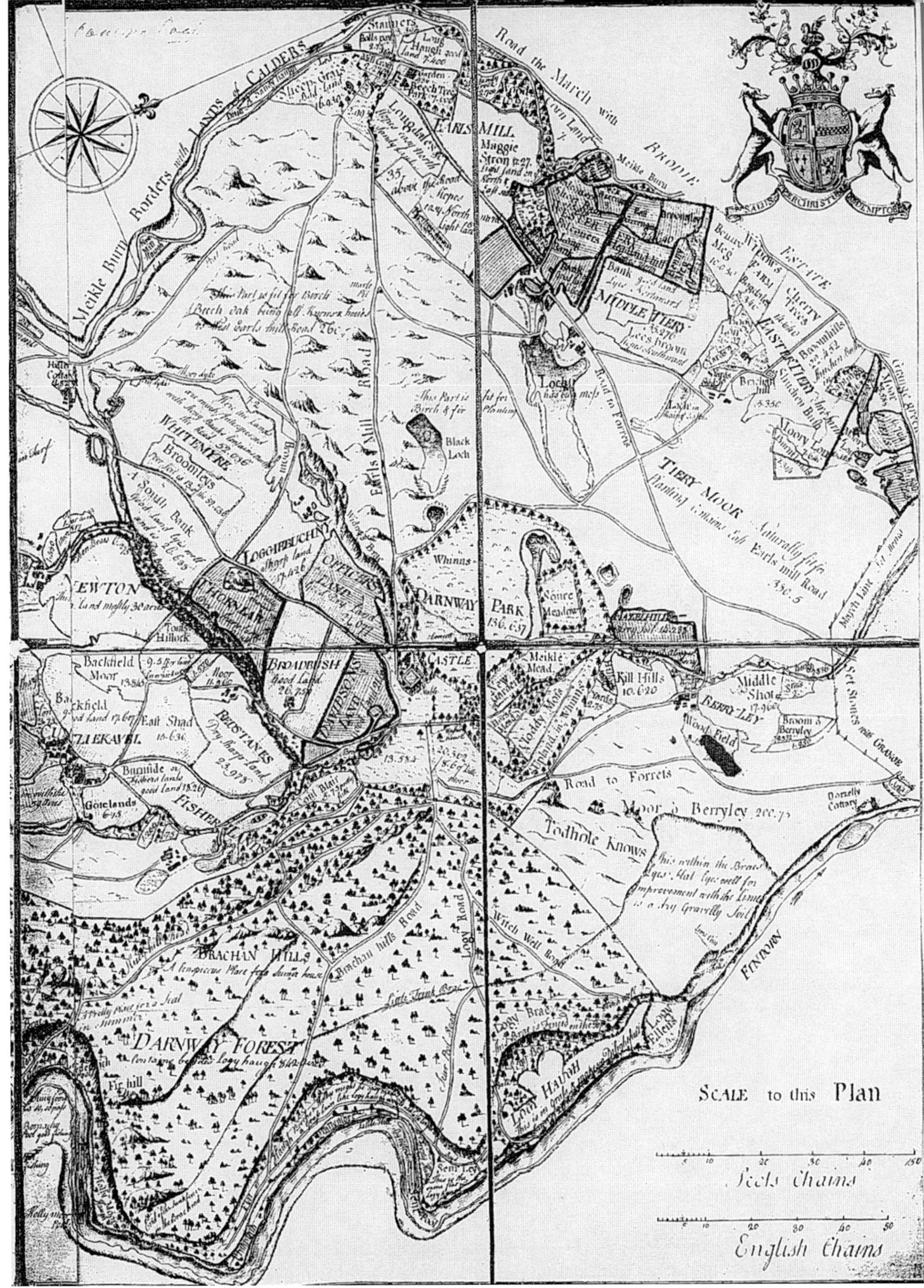

Road the March with
BRODIE
Borders with LANDS of CALDERS
Meikle Burn
EARLS MILL
Maggie Stron
Loch
Road to Forres
TIERY MOOR
Black Loch
Earls Mill Road
NEWTON
DARNWAY PARK 136.657
Whinns
Squire Meadow
CASTLE
BROADBUSH Good land 26.758
Backfield Moor
Meikle Mead
Kill Hills 10.620
Middle Shot
BERRY LEY
Wood Field
Road to Forres
Moor o Berryley
Todhole Knows
BRACHAN HILLS
DARNWAY FOREST
Logy Road
Fir hill
Logy Haugh
FINDORN
SCALE to this Plan
Scots Chains
English Chains

As the century progressed, the word, 'improvement' and the phrase, 'capable of improvement' entered the jargon of the landlord and his agents. Edward Laurence wrote in 1727 *The Duty of a Steward to his Lord* in which he commented: 'That the art of husbandry is of late years greatly improved is an undoubted truth confirmed by every day's experience; and accordingly many estates have already admitted their utmost Improvement'. Others however 'have felt few or none of the effects of modern arts and experiments'. The book, originally written for the guidance of the tenants and stewards of the Duke of Buckingham, included an appendix showing the 'way to plenty proposed to the farmers; wherein are laid down general rules and directions for the management and improvement of a farm'.[32] William Young, the factor on the Duke of Sutherland and Marquis of Stafford's Sutherland estate, wrote on his retirement, 'my favourite object through life has been to drain moors and improve waste'.[33]

From the 1750s, agricultural prices began to show signs of steady improvement and the prospects of raising rents became very real. After the declaration of war on France in 1793 wheat prices rocketed, and there was also the patriotic motive to encourage intensification. It was in the second half of the eighteenth century that the commissioning of reports by owners on how to improve the financial potential of their estates proliferated. There is a certain sameness about them all. Their authors, drawn from the ranks of the emerging profession of surveyors and land agents were unanimous in their optimism. The most unlikely terrain could be made to produce luxuriant crops and the phrase 'capable of improvement' was trotted out at every opportunity. Even on the inhospitable outer Hebridean island of South Uist a sanguine surveyor wrote in 1800 that the ending of an in-field, out-field system and its replacement with a crop rotation including clover and turnips would greatly increase the output. The moors could be 'inclosed by stone dykes, top-dressed with a thick covering of sand and seaware and be reclaimed so as in a short time to produce full crops of grass and enable the tenant greatly to increase his stock of cattle'.[34] Only rarely do we find a more candid opinion being expressed. Robert Cauldwell, the agent for the progressive Holkham estate (Norfolk) was employed in 1780 to assess the potential of de Grey's Breckland lands. He wrote, 'When I rode about your estates, I observed the best soils towards the extreme parts of your land, and if it could be considered to enclose and cultivate for corn and cattle some of those parts and leave the worst for rabbits, it might suit every purpose.'[35] The result was that the more gullible and the most wealthy of landlords, were sometimes duped into schemes that, if they were viable for the very few years of famine prices at the turn of the century, were certainly not in the longer term. The landscape effects of these efforts to bring marginal lands into cultivation will be considered in the following chapters, but it is important to understand the mindset of their initiators before looking at the farms themselves.

Of course only the largest of the capitalistic working farmers ever had the time or inclination for the philosophic writings of the Enlightenment or the classical authors. Their concern was with maximising income from their land and it was for 'practical' men that landlords went looking when seeking tenants for their new farms. This point will be more fully developed in chapter six.

The Age of Science

Changes in agriculture were as much part of the industrialisation of production as those in engineering or the manufacture of iron and steel. The links between the leaders in both fields had long been close. In 1798 the iron master, John Wilkinson installed a steam engine for threshing on his own farm in Denbighshire.[36] The oldest surviving agricultural steam engine, now in the Science Museum, was installed for Sir Christopher Hawkins in 1811 by the famous engineer and inventor of the locomotive, Richard Trevithick, on the Home Farm, Trewithan House, Probus, Cornwall. Once operational, Trevithick received further orders from Sir Christopher's neighbours and so steam chimneys were to be found towering over Cornish farms as well tin mines.[37]

The founding of the Agricultural Society of England in 1838 marked the real beginning of a gradual change in attitude. Its motto, 'Practice with science' is an indication of the emerging appreciation of the importance of scientific knowledge to the development of agriculture, and steam power was very much the icon of the Victorian Age. Its seemingly immense strength heralded an age in which everything was possible and is a symbol of the optimism of the time. An understanding of science was seen as most important in the early days of the marketing of artificial fertilisers. 'Chemical knowledge is the only way we can arrive at the real value of these artificial manures. Our practical ignorance cannot be bliss, unless it is pleasant to buy things at double their value, and lose good crops into the bargain.'[38]

The period from the beginning of Queen Victoria's reign to the 1870s is often known as that of 'high farming' with its mouthpiece, *The Journal of the Royal Agricultural Society*. With more than 5,000 members by 1854, the *Journal* had considerable influence amongst the higher echelons of the farming community. Although the term, 'high farming' is difficult to define, its philosophy was well understood at the time. It embodied the belief that science in its many branches would enable production to increase 'as knowledge itself increases'.[39] Though most of the land suited to enclosure had been brought into cultivation by the end of the Napoleonic Wars, ever more powerful machines would have the strength to tear up stiff moorland, dig deeper drains and remove the largest of stones. Increasing understanding of soil science and manures would mean that soil could be cultivated ever more intensively and appreciation of the nutritional value of newly introduced feeds would allow more stock to be kept and fattened more quickly. It was a period when increased farming profits meant that changes that had begun a generation before were taken up by the majority of landlords and farmers. According to one writer, 'Agricultural improvement, which might hitherto be looked on as a hobby for a few country gentlemen, is now become the unavoidable business of landowners, generally'.[40] Indeed it was the duty of landlords to improve. The

FIGURE 4.
By the 1860s, the ideal modern barn as illustrated had become very much like a factory floor with a wide variety of machinery being worked by belt drives off a steam engine.

(From Copland, *Agriculture Ancient and Modern*, 1866)

god-given right of the landed classes to a superior social and political position was increasingly questioned after the French Revolutions of 1789 and 1830 and the passing of the British Parliamentary reform bill in 1832. 'If the plain means of improvement and employment are still neglected, it will be impossible not to tax the owners of needless deserts with supineness; and difficult to deny that they hold in their hands more of the country's surface than they are able to manage for their own good or the good of the community.'[41] All these efforts were worthwhile because the market expanded as the population continued to rise, doubling from 12 million to 24 million between 1821 and 1881. As more people lived in towns and as the standard of living rose, the market for meat as well as grain increased. The development of the railway also helped farmers by giving them access to urban markets. With only a fifth of the nation's food being imported in 1841, farmers had little to fear from free trade, and after a short collapse in confidence after the repeal of the Corn Laws in 1846, prosperity returned and lasted for another generation. One writer commented that 'Chemistry and mechanisation have beaten politics and protection.'[42] The invention of the drain pipe making machine resulted in the mass production of pipes and the draining of 12 million acres between 1840 and 1880. While the initial cost was eased by government loans, the scale of investment was immense and an indication of the confidence felt in the future. More visible evidence in today's landscape is to be seen in the industrial farmsteads erected on many estates. With their horse engines, complex water systems or chimneys to power an increasing array of machinery (Figure 4), their covered cattle yards to allow for intensive beef and manure production and their industrial approach to time and motion, using tram lines to facilitate the throughput of raw materials, they are impressive monuments to the high farmers. These completely new farmsteads never made up more than a minority of those in Britain, but on the other hand there was hardly a farm which did not undergo major remodelling at this time and it is only in the last fifty years that these buildings have been replaced.

Two of the most influential proponents of the philosophy of high farming were James Caird and Philip Pusey (Figure 5). Pusey was born in 1799 and inherited his family estate at Pusey, Berkshire in 1828, after which he soon became involved in a Parliamentary career, finally becoming an MP for Berkshire in 1835, a position which he retained until 1852. He played a prominent part in the founding of the Royal Agricultural Society and was chairman of its Journal Committee from 1839 and 1854. Both his ideas and his literary style dominated the *Journal* throughout those years. From his family estates he encouraged articles from enthusiastic practitioners who wrote about their experiences of for instance, various drainage techniques and new manures, often adding his own comments as an editorial note at the end. The gradual shift to reliance on scientists and specialists is reflected in the change of emphasis from these short articles based on practical experience to specially commissioned longer contributions; a change begun in Pusey's time, but extended after 1854.[43]

In 1842 Pusey wrote a long and thoughtful essay on what the Society had achieved in its first four years. He saw it as having an important role in both the supporting of scientific work and the spreading of already established scientific advice to a wider audience. He was convinced of the value of improvements such as drainage ('Thorough draining is to land as foundations are to a house'[44]), which was widely discussed in the pages of the *Journal*, and marling. The importance of the analytical approach had been shown in the tests on various types of plough which had been carried out. Improving the seed for cereal crops had made little progress by 1842, but improvements in forage crops and the work of the Smithfield Club had produced breeds that reached maturity at an earlier age. As far as Pusey was concerned high farming meant intensive feeding of cattle in stalls and yards in the east of Britain and folded sheep on the downs of the south. He was much more sceptical about artificial manures, of which 'we have learnt much in the last 4 years, but know nothing' ... 'we have learnt many of the chemical principles on which manures act, but we do not as yet know how to apply those principles'.[45] Although Pusey considered the dissemination of these new scientific advances important, he saw the *Journal*'s promotion as showing of best practice as even more significant. 'I am certain that four years ago no one knew how much good farming there was in the country.'[46] By his death in 1855, many of the new scientific ideas of high farming were becoming more generally understood and accepted and his work in publicising and promoting the Society's motto of 'Practice with Science' had been an important one.

FIGURE 5. Leaders of Farming Opinion: Philip Pusey, Chairman of the Journal Committee of the Royal Agricultural Society 1839–1854, a Berkshire farmer and influential writer and James Caird, most famous for the series of articles he wrote for *The Times* in the 1850s. He believed that the repeal of the Corn Laws was inevitable and farming would have to adapt to remain profitable.

ROYAL AGRICULTURAL SOCIETY AND THE NATIONAL PORTRAIT GALLERY

Like the other great farming name of the time, James Caird, Pusey had been a supporter of free trade and believed that farming would have to become more intensive to stand up to competition. James Caird began life as a practical farmer, being sent to Northumberland from his native Scotland to learn practical farming. Born in 1816, he took on the tenancy of a farm at Baldoon, near Wigtown in 1841. He campaigned for free trade and in 1849 wrote, *High farming as the best substitute for Protection*, which went through eight editions and came to the attention of Robert Peel, who recognised the importance of the support of a practical farmer for free trade. Caird's views were at variance with those of most of the farming community who were complaining of the distressed state of agriculture. As a consequence, he was sent by the *Times* on a fact-finding mission to every county and wrote up his observations in a series of articles for the newspaper, which were subsequently collected into a book entitled *English Agriculture in 1850–51*, published in 1852. In this he stressed both the ability and necessity of farming to adapt to the changed circumstances of the free-trade world. The farmer's business was to grow 'crops of the most remunerative kind his soil can be made to carry, and within certain limits of climate which experience has now defined, the better he farms, the more capable his land becomes of growing the higher qualities of grain, of supporting the most valuable breeds of stock, and of being readily adapted to the growth of any kind of agricultural produce, which railway facilities or an increasing population may render most remunerative. In this country the agricultural improver cannot stand still. If he tries to do so, he will soon fall into the list of obsolete men, being passed by eager competitors, willing to seize the current of events and turn them to their advantage.'[47]

It is this thrusting, optimistic and adaptable attitude which is so much part of the philosophy of high farming. High farming itself can be seen as a state of mind as much as a particular farming system. How relevant it necessarily was to the majority of British farmers will be considered later in this book, but, as we shall see, it has certainly left its mark on the landscape.

Caird himself became an MP in 1857 and supported bills proposing the yearly collection of agricultural statistics, which finally began in 1866. In 1860 he bought an estate at Cassencary, Kirkudbrightshire and gave up his tenancy at Baldoon, but continued to be an active farmer and write on agricultural matters until his death in 1892.

The economies of high farming were based on the belief that there would be an ever-increasing demand for British produce by an expanding population. The limited impact of the repeal of the Corn Laws strengthened this assumption. However in the 1870s this situation began to change. 1874 saw the first of a series of poor harvests, but at the same time prices did not rise to compensate. Instead imports from North America rose. The end of the American Civil War in 1865 brought in a period of expansion west across the continent, accompanied by a rapid extension of the railways. From 1860 to 1880 American wheat production rose from 20 to 60 million quarters. In a single year the wheat acreage was increased by an area equal to Britain's total. The cost of transport fell from 2*d.* a ton to 0.25*d.*[48] Whilst the impending disaster had been foreseen by a few commentators, it took most farmers in Britain by surprise and there followed a long period of re-adjustment while the confidence of the high farmers was shattered and the concept of improvement was replaced by that of retrenchment. Even Caird admitted that land had been ploughed up which never should have been. 'There is no doubt that vast areas of poor down and heathland in the south of England, were converted to arable at the beginning of this century – land that cannot be tilled profitably now and that cannot be restored to its former condition within any reasonable limit of time, if ever.' In just over a century farming priorities had gone full circle with a return to the belief that 'Great Britain is naturally adapted to the position of a grass growing or pastoral country.'[49] It is with this brief period of less than two centuries – in which corn was king, albeit within a mixed farming system – that this book is primarily concerned.

CHAPTER TWO

Landscapes of 'Improvement' to 1830

The previous chapter has shown how the ideas supporting agricultural 'improvement' were in place by the early eighteenth century, but even if the moral duty to produce more food was accepted in theory, change was not likely to take place on a general scale unless it was seen to be profitable. Technical ability was not enough; it was the profit motive that drove forward progress. As the editor of the Royal Agricultural Society's *Journal*, Philip Pusey, wrote in 1849, if it were profitable to put a canal through the isthmus of Panama or at Suez, someone would have found a way of doing it.[1] It is not surprising therefore that the progress of enclosure, the most striking type of landscape change resulting from the ideas of the 'improvers', was governed by the changing balance of profits between pastoral and arable farming and by progress in farming practice, which influenced the profitability of conflicting farming systems within open fields. However, enclosure should be seen as just one stage in the process. Once divided into fields, the land had to be drained, limed or marled to bring its productivity up to a level that would justify the expense involved.

FIGURE 6
(*opposite, top*)
Field patterns of early enclosure: the area around Worthy and Abbots Beckington, north-east Devon. The first edition Ordnance Survey map (Devonshire 39NW) shows an irregular pattern of small fields with some commons and woodland surviving along the valleys.

FIGURE 7
Field patterns of the South Elmhams (Suffolk). The early Ordnance Survey map (Suffolk 17 SE) shows an unusual field pattern of rectangular fields showing a distinct north-south, slightly curved alignment. Most have now disappeared but they may be of Iron Age, Roman or early medieval origin.

Yeoman improvement up to 1750

As late as 1688 it is estimated that a third of England was still owned by small-scale freeholders. By 1800, this had dropped to 10 per cent. Many others farmed on life tenancies where the landowner exercised very little control over what happened on the land and so perhaps a further third of the country was farmed by a virtually independent group. Together these two groups can be called yeoman. It was these people who were behind much of the farming change up to the early eighteenth century. It can be argued that from the end of the seventeenth century they were gradually eliminated, as the large estates embarked upon both a long-term policy of acquisition of land and a programme of replacing life tenancies by a more restrictive system of yearly rents and leases.[2]

Enclosure has long been seen as the most fundamental landscape change of post-medieval times. However, it cannot be regarded as a single process and attitudes towards it changed considerably over time. This variety in history and motivation can be seen, if not in the modern landscape (much of which has gone through a more drastic period of change over the last forty years), at least in war-time aerial photographs and earlier editions of large-scale ordnance survey maps (Figures 6 and 7).

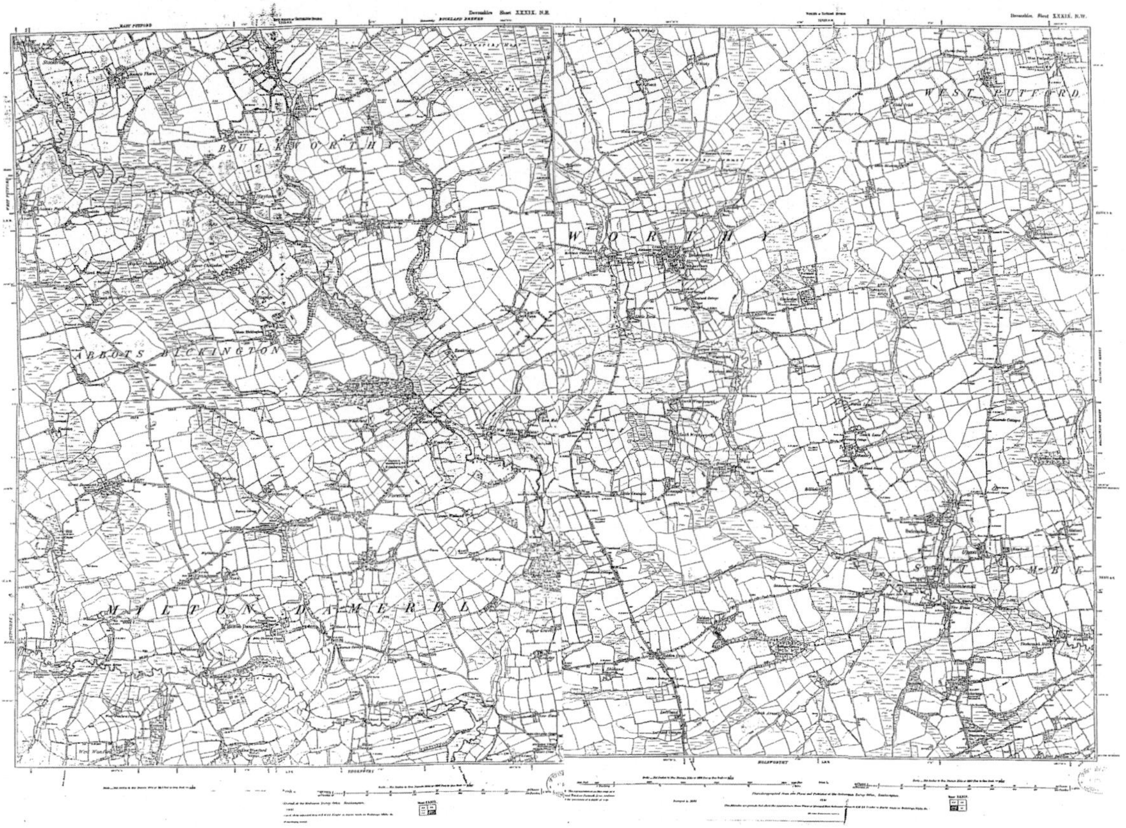

Devonshire Sheet XXXIX. N.E.

Devonshire Sheet XXXIX. N.W.

BULKWORTHY

WEST PUTFORD

WORTHY

ABBOTS BICKINGTON

MILTON DAMEREL

SUTCOMBE

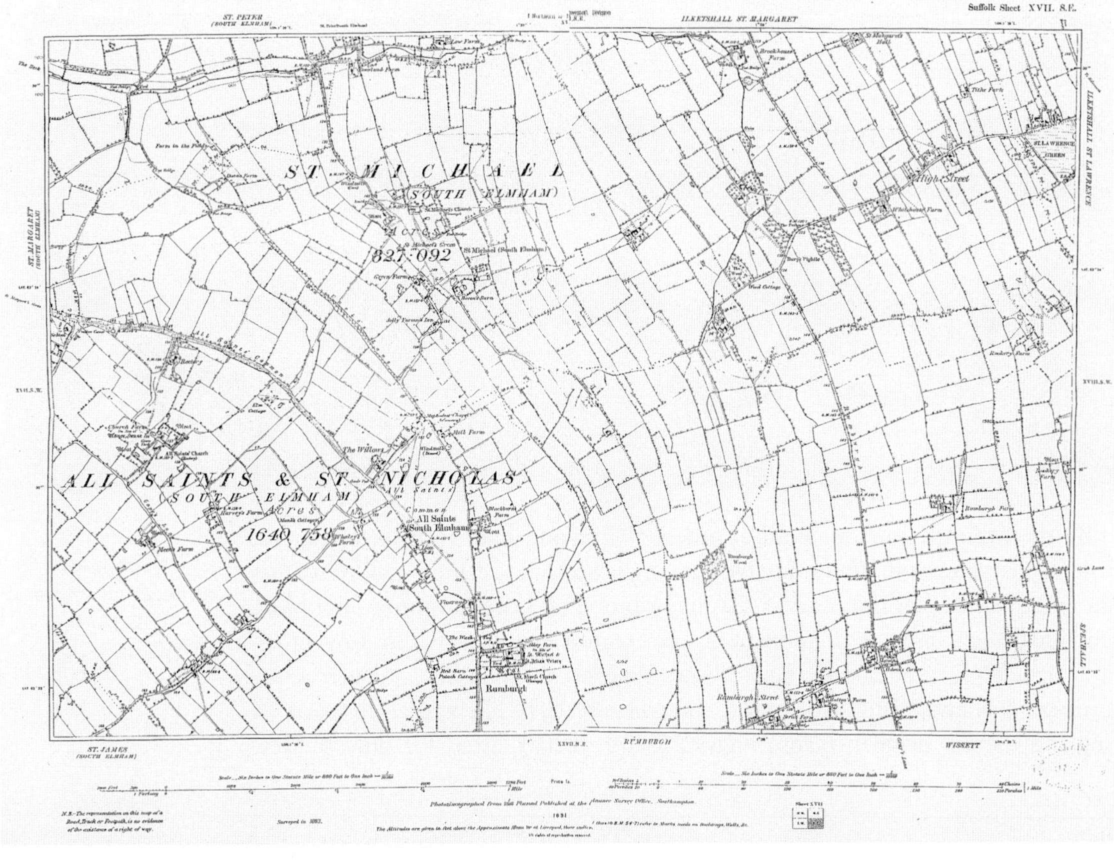

Suffolk Sheet XVII. S.E.

ST. PETER
(SOUTH ELMHAM)

ILKETSHALL ST. MARGARET

ILKETSHALL ST. LAWRENCE

ST. MARGARET
(SOUTH ELMHAM)

ST. MICHAEL
(SOUTH ELMHAM)
Acres
327·092

Low Farm

Brookhouse Farm

St Margaret's Hall

Tithe Farm

ST. LAWRENCE GREEN

High Street

ALL SAINTS & ST. NICHOLAS
(SOUTH ELMHAM)
Acres
1640·758

All Saints South Elmham

Rumburgh

Rumburgh Street

XVII. S.W.

XVIII. S.W.

SPEXHALL

ST. JAMES
(SOUTH ELMHAM)

RUMBURGH

WISSETT

Scale.—Six Inches to One Statute Mile or 880 Feet to One Inch — 1/10560

Photozincographed from the Plan Published at the Ordnance Survey Office, Southampton

1891

N.B.—The representation on this map of a Road, Track or Footpath, is no evidence of the existence of a right of way.

Surveyed in 1883.

The Altitudes are given in feet above the Approximate Mean Water at Liverpool, those indica...(thus B.M. 54·7) refer to Marks made on Buildings, Walls, &c.

FIGURE 8.
The open fields:
a) ridge and furrow at Little Lawford (Warwickshire).
CUCAP

By the beginning of our period, much of England had been enclosed, but little of Scotland and Wales outside the anglicised areas. Open arable in areas like west Pembrokeshire, coastal Cardiganshire and eastern Montgomeryshire remained unenclosed at the end of the eighteenth century,[3] whilst Roy's map of Scotland surveyed in the 1750s shows patches of enclosed land across the southern lowlands, but little more. In contrast it is likely that in parts of England the era of open fields (Figures 8 and 9) had lasted for only the few

b) open fields at Laxton (Nottinghamshire). Laxton is one of the few surviving open field parishes in England and the curves in the strips, resulting from the turning of medieval ploughs, can clearly be seen.

hundred years of greatest population pressure in the early middle ages. It disappeared as population fell, making grain production on land more suited to pasture unprofitable by the fifteenth century.

The most publicised of the early enclosures were in the midlands and were undertaken by large-scale sheep farmers involving the removal of the last few houses from already largely depopulated villages. Anti-enclosure acts were passed in 1489, 1515, 1533 and 1555, but the fact that these resulted in very few prosecutions suggests that the issue was already no longer an important one and wholesale enclosure for sheep was already declining. At least 64 per cent of open-field parishes in Nottinghamshire still remained to be enclosed after 1720 (Figure 9).[4]

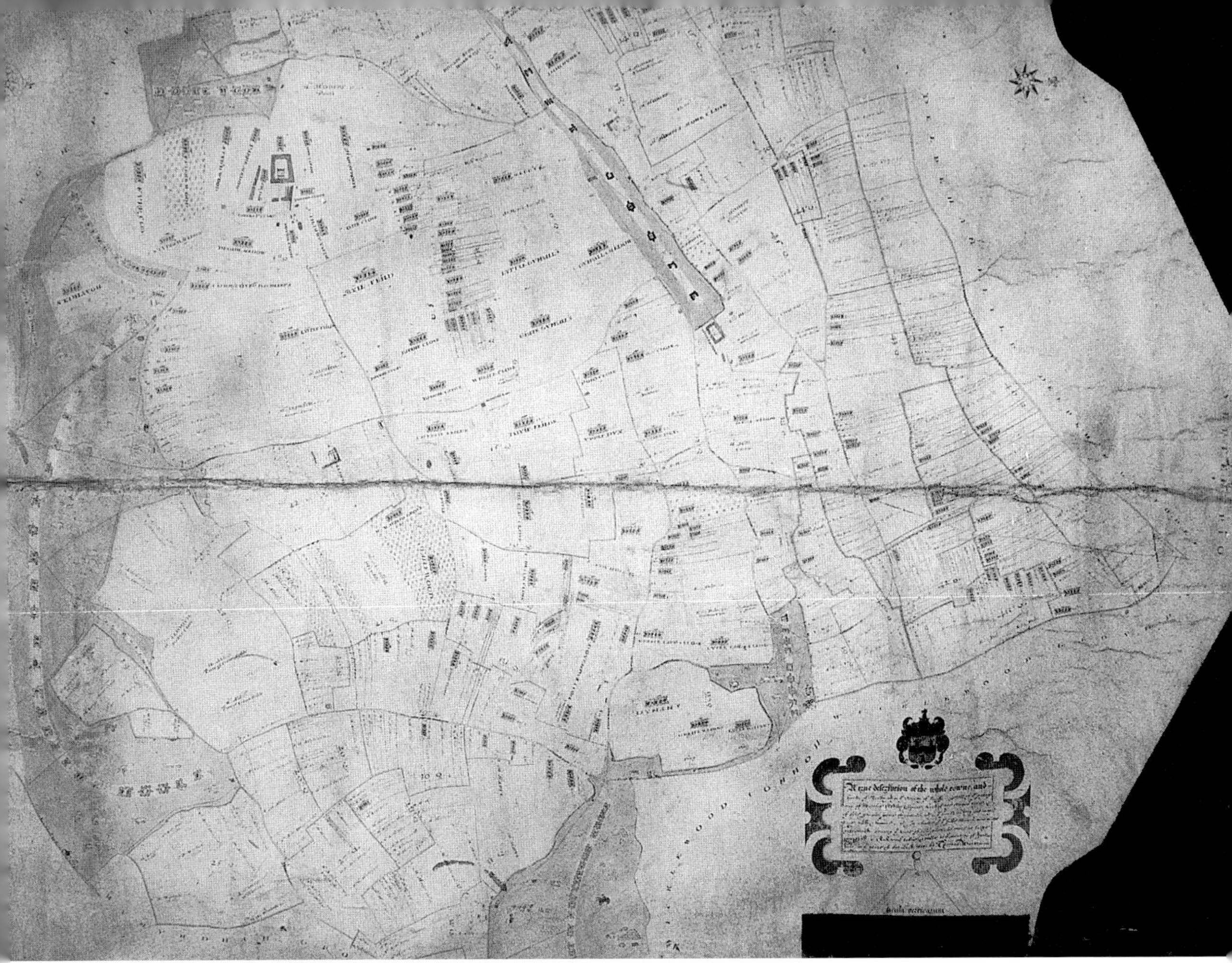

Much more widespread, if less publicised, was enclosure mainly for cattle in the south and west. By 1600 the pastoral counties of Cornwall, Devon, Cheshire, Lancashire and western Monmouthshire were described as 'wholly enclosed' while Shropshire, Hereford, Sussex, Suffolk, Somerset, Dorset and parts of Northumberland and North Yorkshire were 'heavily enclosed'. Somerset indeed was described as 'prosperous through enclosure', although in fact it was the mainly pastoral Vale of Taunton and the lower Mendips which were enclosed early, with the rough uplands remaining open until the end of the eighteenth century. While this had all been enclosure for pastoral farming, counties such as Kent, Essex, and north-east County Durham had been enclosed for commercial production for London and the increasingly urbanised north-east coalfield. Enclosure continued throughout the seventeenth century in the pastoral areas with 47 per cent of Leicestershire in hedged fields by 1710. However there was a difference between this and the work of the Tudor landlords in that it was mostly by small farmers rather than squires and landowners.[5]

The identification of areas of enclosure by county is an oversimplification. More helpful would be a study by farming regions. In Wiltshire for instance, the butter and cheese producing region of the clays was mostly enclosed in the seventeenth century whilst the light chalkland sheep and corn country

FIGURE 9.
The open fields
a) (*opposite*)
Seventeenth-century map of Colkirk, Norfolk, showing the strips within open fields subdivided into furlongs.
NORFOLK RECORD OFFICE
b) Map of Nottinghamshire showing parishes and the dates of enclosure. It is clear that here the majority of parishes remained open until the eighteenth century.
PHILLIP JUDGE, REDRAWN FROM D. HALL (2001)

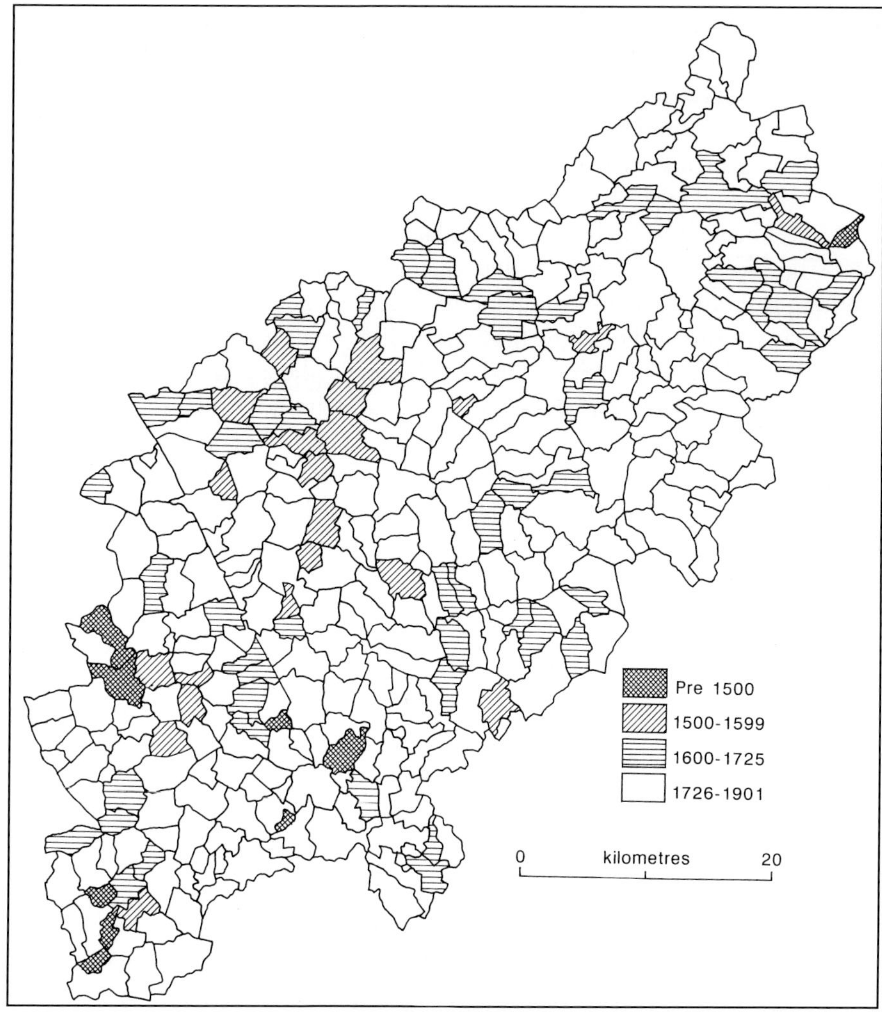

dominated by great estates remained open until the end of the eighteenth century. In Warwickshire it was the wood-pastures of the Forest of Arden which were enclosed by 1700, leaving the rest of the county to later improvers.[6] In many areas, it is even more complicated with both open and enclosed fields existing side by side.[7]

There were various processes by which enclosure was undertaken. Although we know most about Parliamentary enclosure because of the amount of documentation it involved, non-Parliamentary types were nationally the dominant form and remained highly significant even in the eighteenth and nineteenth centuries.[8] Piecemeal enclosure took place over a long period of time as farmers exchanged land with their neighbours to create larger holdings within the open fields. In 1763 Robert Knopwood of Tottington (Norfolk), the owner of about 80 acres and the second largest proprietor in the parish agreed to exchange land with the largest owner, Thomas De Grey: 'Whereas … such lands … do lay intermixed with and are inconvenient to each party and at a great distance from their several farmhouses and for the better convenience and improvement of their said estates ... agree to exchange such lands as lay convenient and contiguous to the inclosed lands of Knopwood as lay convenient and contiguous to and intermixed with the land of the said Thomas de Grey.'[9] It was arrangements such as this that gradually led to the disintegration of the whole open field structure but frequently the old system would be preserved in a simplified form in the field boundaries of the emergent landscape, with long-strip-like fields, often with the remains of the reversed S curve in them, resulting from the plough-turning methods of the open fields (Figure 8). Much of this pattern survived until the field rationalisation campaigns after the Second World War. Because of their gradual development, there is very little documentation to illustrate the change taking place and its importance is only now beginning to be appreciated. In Hampshire 51 per cent of the open fields existing in 1700 were later enclosed by this means.[10] The new fields were created by small farmers for mainly pastoral systems to which small enclosures were eminently suited. However, they were already being eroded in the nineteenth century as mixed arable systems requiring larger fields took over. Hedge removal was already an issue in the mid-nineteenth century.[11]

A second form of enclosure was that undertaken by general agreement between the farmers within the open fields. It was therefore most likely where only a few people had to agree to the change or where piecemeal enclosure had already undermined the open field system. The seventeenth century saw the consolidation of estates which helped the progress of enclosure. It involved a once and for all total re-organisation of the landscape. Families who owned large parts of one or two parishes would engross further land and create large farms within their newly laid out fields. Because it was an informal arrangement, there is often no documentation, although its legality was often tested in the courts, and enrolled in the Court of Chancery, resulting in an official record surviving.[12] These enrollments are difficult to locate and no complete list of them has been compiled, but it is likely that the counties most affected were the midland ones of Leicestershire, Northamptonshire and Warwickshire, with Lincolnshire and Yorkshire to the east. Blake Tyson's studies in Cumbria show that open-field arable had existed there, but had all gone through non-parliamentary enclosure by 1750.[13] Here it was likely that the field boundaries would be entirely redrawn and a more formal field layout would emerge. Both piecemeal enclosure and enclosure by agreement were increasing in importance during the late seventeenth and early eighteenth century as a slow transition from mainly open-field semi-subsistence farming in which market influences were local, to a market economy whose prices were dictated by the needs of an urban population was taking place. Initially some of these enclosures on the heavy clays may have been to support a mixed farming system in which grain was alternated with pasture to create an integrated system in which the animals helped keep up the fertility of the soils. However, as grain prices slumped in the early eighteenth century and yields on the light lands were increasing with the introduction of new rotations not suited to heavy soils, the clayland farmers shifted into systems dominated by permanent pasture. This was favoured by landlords as rents for pasture were higher and investment in buildings was less than that for arable farms.[14] It is also likely that pressure was being put on the common grazings as individual farmers attempted to intensify production and so enclosure to provide more pasture was seen as a solution.[15]

Enclosure was not necessarily followed by new farming practices, and progressive farming systems could be operated in open fields.[16] 'The inefficiency of the open-fields is by no means as plain and obvious as it once seemed.'[17] At Ashley, near Scunthorpe (Lincolnshire) in 1784, the landowners and occupiers drew up an agreement 'for the Improvement of Lands in the several open arable fields'.[18] A lease for a farm in the north Norfolk parish of Burnham Westgate in 1737 for 70 acres* of 'parcels of land laying dispersed in the several fields' stated that not more than two corn crops could be grown in succession and another stipulated that at least half the temporary grass leys should be in the open fields, suggesting firstly that there was no difference in farming practice between the open and closed fields and secondly that there was a need for further livestock provision.[19] After enclosure, the farmers were the same people on the whole as before, and so with the same outlooks. It would be surprising therefore if agricultural methods on most holdings had suddenly changed.[20] On the other hand, 'it is difficult to imagine a *major* agricultural reform movement developing with any success in a region where open field farming and rights of common remained ... it was part of a structural revolution of major proportions which heralded the beginning of a substantial transformation of the English countryside'.[21]

Enclosure in this early phase was dominated by agreement between farmers, rather than imposition by landowners. Indeed, there is an example of a Gloucestershire farmer pointing out the advantages of enclosure to Lord Harwicke's agent.[22] It was to be found predominantly on the claylands where it allowed for the creation of more pasture for intensive livestock production, on land more suited to pastoral than arable farming and so where grain production was not profitable in periods of low cereal prices. Fields were smaller (under 30 acres) than those of the later enclosures. It rarely included the enclosure of commons and waste.

Other than enclosure, the most significant land improvements of this early phase were also to enable more intensive livestock husbandry. These included the creation of water meadows, discussed in the previous chapter and the first stages of the draining of marshland. Work had begun on the Isle of Axholme, Hatfield Chase, Holderness and the Hull valley, the Somerset Levels and the marshes of Lancashire. Many of these were only of temporary success and their completion had to await the period after 1750. The most

* Area measurements figure prominently in this book. I have chosen to use the acre – the unit used in the sources – rather than to include metric conversions, which would weigh down the text with parentheses.

successful was the Bedford Level in the Fens, but even here the shrinking of the peat as it was drained meant that inundations were frequent and stronger pumps would be required.[23]

Under-draining of the heavy clays was also beginning before 1750 with Walter Blyth describing in 1649 a method of 'hollow draining' whereby drains could be dug out and filled with stones and bushes before being covered over. Richard Bradley described a similar method in 1727 which was 'chiefly practiced in Essex, although by 1750, it was to be found throughout East Anglia and into Hertfordshire'.[24]

The landscape of Britain in 1750 would have presented many contrasts. The fields in the river valleys and on the heavy clays would have been far wetter in 1750 than 1900. There were inumerable ponds and boggy patches with meandering rivers and ox-bow lakes. The map of Devon remained into the twentieth century very much as it had been in 1550, whilst that of the Yorkshire Wolds was completely remodelled during the eighteenth century. Much of the old open arable, particularly in the areas more suited to livestock farming, would have been enclosed by 1750, either into regular fields under enclosures by agreement or into more random and usually smaller, often linear fields where the change had been piecemeal. Here farmers would have practiced a mixed system in which animals would have alternated with crops which might include fodder as well as grain. Some farmers, particularly on the heavy East Anglian clays were experimenting with underdrains, but elsewhere, where open fields persisted, farmers relied on ridge and furrow to take away excess water. River valleys of the southern chalklands would have been dominated by water meadows. Elsewhere, particularly in the midlands, on the rich arable lands such as the good loams of east Norfolk, and on the light chalks which relied on the folding of sheep on the open fields to keep them fertile, the old communal fields which could be anything up to 2,000 acres, remained. Commons and heaths also survived and marshes remained undrained. There was still plenty to keep improvers busy over the next eighty years.

Whig improvement, 1750–1830

The years from the mid-eighteenth century until after the Napoleonic Wars saw dramatic changes in the farming landscapes in many areas of Britain not already affected by enclosure, and in most cases, this was led by the increasingly powerful landlord class, encouraged by some of their tenants and the emerging profession of land agents who were taking over duties traditionally handled by the family lawyer, or the land steward of the larger estates.[25]

The extension of influence of the large estates alongside the ending of life leases to be replaced by shorter ones allowed the landlord to reflect the rising agricultural prosperity in the rents he charged. At the same time the amount of land owned by the estates was increasing. According to Gregory King's estimate, peers controlled about 2.5 per cent of the total income from land of all classes while a hundred years later at the end of the eighteenth century the

FIGURE 10.
Eighteenth century map of Hall Farm, Earsham (Norfolk). This map shows the old deer park enclosed by the eighteenth century. Land is being ploughed and turnips lifted to feed to cattle in the field.

NICHOLAS MEADE

great landowners owned about 20 per cent of England. By the late nineteenth century this had risen to 24 per cent.[26] A growing interest in agricultural improvement as grain price rises outstripped those for livestock meant that landlord-led enclosure for arable rather than pastoral farming increased in importance. At the same time there was an increasing understanding of soils and regional differences. Darby quotes an early seventeenth-century description of Dorset which merely differentiates between the clays and chalks. By 1774, down, vale and heath are all recognised as specific regions. The Royal Society of Arts offered awards for county maps at a scale of one inch to the mile from its foundation in 1754[27] and the Board of Agriculture's county *General Views*, published from the 1790s, mostly contained a soil map. That for Hampshire divides the county into eight very distinct districts by soil, taking up the first 40 pages of the volume.[28] New farming practices were entering the country from the Low Countries, mainly through East Anglia. Most significantly, these emphasised the importance of getting rid of the fallow year by growing instead a crop of 'artificial grass' such as sainfoin or nitrogenous clover providing both a break crop between cereals on which animals could be grazed, and a more nutritious hay crop. Also important was the introduction of the turnip to replace the fallow year (Figure 10).

Turnips provided animal fodder which could be fed on or off the field and was a 'cleaning' crop, because, when drilled in rows, it was possible to hoe out the weeds between. However the growing of turnips was most suited to the light-land regions of the east and allowed for increased grain productivity and the fattening of more stock. Much of this region had remained open sheep walk until the early eighteenth century and as such land was cheaper

improved'.[34] Jackson's map of 1773[35] shows Redcar, Marske and Upleatham enclosed in regular linear and often slightly curved fields following the lines of the old strips, most of which survived until the six inch to the mile Ordnance Survey map of 1857 and can still be identified in the street pattern of Redcar. The only changes were on the newly enclosed moorland where some of the regular field boundaries have been slightly altered and three new farms created. Two areas were commented on particularly favourably by Arthur Young after his visit in 1769. The estates of Charles Turner adjacent to the Dundas lands around Kirkleatham (Figure 11) had been reorganised, so that the fields worked by each farm were in a block rather than scattered across the parish. However, the fields themselves were not altered but retained their earlier linear form. Turner had taken farms in hand, brought them into a 'proper state' and rebuilt the farmsteads before reletting. Sir Walter Blackett on the other hand had laid out new regular rectangular fields and farms as well as built roads on his estates around Cambo in Northumberland (Figure 12).[36]

FIGURE 12.
The re-arrangement of the landscape by landlords.
Map of the Cambo and Wallington area showing the straight roads and regular fields laid out by Sir Walter Blackett and which impressed Arthur Young when on his Northern Tour (OS Northumberland 62SW).

One of the earliest of the new profession of land agent was Edward Laurence who wrote *The Duty and Office of a Land Steward*, first published in 1727 'for the tenants and stewards of the Duke of Buckingham' (Figure 13). In it he advocated enclosure and farm amalgamation, but not to the detriment of the small tenant. Amalgamation was only possible at the end of leases when farms

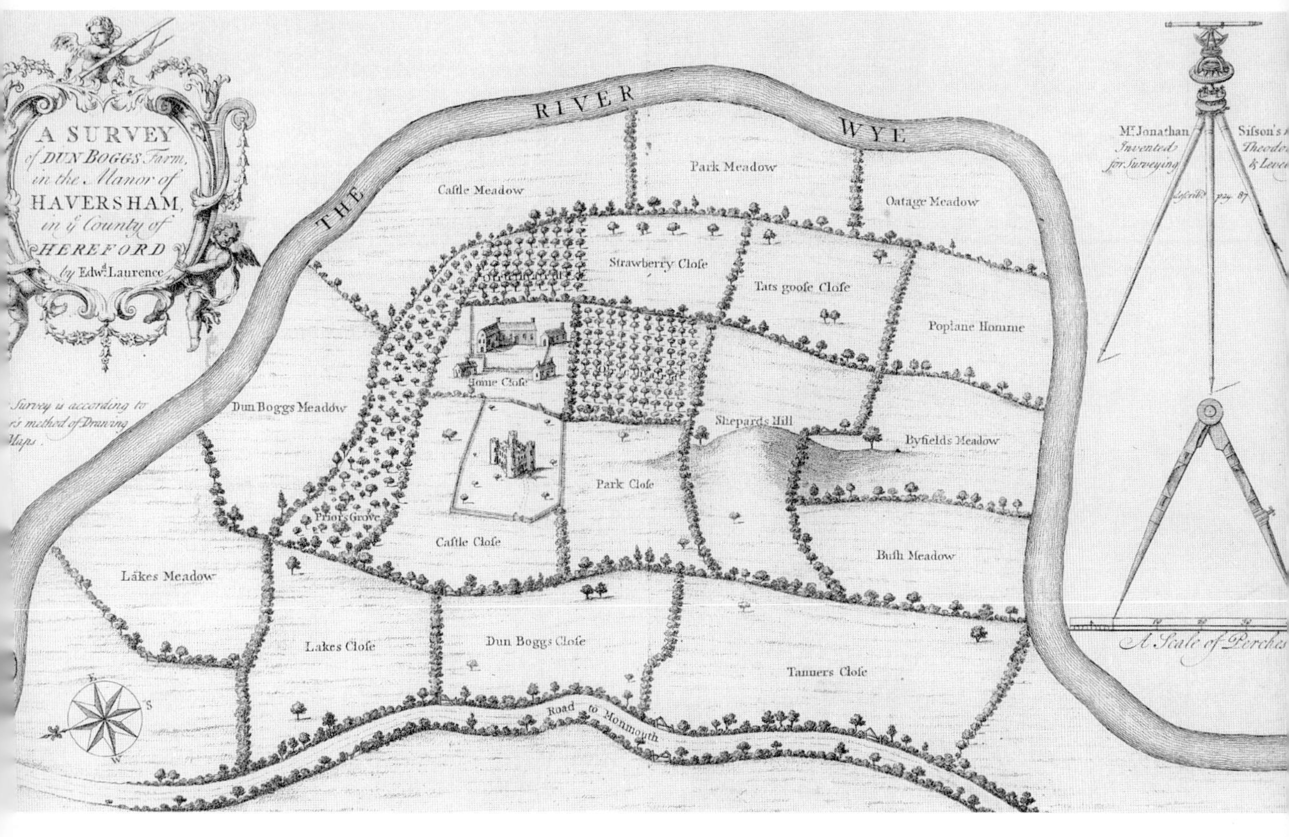

FIGURE 13.
Map of Haversham (Herefordshire). This map, drawn by Edward Laurence, author of *The Duty and Office of a Land Steward*, published in 1727, shows a typical early enclosed pastoral farm. Orchards were already very much part of the Herefordshire economy; fields were hedged and meadow makes up at least half the farmland.

SYNDICS OF CAMBRIDGE UNIVERSITY LIBRARY

became vacant, for it would raise too great an odium to turn poor families into the wide world by 'uniting farms all at once'. He believed in strict husbandry leases to ensure that land was not exhausted through over-cropping. At this early date it was the enforcement of a fallow year, rather than the encouragement of the growing of break crops such as grasses and turnips, which was to be stipulated. He knew of the value of these crops and discussed them in detail later in the book.

Enclosure by agreement continued to be important throughout the eighteenth century and landowners often tried to buy out their neighbours so that they could enclose without the expense of a parliamentary act. However, where this was not possible, resort had to be made to Parliament and during the 1760s and 1770s much of the remaining open field on the midland clays was enclosed, mostly for pastoral farming, as the survival of the earlier ridge and furrow in many of the new fields shows (Figure 8).[37] In most cases the open fields had been farmed continuously since before the Norman Conquest and in spite of regular fallowing, the soil was becoming exhausted. Attempts to grow turnips and introduce the new rotations in the newly enclosed fields of Swithland, Leicestershire failed because 'the light meagre soil was worn out by perpetual tillage'.[38] The swing from open-field arable to enclosed pastoral in the middle years of the eighteenth century allowed landlords to put up

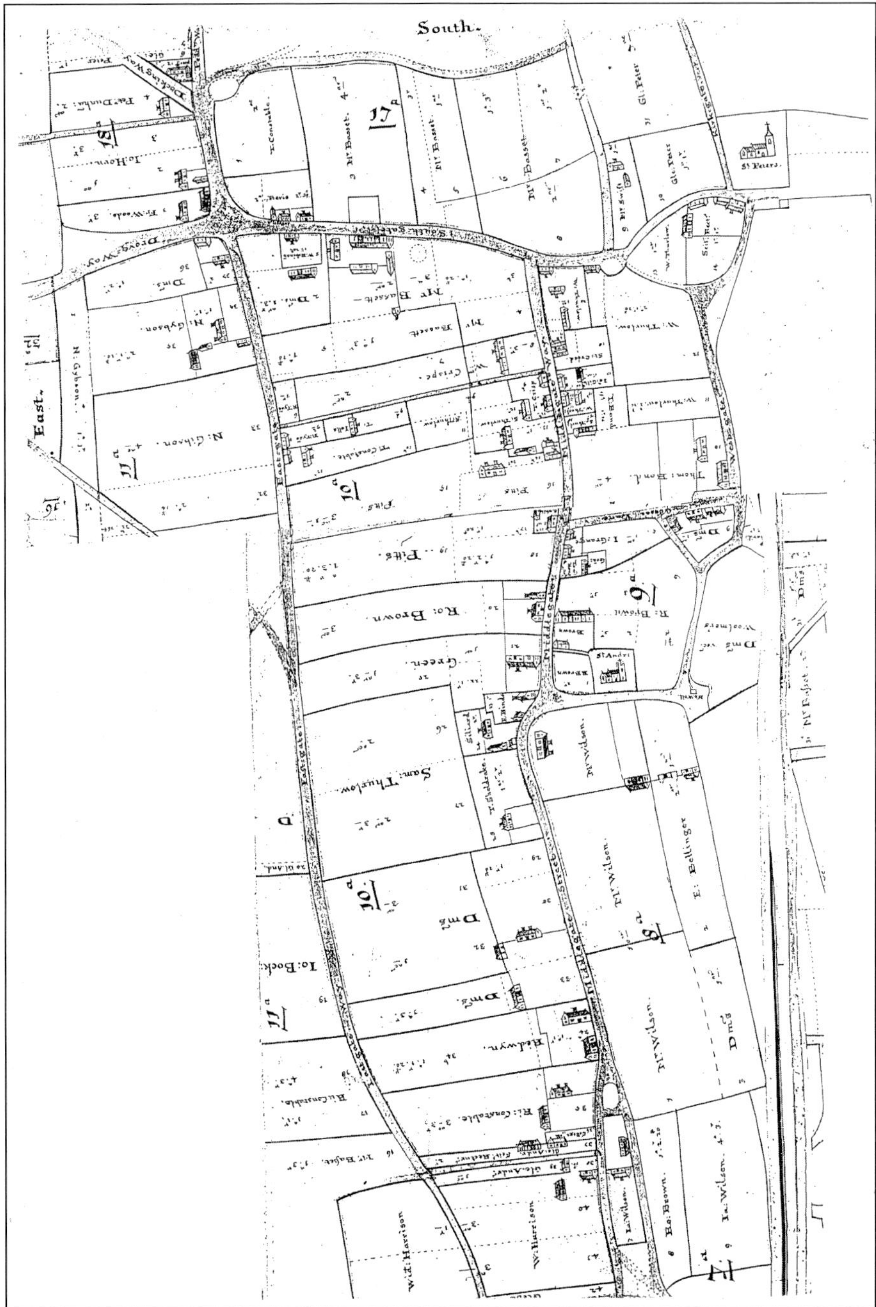

FIGURE 14.
Ringstead (Norfolk) before and after enclosure.
These two maps of 1690 (*left*) and 1820 (*opposite*) show how, before enclosure the farmhouses and barns were along the village street, but with enclosure the number was greatly reduced and several were rebuilt in the centre of their fields.
NORFOLK RECORD OFFICE. LE STRANGE COLLECTION

their rents, which were always higher for pasture than for bare arable. Profits for livestock, particularly dairy farming, held up better in the years of stagnation up to 1760. As a result Leicestershire, which had been a corn county before enclosure 'does not now keep itself in bread'.[39] However, as Tom Williamson points out, there may have been motives other than economic ones for enclosure for pasture. Aesthetic considerations, the increasing fashion

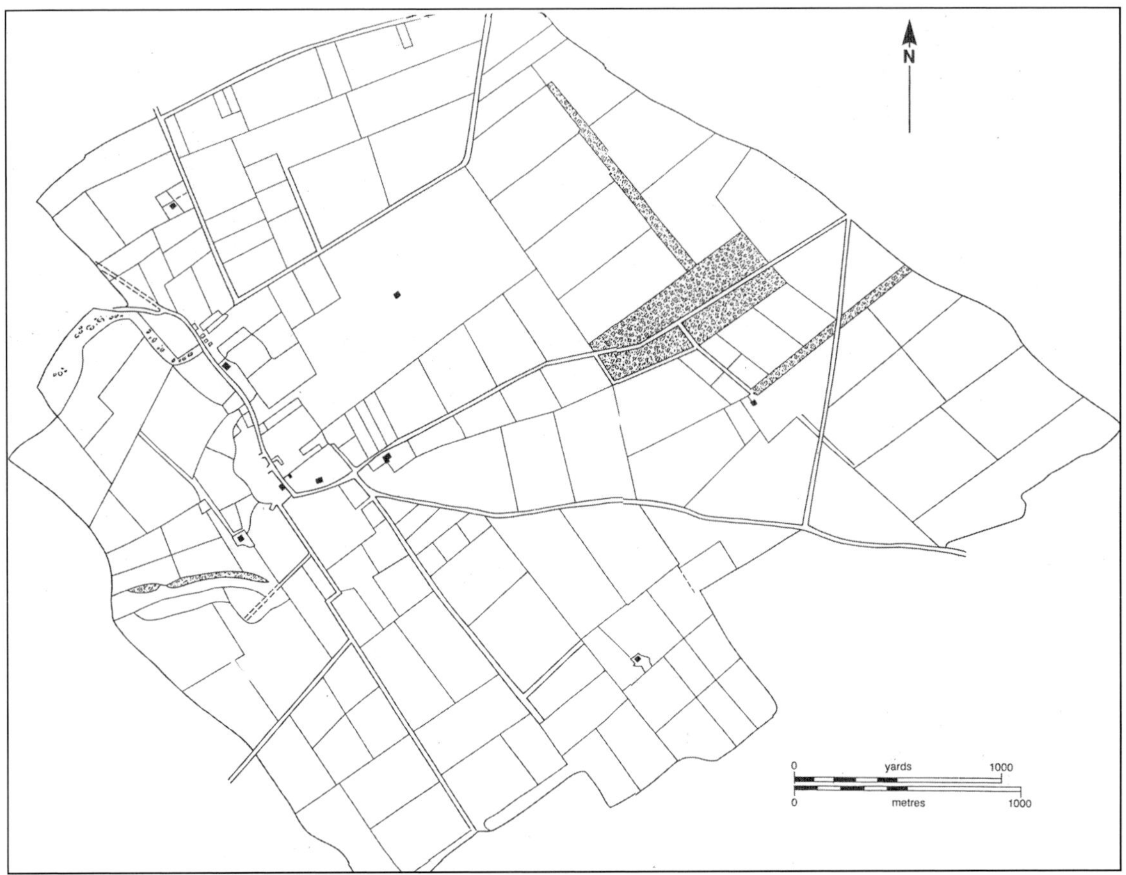

for hunting, ease of management and a desire to reduce population may well all have played a part.[40]

Elsewhere, declining wool prices from 1750 encouraged the light-land farmers to enclose sheep walks for arable, resulting often in a doubling of rents.[41] While the first peak in parliamentary enclosure was between 1760 and 1780, when most of the remaining open field disappeared, the second peak covered the years of increasing grain prices during the Napoleonic War and involved the enclosure of light land and commons for arable farming. Altogether, about 6.8 million acres of England was affected by parliamentary act (20.9 per cent of the area of the country). Of the 5,265 acts, 3,828 were passed between 1750 and 1819, with more than 50 per cent of the land area of Oxfordshire, Cambridgeshire and Northamptonshire enclosed at this time. However it is dangerous to assume that the existence of an act means that there had been little enclosure before, as examples from north-west Norfolk show.[42] In Cornwall, the Welsh marches and the south, less than 10 per cent of the land surface was affected.[43]

There were few parts of the country where enclosure would have been an unfamiliar process by 1750 and in some places farmers feared the results. There has been much debate over the effect enclosure had on the small farmer.

William Gardner told the Earl of Huntingdon that: 'the farmers will all be against it, as they know it will cause some of them to seek farms in other places',[44] and as we have seen, the turning out of small tenants was a concern of the land steward, Edward Laurence. The parish of Ringstead (Norfolk) was enclosed in several stages, with the final phase involving the enclosure of the common at the end of the eighteenth century. A map of 1690 shows the open-field parish with small enclosed strips behind the houses in the village. There appear to be at least 22 farms along the village street. After the final enclosure, the fields were completely re-laid out and the number of farms reduced to seven, all of them over 100 acres (Figure 14).[45]

However, it is important not to exaggerate the importance of enclosure in the general eighteenth-century move towards large farms. Farms in the open fields as well as the newly enclosed areas were also increasing in size,[46] while in the newly-enclosed areas of the south midlands, enclosure seems to have had little effect on the number of farmers.[47] It is likely that it was the type of farming practiced rather than the enclosure itself that resulted in a change in farm size. Economies of scale were not so obvious in pastoral as in arable farming. It is also dangerous to assume that the owners of small patches of land also farmed them. Often they were let to neighbouring farmers and farmed as part of the same holding. Rather than being losers, selling out at the time of enclosure could be highly profitable. At the time of the Tottington (Norfolk) enclosure, Lord Walsingham was keen to buy out the small owners to simplify the enclosure process. Mrs Duffield owned 43 acres in 33 separate pieces and struck a hard bargain because, as the agent wrote, 'she says (and with some truth), she can increase the rents, though I cannot, because she can let her little scraps to such tenants of mine with whom they are intermixed and they must give her a full price or suffer by the refusal'.[48] Of the four other small owners who remained at the time of the final enclosure, two were described as 'yeoman' and one as a 'gentleman'. The fourth was a carpenter. Only one lived in the parish. It is probable, therefore that they had always let their land in the parish and may well have owned land elsewhere as well.[49] Furthermore, it is clear that the survival of the separate ownership of strips did not always affect the actual cultivation of the soil. The implications could be purely legal. At Kempstone (Norfolk) land owned by the tenant of the farm was intermingled with that of his landlord, but the fields were farmed as single enclosed entities.[50]

The preamble of Parliamentary acts always listed the disadvantages of open field farming in a formal manner and great claims were often made for the benefits of enclosure to both tenants and landlords. Productivity could sometimes be doubled and rents went up by an equivalent amount. Certainly enclosure gave farmers greater freedom in the use of their lands, but it was the nature of the soils rather than the enclosure itself which was crucial. Arable could be extended into the light soils as a result of new husbandries rather than enclosure itself and in some places post-enclosure farming was little different to that practised before.

The light soils of the Yorkshire, and Lincolnshire Wolds were mostly controlled by great landlords and this was an area particularly dramatically affected by enclosure. The rediscovery of the art of making dew ponds allowed much of the Yorkshire Wolds to be enclosed for arable farming, relying on the folding of sheep on the turnips for its success. Sir Christopher Sykes continued the work of his predecessors, developing the Sledmere estate in the 1770s, creating new farms in the fields in the parishes of Sledmere, Garton-on-the-Wolds and Cottam. Many of Sykes' neighbours were also busy. The Duke of Devonshire owned much of the neighbouring parish of Middleton-on-the-Wolds where an enclosure act was passed in 1805. Here the six open fields were enclosed, new farms created and seven sets of farm buildings built away from the village in the centre of their fields. Further north, the Birdsall estates of the Willoughby family (later Lords Middleton) and further south the Yarborough estates of the Pelhams also provide examples of extensive re-shaping of the farming landscape as large rectangular fields surrounding new farmsteads were created on the light wold soils. These nineteenth-century fields were larger than those created in the century before with those on the Yorkshire chalks varying between 30 and 70 acres and those in Lincolnshire sometimes as large as 100 acres. The hedgerows of hawthorn and blackthorn thickened up to form ideal barriers for stock, but provided little hedgerow timber or kindling. As coal became more generally available locally gathered fuel was less important and timber was grown in plantations rather than hedges.[51]

Whatever were the effects on farming practice, the framework within which

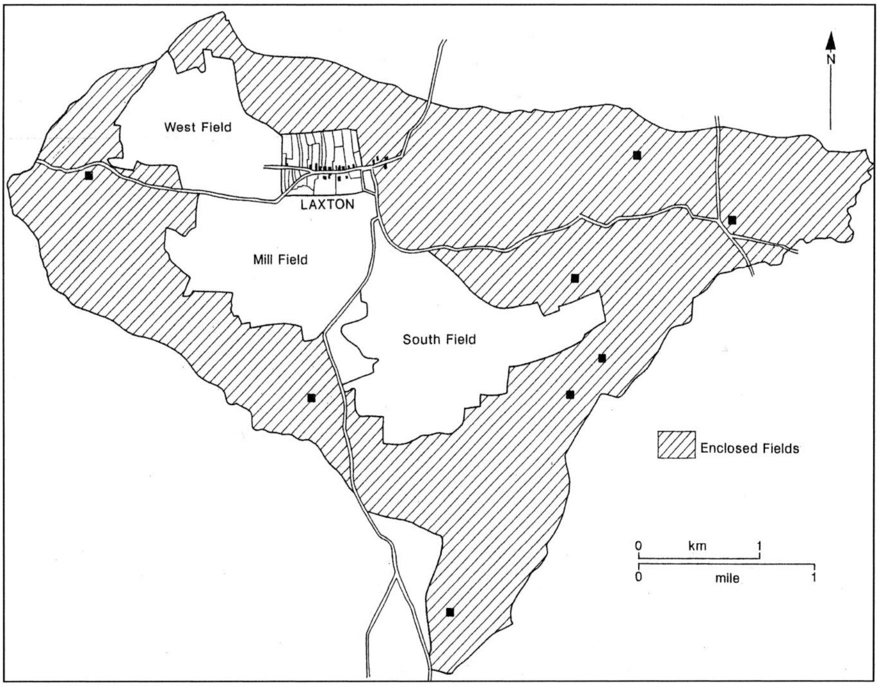

FIGURE 15. The parish of Laxton (Nottinghamshire). The distribution of settlement within the parish has clearly been influenced by field patterns. In the enclosed area of the parish farmsteads are scattered across the fields within their ring-fenced holdings. In contrast, where the fields are still open, the farmsteads are concentrated in the village with barns along the street.
PHILLIP JUDGE

farming operated was altered drastically. Middleton was typical of many villages where the centre of gravity of farming life moved from the nucleated village out onto isolated farmsteads (Figure 15).[52] The landowning structure of the manor was dismantled and replaced by one based on private ownership. The farmer could no longer regard the strips which his family may have worked for generations as his own. There might well be a period in which he had no idea where exactly his new holding would be. In 1813 a farmer in Gravenhurst (Bedfordshire) explained that he had drained four or five acres in the open fields, 'but as an enclosure was in agitation, he apprehended he should loose the ground before he received any benefit'.[53] One of the duties of the commissioners appointed to oversee the enclosure was to organise farming throughout the enclosure period, which could well take several years. They would be responsible for buying seed, allotting land, paying compensation and establishing a final date for the changeover. Only then would their task be completed.[54] The costs of the whole process could seem very great, and were certainly only worthwhile when likely returns were high. In some cases land was sold to defray expenses resulting in a more diverse ownership pattern in the parish. Most landowners however were more interested in consolidating their power and so paid from their reserves. The cost to Lord Walsingham, by far the largest owner in the 2,265-acre parish of Tottington (Norfolk) was £500 to the solicitor, £200 for making fences and £50 for roads.[55] It has been calculated that the national expenditure on Parliamentary enclosure was somewhere between 13 and 30 million pounds – an enormous sum for something that only affected about a quarter of the land area of England and Wales.[56]

There were significant differences in the effect of enclosure on the heavy clays and the light chalks. Early enclosure on the clays, as we have seen, was mainly for pasture. However, as grain prices rose this land could be converted back to arable, and individual ownership provided more scope for the drainage of the new fields. In the open fields ridge and furrow had been the usual method, and ridging in some form continued in use in some enclosed fields. However, it gradually lost favour and during the eighteenth century began to be replaced by various forms of underdraining.[57] By 1769 the Marquis of Rockingham at Wentworth had replaced ridge and furrow drainage 'a practice highly destructive of profit and detestable to the eye', with deep ditches connected to covered drains full of stones.[58] The extent of drainage is described in the county *General Views* and was certainly regarded as a valuable improvement. As well as the digging of ditches and straightening of water courses it usually involved the creation of drains (described as 'hollow drains') into which stones and bushes were thrown, the drain was then covered and expected to remain serviceable for up to 30 years. The *General Views* suggest that underdrainage around 1800, when grain prices were at their highest was mainly confined to the areas of its original development in the heavy lands of the arable east through Essex, Suffolk, and parts of Norfolk, Cambridgeshire and Hertfordshire. However, scattered examples were to be found, particularly in south Derbyshire and the Severn valley in Gloucestershire.[59] In Cornwall the importance of draining was said to be 'long understood',[60] while in Cheshire it was recognised that the more general adoption of hollow drainage would 'constitute undoubtably one of the most important and valuable improvements in modern agriculture'.[61] Of course, the reporters for the *General Views* tended to confine their investigations to the gentleman farmers, but as drainage was admitted to be an expensive business, limited to the 'opulent landlord; a tenant on a short lease has no encouragement to undertake it',[62] it may well be that they were the only ones who could afford it. However, Suffolk evidence would suggest that here it was small farmers and tenants who undertook these improvements. Indeed, in many parts of southern England the heavy lands were dominated by small farmers and owners.[63] Glyde, writing of Suffolk in 1856 reported that 'draining has been effected at enormous outlay, but from the great increase in production no one questions the propriety of the expenditure'. The advantage was that its immediate results justified the expense and the benefits could be seen in the first crop. Glyde believed that in Suffolk wheat yields had increased by one third between 1750 and 1830.[64]

Tile drainage began to replace bushes in the early nineteenth century, but although longer lasting this was even more expensive. Earthenware horseshoe shaped tiles which were placed on flat tiles to form a tunnel were introduced from Staffordshire to Cumberland in 1819 by Sir James Graham of Netherby who was also one of the first landowners to build a tile works on his estate.[65] Between 1822 and 1846 4,800 acres of the Netherby estate were drained under the supervision of Sir John Graham's agent, John Yule, but mostly jointly financed by the landlord and tenant.[66] The main period of tile drainage was, as we shall see, not until after 1840.

From its outset, enclosure on light land was mainly for arable, and here marling was likely to be important (Figure 16). The spreading of a chalky-clayey subsoil at a rate of anything up to 75 loads per acre was usually the tenant's responsibility and he might be expected to complete the marling of the entire farm within the first five years of his tenancy. Marling was regarded by Arthur Young as an essential element of the improved Norfolk husbandry and the distribution of marl pits across the light lands of East Anglia is an indication of the amount of effort that went into this operation. Again the extent of marling was commented upon by the reporters for the *General Views* and seems to have been carried out wherever there was a suitable subsoil. Most of the improvements in Lancashire were said to owe their origin to marl[67] and the heathy lands around Christchurch (Hampshire), were marled at a rate of about 40 tons an acre. The results were 'truly astonishing. It gives that consistence to the soil so much required in these lands.'[68]

Where marl was not available and the soil was naturally heavier, chalk was either spread untreated or burnt in limekilns before spreading on the land. Sir Thomas Dundas' agent wrote in 1809 to his employer commenting on the farming methods on his experimental farm at his Marske (Cleveland) estate. 'Many have criticised the amount of lime put on, but they are now

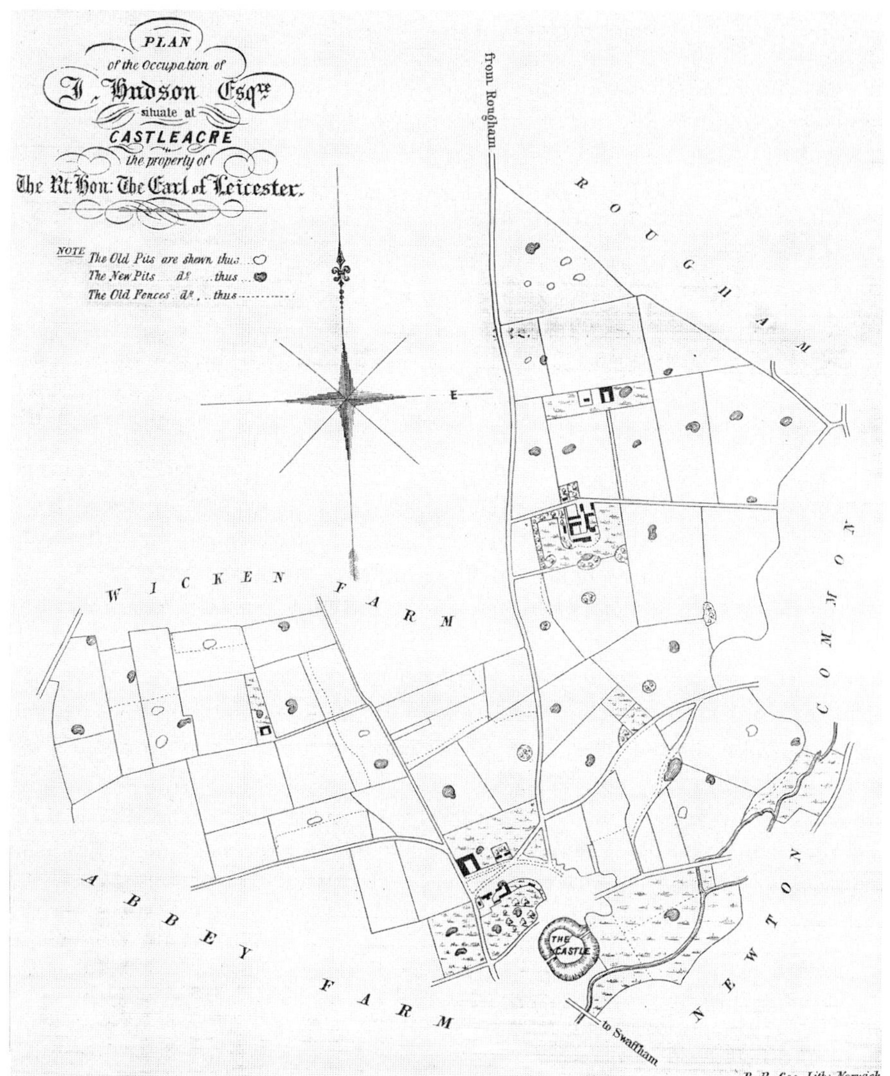

FIGURE 16.
Plan of John Hudson's farm at Castle Acre (Norfolk). This plan, published in Bacon's *Norfolk Agriculture* in 1843 shows a well-laid out farm with farm buildings at the centre of the farm and marl pits in nearly every field.

silenced.'[69] Later, in 1813 he wrote, 'When the tenants are assembled on rent day they will be told how much lime and manure they must put on fallows. They will be allowed to claim back the cost of lime if they can produce the receipts.'[70] In Hertfordshire 60 loads of chalk to the acre was often spread from pits that could be dug down ten feet before they reached the chalk.[71]

Landscape change of the period of agricultural improvement must not only be seen in terms of field boundaries and the creation of new farms, but also in the alteration of the very character of the soils themselves. There was a significant reduction in water-logged land and an improvement in the quality of light and acidic soils. While it was primarily the landlord who was responsible for the initial re-organisation of the fields and farms, it was the tenant who undertook the equally important and often expensive work of creating a productive soilscape within which to work. An example of a 'landscape of improvement' on a small scale created almost entirely by the tenant is that at Grenstein Farm, Mileham (Norfolk) on the Holkham estate. The initial creation of 200-acre farm from outlying parts of other holdings and 40 acres of bog and common followed an enclosure of 1814. However, it was the tenant who re-arranged the fields within the farm, straightened the stream and drained the bog. He also marked the farm by digging marl pits in nearly every field. The work of reclamation was said to have cost the tenant £500.[72]

The new farming practices and their rotations were suited to the lighter soils. As early as 1701, Richard Morden wrote of the chalky belt of land between Royston and Newmarket that sainfoin 'does wonderfully enrich the Dry and Barren grounds of that county'. Defoe saw the same results on the Downs of Hampshire, Wiltshire and Dorset.[73] It was not only the fact that the fields were open which had held up the introduction of fodder crops in them, but the fact that during the winter the fields were opened up for sheep to graze on the stubbles (the so-called fold cource system). In the past this had been seen as a good way of manuring the land, but as ever heavier crops of grain were aimed at, more stock needed to be kept than could be supported by the stubble. Heavier crops would mean higher rents and so there was an incentive for the landlord to bring the old fold course system to an end and replace it with single-tenancy consolidated farms. In fact in some cases the old rules had been broken and tenants were growing turnips in small fenced-off closes in the open fields. Witnesses in a disputed case at Thetford (Norfolk) in 1724 claimed that some occupiers of the field had been sowing turnips for 25 years and shepherds had kept the sheep off them 'until last year when the sheep ate the defendant's turnips'.[74] A similar undated case at nearby Ashill involved the growing of turnips in an open field where fold-course rights existed. Here 'Sir Henry Bedinfield's descendants and daughters who lived near the parish and were acquainted with the customs of the said manor did for more than 40 years acquiesce and no way oppose the landowners inclosing and sowing the said pastures with turnips'.[75] Test cases such as this were frequently brought in the final days of the fold-course system and show that, with or without enclosure, changes had already been taking place. The Napoleonic Wars saw the final enclosure of these dry light lands and the creation of large ordered fields across the chalk downlands of southern England and the Wolds of the east. Owned as they were by some of the most publicity conscious landlords such as the Duke of Yarborough (Lincolnshire) and Thomas Coke (Norfolk) they were recognised as the centres of the new agriculture and the four-course system, relying on flocks of turnip-fed sheep and stall-fed cattle to keep up the fertility of the soil.

When the open fields had been enclosed, interest shifted to the wastes and commons, and here it took on a further significance for the increasingly powerful landowner-class. The commons were the only areas which had remained outside landlord influence and their enclosure emphasised a desire for prestige and order, and the link which the establishment saw between the two. It was often this rather than the profit motive which drove the gentry and aristocracy in their efforts to enlarge their estates.[76] It was a key aspect in the development of a capitalism which saw the landowner at the head of the system.[77] The commons had long been regarded as the resort of itinerants and lawless people and the bringing of these areas into a state of order was part of this process. In 1774, Thomas De Grey, managing the sandy Norfolk Breckland estates for his brother wrote, 'the great expense (of land reclamation) would but ill answer, unless there was real satisfaction in employing labourers and bringing forth a ragged dirty parish to a neatness of cultivation'[78] – a sentiment which drove British empire builders and missionaries in their efforts around the world. Arthur Young was only too aware of the 'many millions of acres' of wasteland still surviving in Britain in the 1770s and had extremely optimistic views of the possibilities these presented for increasing the area of cultivation. 'We are daily told of the emigration to the colonies depopulating us; why should not these emigrations be to the moors and heaths of Britain instead of the swamps and forests of America?'[79]

A great variety of land is covered by the general term, 'wastes', from the relatively small areas of greens and common to be found in mainly arable parishes to huge areas of heath, moor, mountain and fen to be found in lowland and upland areas of Britain (Figure 17). How extensive this wasteland was is very difficult to estimate but Gregory King calculated that in 1696 it made up 10 million acres of England. The authors of the *General Views* were asked to ascertain the area of waste in each county which they did with no doubt varying accuracy and came up with a figure of 6,179,590 acres for England, 1,628,307 for Wales and 22,026,121 for Scotland.[80] There are problems with these figures but by using them it appears that the distribution of waste bears a simple relationship to physical geography, the largest areas being found in the upland areas. Most survived in Scotland, where as much 95 per cent of Sutherland was still unenclosed with cultivation confined to the east coast and flat floors of the inland straths. Only in the small eastern lowland counties of Fife and West Lothian, and the western county of Renfrewshire, was less than 20 per cent of the land surface common. To the south, 450,000 acres of Northumberland was regarded as mountainous and 'improper for tillage', while 80 per cent of Westmorland, was described as waste. Of the Welsh counties, 70 per cent of mountainous Brecknockshire was waste, with between a third and a half of Cardiganshire, and Carmarthenshire also unenclosed. There were also lowland wastes. A third of Cambridgeshire was open fen and common with Peterborough Fen covering between 6,000 and 7,000 acres. Peat bogs and sea sand in Cheshire accounted for 60,000 acres and Charnwood Forest in Leicestershire covered 16,000 acres. Away from this area, if the statistics are to be believed, there were very few large commons in Leicestershire, the total commons area being only 5 per cent of the county. Much of the 10 per cent of Somerset which was unreclaimed would have been on Exmoor and in the Somerset Levels, although work there had already begun to drain the 512,000 acres of Sedgemoor at the cost of £30,000.[81] The only counties with little (under 10 per cent) left to enclose were in the relatively flat and

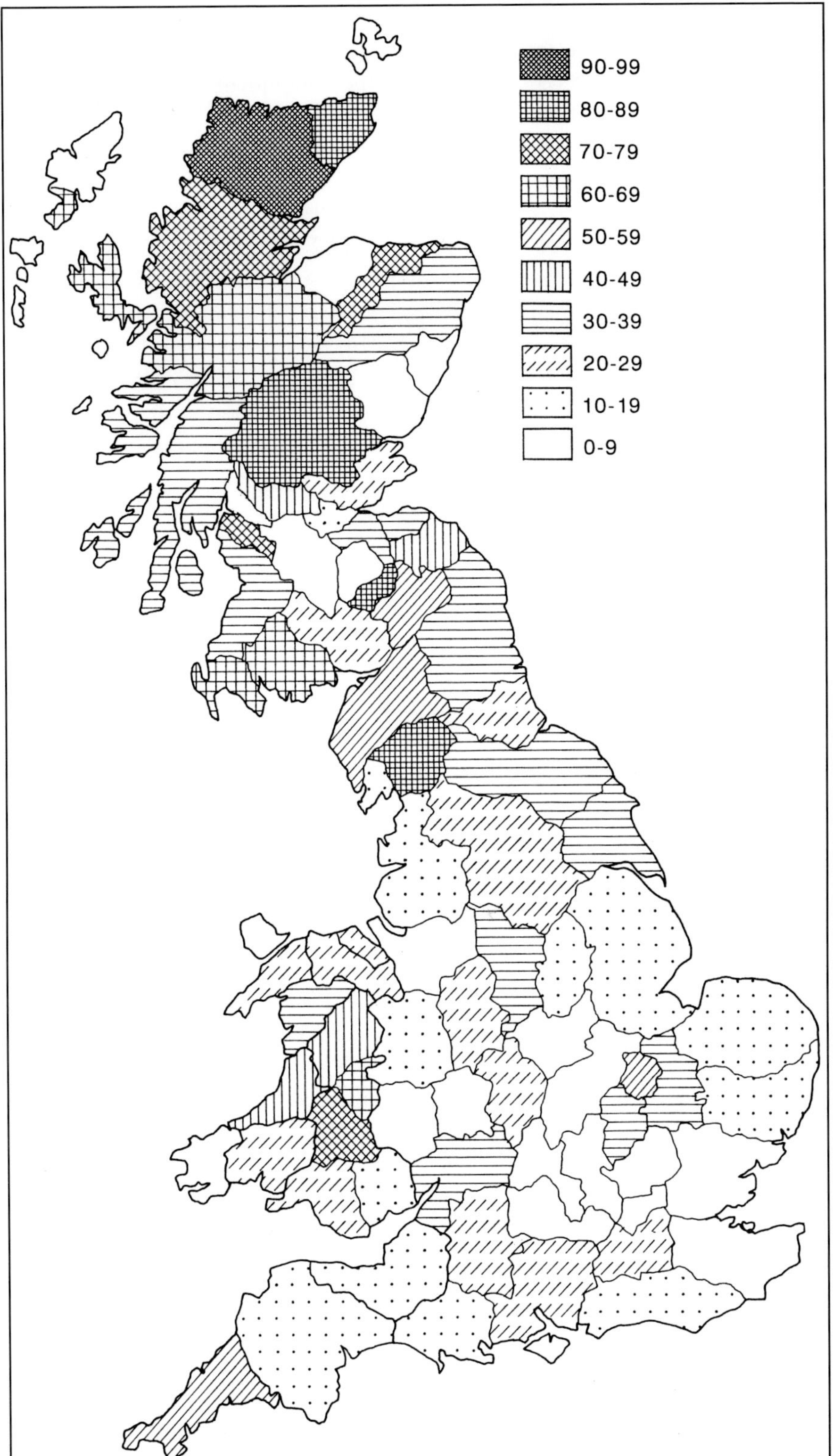

FIGURE 17.
Distribution of waste land in Britain as a percentage of the county total, calculated by Arthur Young in the 1790s.
PHILLIP JUDGE

fertile counties of East Anglia, the south-east, parts of the midlands, Cheshire, Herefordshire and Worcestershire.

With the outbreak of war in 1796, and the consequent rise in grain prices, interest in reclamation rose. The conquest of waste and the conquest of France became synonymous. As Sir John Sinclair wrote in 1803, 'Let us not be satisfied with the liberation of Egypt or the subjugation of Malta, but let us subdue Finchley Common; let us conquer Hounslow Heath, let us compel Epping Forest to submit to the yoke of improvement.'[82] Epping was only saved after a major legal battle and the passing of the Epping Forest Act in 1878. As a result of the efforts of nineteenth-century enclosers the amount of open waste in England had dropped to 383,407 acres by 1873. Virtually all the lowland waste had gone and the percentage of the total land surface of England so defined had gone down from about 21.3 per cent in 1800 to 6.4 per cent in 1873, although the two sets of returns from which these figures are calculated are not entirely compatible.[83]

The enclosure of wasteland in general can be divided into several categories. Firstly there was the enclosure of the greens and commons which had played such an important part in the traditional farming systems. The commons were the property of the lord of the manor and those with commoning rights were entitled to graze a certain number of animals there. It has been suggested that one of the reasons for early enclosure of the arable was because of pressure on the commons and the need to find additional grazing.[84] While enclosure of the open fields could frequently be carried through by agreement, especially when few landowners were involved, that of the commons could be a different matter and usually involved an enclosure act. This was because it was not only farmers who had rights on the commons, but also cottagers, for whom the common could be an important source of fuel. Wild fowling and peat cutting could be profitable occupations on the wetter lands, and although there were attempts to make good some of these losses in the form of fuel allotments, others were irreplaceable. Any rights on the commons the poor might have had were not so much manorial, as ones which had grown up as a result of the poor laws and attempts to keep rates down by allowing the poor such concessions as fuel gathering.[85] Much has been written about the fate of the cottagers when the commons were enclosed but what perhaps is most significant about the Parliamentary system of enclosure was the fact that cottagers' claims were largely accepted. However, it 'may be regarded as a landmark in the recognition of the rights of small men ... but ... the landed class taken as a whole, and Parliament as its legislative body, failed to ensure that the essential modernisation of a large part of English agriculture did not leave in its wake a trail of dispossessed'.[86] Usually written proof of commoning rights was required but on rare occasions attempts were made to compensate in instances where this was not forthcoming. Mr Algur, a commissioner working widely in Norfolk did not require proof of the legality of the claims of the poor, but 'if it has been considered a right of common is allotted accordingly'. However in Norfolk, as elsewhere, there were plenty of examples where the poor suffered the loss of rights, particularly cow-keeping, which had provided an important subsidiary income for many.[87]

Unlike earlier enclosures, the commons and greens were taken into cultivation during the period of high grain prices to increase the output of cereals. Many of them were the poorer land in the parish and therefore could only be profitably cropped when wheat prices were exceptionally high, as they were during the years of the Napoleonic Wars when Parliamentary acts for the enclosure of commons reached a peak. Where enclosure was delayed until the end of the war, the costs could be prohibitive. The Holkham estate initiated the enclosure of the common land in Longham (Norfolk) in 1815, and whilst the initial enclosure was the responsibility of the landlord, the improvement of the soil by marling and ploughing was the responsibility of the tenant. As grain prices fell at the end of the war, the cost was uneconomic. The tenant, described as 'zealous' and 'industrious' was said to be 'heart-broken by his present undertaking' and it was only as a result of support from the landlord that the reclamation was completed.[88]

There were the great heaths and warrens which made up a large proportion of many light-land parishes where rabbit warrens and extensive sheep grazing were seen as the most economic use of land, so long as grain prices were low. The fact that turnip husbandry was particularly suited to light land made the reclamation of these soils possible, while allowing at the same time for the keeping of larger flocks of sheep than before. As Thomas Davis wrote of Wiltshire in the years of high grain prices, the principal purpose of keeping sheep is undoubtedly the dung of the sheepfold.[89] As we have seen, much of the open wolds of Lincolnshire, and Yorkshire as well as the Cotswolds was brought into cultivation at this time, and this involved the enclosure of both open field and heath. Not only was previous heath land enclosed but new farms had to be built by the landlord, resulting in a regimented and planned landscape of fields and buildings. But from this stage on, reclamation was the responsibility of the tenant. Not only did the internal fences of the farm have to planted and maintained, but the land needed heavily marling, ploughing and manuring. It could be several years before it was brought into a fertile enough condition for a grain crop to be taken. This was an expensive business and tenants prepared to risk the capital needed could be difficult to find.

Some of the poorest light soils to be brought into cultivation at this time were the sandy wastes of Norfolk and Suffolk Breckland. Much of the area was in the hands of large estates which, as farming profits began to rise, looked for ways of bringing their lands, which had been farmed as extensive sheep walk or let out as warrens, into cultivation. 'A great part of the land is capable of improvement', Thomas de Grey wrote optimistically to his brother in 1769 of some of the poorest soils on his 12,120-acre Norfolk estates. Unperturbed by the pessimistic view of Ralph Cauldwell, de Grey pursued a policy of enclosure, where possible by agreement, but if necessary through a Parliamentary act.[90] Traditionally Breckland had been divided into commonland, where the lord of the manor sometimes had sole right to graze his sheep, and half-year land which was cultivated for part of the year and open for the lord's sheep for the rest. The farms were large, often over 500 acres. The enclosure of the land was only the first phase of improvement. The tenants of the newly arranged farms were expected to continue the work. On the very poor soils of Stanford, the new farms were let in 1780 at the low rent of four shillings an acre. The tenant was to bring 100 acres of the newly enclosed heath into cultivation every year. This would involve heavy marling of the soil. Amounts stipulated in leases were about 75 loads per acre. This labour-intensive work was difficult to enforce. Tenants were convinced that it was the change in the soil chemistry which these heavy applications brought about that caused abortion amongst their ewes. They knew that, even in the years of high grain prices, it was sheep that were really the mainstay of Breckland farming. In spite of the removal of commons and half-year land, much of the area remained heath and rabbits remained an important element in the region's economy.[91] Enclosure alone could not force improvement on these very sandy soils.

As well as the lowland heaths, enclosure also penetrated the moorlands. Twenty acts covering parts of the North York Moors were passed before the main push into less hospitable regions after 1793 and the optimism which drove on these enclosures is difficult to understand. Most acts referred to the desire to 'improve' land and the incentive of increased rents on reclaimed land was certainly a factor. The results can be seen at Duncombe and Pickering. The careful spacing of farms on Pickering High Moor and Muffles Rigg, Cropton suggests that reclamation of the intervening areas was the eventual aim. Certainly some over-ambitious schemes were being put forward. Secondary considerations may well have been the regularising of the tithe situation, which was difficult to establish with flocks wandering across open moor covering several parishes, as well as the securing of rights over game shooting. One solution to the problem of the expense of enclosure was the unusual recourse to 'permissive enclosure' which did not limit the landowners to a specific time scale for the erection of fences. Some of these long-term projects were eventually more successful than those immediately following an act, creating grid-iron patterns of fields with a new centrally placed farm.[92]

Equally formidable were challenges presented by Dartmoor, much of it the property of the Duchy of Cornwall. Enthusiasm for improvement, inspired by the Prince of Wales, began in the 1780s and led to the enclosure of about 14,000 acres. Much of the effort was centred on Tor Royal and Princes Hall where Thomas Tyrwhitt founded Princetown village and built cottages. The work involved in breaking up the moorland proved extremely labour intensive and during the Napoleonic Wars, Tyrwhitt offered Princetown to the government for housing French prisoners of war who could then be put to work on the land. Finally the project of reclamation was abandoned and the moor has remained open common with rights of pasturage divided amongst neighbouring parishes.[93] New holdings were also created on Bodmin Moor by enclosure, often in remote and exposed positions. Many are now deserted as the struggle to keep them productive has proved too great.[94]

Commons were often the wettest land in the parish and here the poor probably had the most to lose, with the complete disruption of a way of life in which the exploitation of wildfowl played a part. At Martin Mere (Lancashire) decoys had allowed the taking of wildfowl, and fish were also caught. Reeds, rushes and marsh hay were harvested and peat dried. The area also provided summer grazing.[95] After enclosure, an administrative system had to be set in place to keep the drains of a wet area working and Parliamentary acts were the mechanism normally used. Perhaps not surprisingly it is in these areas that rioting was most frequent. The rent on Hatfield Chase (Yorkshire) was raised from sixpence to ten shillings an acre as a result of drainage, and the work met with violent resistence from the inhabitants.[96] On Otmoor (Oxfordshire) enclosure and drainage was first proposed in 1787 and resulted in trouble; bridges and hedges were damaged on and off until 1835.[97] On Sedgemoor in Somerset the commoning rights of peat digging, fishing, fowling, reed cutting and the keeping of geese for their feathers all came to an end with enclosure, but not without the opposition of the commoners who mobbed and burnt effigies of the promoters of the bills.[98] Much of this work was inspired by Richard Locke of Pillmouth Farm, Burnham, who, having improved the meadows of the coastal clays by better surface drainage and manuring, turned his attention in 1769 to the peat moors themselves. He bought a small estate in Churchland Moors where he began work and then wrote pamphlets and articles in the *Bath and West of England Society Journal* to convince others of the profits to be made. He claimed to have had the satisfaction of knowing 'that the neighbourhood is two millions the richer' as a result of his encouragement for the enclosing of 45,000 acres of peat.[99]

In the Hull valley wild fowling, swanning and fishing as well as the collecting of brushwood, thatching materials and fuel were all important and disputes arose over the use of the land for summer grazing before the nesting birds had left.[100] However, this aspect was never dwelt upon by the improvers who were merely interested in the increase in rent that might result from their new farms. Arthur Young described the drainage of 40,000 acres to the east of the river Hull which was carried out after an enclosure act in the 1760s. As a result good crops of oats and rape, which was fed off for sheep, were grown.[101]

Enclosure acts only provided an administration responsible for the main drains. There was also a need for Internal Drainage Boards, and the earliest of these was set up at Haddenham, Cambridgeshire in 1727.[102] As the techniques of drainage changed little from the middle ages until the introduction of steam power, the pace of activity was governed entirely by economics. As prices, firstly for livestock and then for grain began to rise after 1750, the speed of activity accelerated, with more land being reclaimed in the 100 years after 1750 than in all previous centuries. As well as the major undertakings described above, the great mosses of Lancashire, the carrs of north Shropshire and the fens and marshes around the Wash and Kent coast were all the subjects of drainage, often preceded by enclosure acts, although the successful completion of many of these schemes had to await the arrival of steam power later

FIGURE 18.
Land drainage: a map to show the reclamation of Kinnersley Moss (Shropshire). It is worth noting the number of place-names including the word 'moor'. The arrows on the boundaries show the direction flow of water in the drainage ditches.

PHILLIP JUDGE

in the century. In areas controlled entirely by one landowner, there might be no need for an act. The Marquis of Stafford drained and divided into fields 1,200 acres of black peat centred on Sydney Farm in Kinnersley and Crudgington as part of his major land re-organisation of his estates around Lilleshall in the years before 1820 (Figure 18).[103]

All this activity was extremely expensive and rarely produced an economic return for the landlord. As Mr Jorrocks commented in Surtees' *Hillingdon Hall* 'Landowning is werry poor trade'. Whilst very wealthy landowners such as the Marquis of Stafford could recycle their industrial wealth into agriculture, others had to borrow money, often from insurance companies. 'The mortgage books of the Equitable looked like a roll-call of the British peerage'. By 1838, the Equitable had lent £200,000 to Sir James Graham at Netherby at 3.5 per cent for new buildings, drainage, roads and bridges.[104] However, as was noted in the previous chapter, 'at the bottom it was not only the pursuit of profit that informed the agricultural enterprise of a great agricultural estate. Instead, what moved it was a traditional hierarchical society.'[105] Whether this money was well spent is a different question.

The landscapes created by the improvements of this period of widespread change are familiar to all. Whether enclosure was by agreement or parliamentary act, the new fields were regular and surrounded either by stone walls or hawthorn hedges. In good conditions, hedges grew fast and within seven years all evidence of the open fields had been obliterated.[106] In the wetlands, it was the drainage ditches which formed the new boundaries. The roadways were also straight, often with wide verges, and new farmsteads were built out in the fields. This regimented landscape could be more varied where physical features such as rivers, valleys or upland imposed itself and fields too could show some individuality where enclosure was a slower process over a longer period. This can be seen clearly on the Somerset Levels where the fields on the older settled lands on the clay belt are larger (20–40 acres) than those in areas drained after 1770 (Figure 19).

Here, where there were large numbers of claimants to the land, as in the

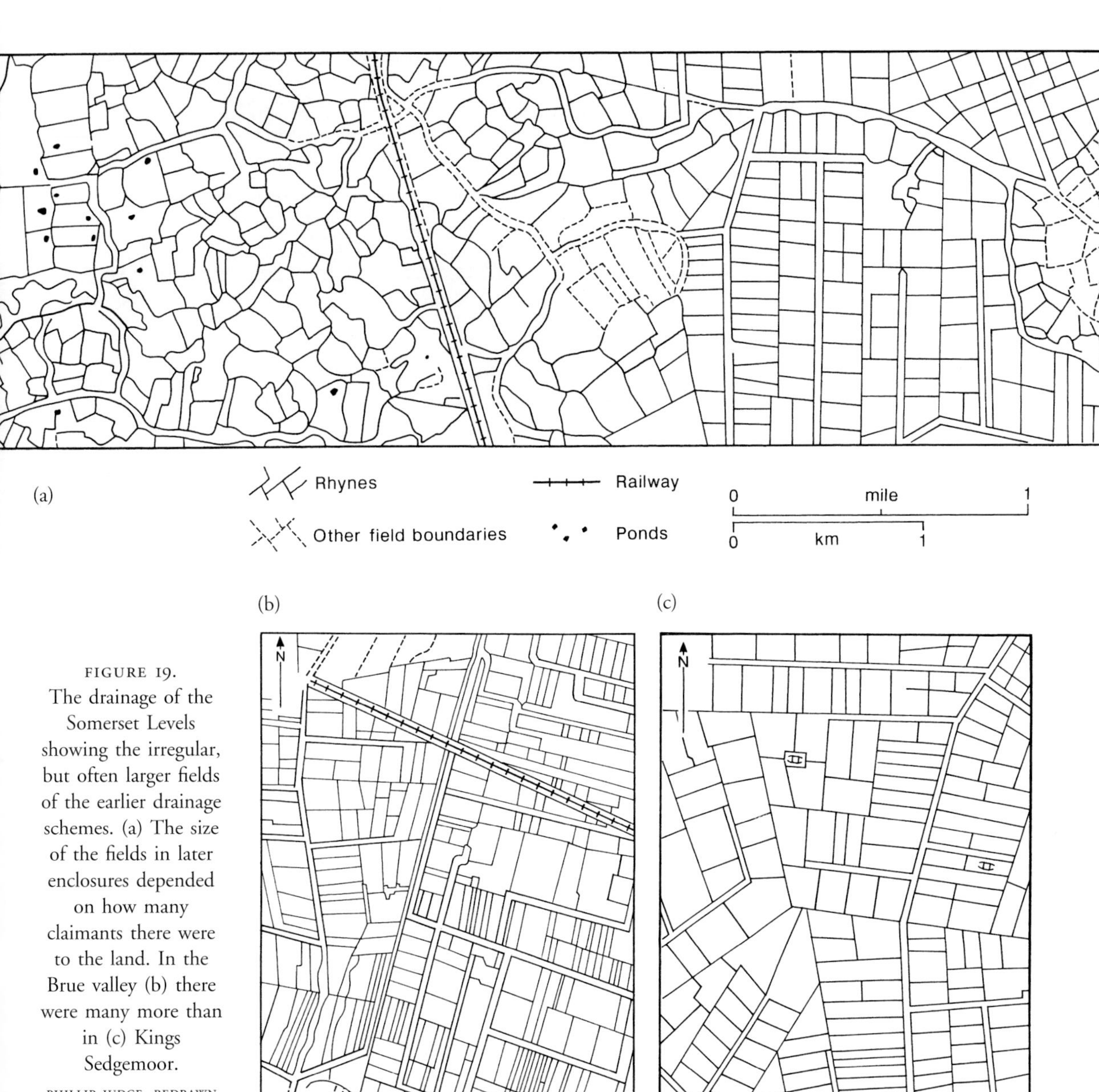

FIGURE 19.
The drainage of the Somerset Levels showing the irregular, but often larger fields of the earlier drainage schemes. (a) The size of the fields in later enclosures depended on how many claimants there were to the land. In the Brue valley (b) there were many more than in (c) Kings Sedgemoor.

PHILLIP JUDGE, REDRAWN FROM WILLIAMS (1970)

Brue valley, some fields could be as small as five acres. On Kings Sedgemoor in contrast, there were fewer successful claimants and fields ranged between 10 and 15 acres. All these fields are in sharp contrast to the irregular enclosures of the medieval reclamations. The area of Norfolk marshland around the Great Smeeth shows even greater variety. (Figure 20) Here, in the area west of Kings Lynn the early settlements were along the coast and surrounded by irregular fields. Gradual reclamation to the south into the marsh resulted in ever more regular fields intersected by droveways for cattle to be taken to the remaining open marshland in the Smeeth, which remained until after 1794.[107] It was finally drained and divided into regular fields during the Napoleonic Wars.

The pace of change in Wales and Scotland was somewhat different to that in England. Infertile soils and distance from markets, hampered by poor communications meant that by the standards of the improvers, Welsh agriculture was seen as strikingly backward in 1750. Farms were still small, averaging between 30 and 60 acres, although some were larger in the 'English' areas such as south Pembrokeshire. In spite of a certain amount of exchange and consolidation of land, many were fragmented and intermixed. A small minority of landowners were encouraging the new farming methods by the early eighteenth century. In north-east Wales in particular Sir John Trevor on his estates near Wrexham, Sir Richard Myddelton and the steward of Joshua Edisbury at Erthig were all trying the new artificial grasses and clovers. Turnips were also being grown by the 1730s with twenty wethers being bought to Wynstay 'for feeding on turnips' in 1743. Elsewhere there was some evidence of change across north Wales and a general spirit of improvement was said to prevail in Anglesey. In south Wales, too there were some 'spirited improvers'. Clover was said to have been introduced into Glamorgan in the 1680s where it was taken up by small yeoman farmers.[108]

By 1810 there had been a considerable amount of farm amalgamation and Walter Davies could write 'In the beginning of the eighteenth century, farms were much smaller than they are at present. Since that time, the practice of reducing three or four, or in some instances, nine or ten tenements into one, has become prevalent'. By the 1850s farms were averaging between 36 and 188 acres in the various counties of the principality.[109] By the 1840s farms were twice the size they had been in the seventeenth century. One reason for this was enclosure. Much of the lowland across the coastal plains of south Wales had been enclosed by 1640, but open arable remained in Pembrokeshire, coastal Cardigan and the eastern vales and plateaus of Montgomeryshire until the 1790s. So also did much of the high moorland and wet lowlands. In Flintshire some marshlands had been drained and a beginning had been made in the lead-mining districts bordering Cheshire. More distant from English influence was Anglesey where, too, there had been some enclosure and drainage of Malldraeth Marsh before 1800.[110] Indeed as late as 1795 a third of the total acreage of the country was unenclosed. The years of the Napoleonic Wars saw the enclosure of most of the remaining open arable as well as 200,000 acres of the wastes and common, with almost the whole of Flintshire enclosed by 1815.[111] The largest area to be enclosed by a single act was 40,000 acres of Fforest Fawr in Breconshire but several others covered more than 20,000. Most of this land was then added to existing farms and few new ones were created. While the upland economy was based on sheep and oats, more mixed systems were to be found in the lowlands. However, the small size of many farms and the isolation in which many operated, meant that traditional subsistence methods lasted longer in Wales than in much of the rest of the United Kingdom. The prevalence of impoverished small estates let to small tenants resulted in a lack of capital for investment and meant that the lifestyle of the farmer differed little from that of the landless labourers.

FIGURE 20. Map to show the gradual draining of Marshland Smeeth (Norfolk). The earliest fields are the smallest and gradually reclamation penetrated deeper into the marsh, with the drove roads surviving into the nineteenth century.
NORFOLK MUSEUMS AND ARCHAEOLOGY SERVICE

Scotland is perhaps the area where change was most dramatic in the period 1750–1815. A largely feudal society where land was held jointly by a township of tenant farmers who paid much of their rent in kind and in services, was transformed into one in which farms were held in severalty with land held under leases and rent paid in money. Farming became a commercial rather than subsistence occupation. The '45 is often seen as the moment when farming methods from the south really found root in Scotland, but change had already begun before Culloden, particularly on the southern estates and amongst those lairds who had travelled south to the Stuart court and wished to increase their incomes to pay for the more extravagant lifestyle of which they wished to be part. By 1700 the demands of the southern markets had meant that livestock production in the borders was becoming commercialised and large cattle and sheep farms were being created there, resulting in the sort of population displacement which was typical of the Highland Clearances a century later. The house of Argyll was one of the first to see a solution to its financial problems in the reorganisation of its estates. The second Duke drastically altered the whole basis of land tenure on much of his island and mainland estate, which extended across 500 square miles. On the island of Tiree land was allocated, not on the basis of kinship but on the ability of the tenants to pay rent and as a result rents doubled between 1703 and 1736. In 1737 the old system of 'tacksmen' who were middlemen between the laird and his tenants and were usually members of a junior branch of the family, were abolished.[112] Instead the land was let directly to the tenants on long leases and by 1798 much of Kintyre was let in individual small farms.[113] However these changes were no means universal. In 1770 half of Tiree was still held by 14 large farmers whilst population increase had meant that the rest was divided into 45 joint farms.[114] In the Argyll parish of Craignish, as elsewhere in the county there were still no leases and feudal services were exacted, only one farm was enclosed and 'in proper order of improvement', and the people had 'neither the skill or the encouragement to attempt material change'.[115] Roys' map of Scotland, surveyed between 1752 and 1754, shows patches of enclosed land around the lairds' great house, but most of the rest of the farmland in open strips.

The real period for change was after 1750 with many landlords embarking on the improvement of their estates. The Roxburghe estate in the borders was creating new farms and looking for tenants for them in the 1760s. The Duke of Roxburghe spent most of his time in London and wrote to his agent at the time, 'I am glad Mr Scott has paid his rent – there is a great advantage in having substantial tenants of his skill in husbandry and intention to improve the land.' A later letter refers to Mr Scott's intention to enclose 200 acres for which the estate would take responsibility so long as Mr Scott paid the 5 per cent interest 'as agreed'. As in England we find that although the initial impetus for change might come from the estate, it was the tenants who were often responsible for the implementation of the work. The Duke was also encouraging improvements on his home farm. He wrote in 1758, 'I am very sorry to hear that your sheep will not eat turnips; for if they would, I think it

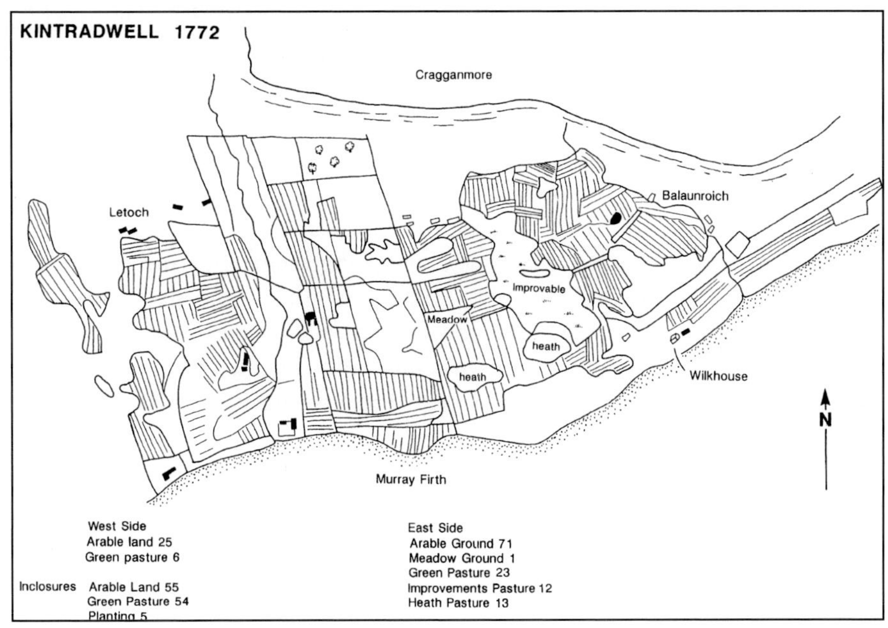

FIGURE 21. Kintradwell (Sutherland) before and after enclosure. By 1772 some new fields were being laid out over the old rigs, but small townships were scattered across the area. By 1874 new fields had been created, the burn straightened and a single farm created.

PHILLIP JUDGE

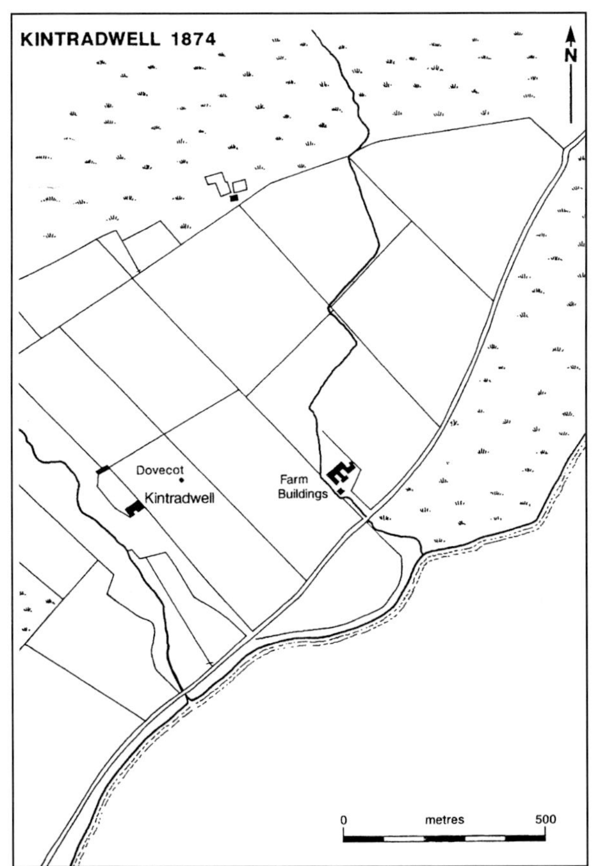

would turn to as good an advantage as in England.'[116] In fact turnips had been grown in the 1730s but on a small scale. They were still 'not generally grown' in the 1790s.[117]

The gradual changes introduced by James Wright in Menstrie Glen, near Stirling, must be typical of those of many a small, often unknown land owner in Scotland. The area was mainly a sheep walk at the end of the middle ages, but as population rose in the seventeenth century, it was transformed into an area of communal farms, being split up as more land was taken into cultivation, the earlier farms being in the most favourable positions. From 1750 improvements were under way. Drainage and liming began, and potatoes and improved grasses planted, but at first there was no change in the management and layout of farms. This began in the 1760s with the building of boundary walls, the creation of sheep walks and the removal of tenants. Sheep became increasingly important, although some crops continued to be grown on the lower ground. The number of farms was slowly reduced from twenty in 1750 to four by the early nineteenth century.[118]

Nearly all enclosure activity in Scotland was accompanied by the need to drain. The *General Views* for the country all contain discussion on the best methods of draining and of coping with both lowland and highland accumulations of peat. The much publicised activities of the Marquis of Stafford (who was also, through his wife, Duke of Sutherland) included the laying out of 36 farms on the lowland north-eastern coastal strip of Sutherland between 1800 and 1829 (Figure 21). The external boundaries of the farms, mostly between 150 and 200 acres, were laid out by the estate, but the tenant was responsible for the internal fences as agreed with the landlord. He also had to drain the land by straightening the burns, which were often utilised for driving a water-powered threshing machine, and digging drains, frequently huge structures, lined with Caithness flags. Land would have to be limed and planted with grasses for the first three years, before a rotation including cereals could be adopted. Because of the work of reclamation demanded of the tenant, very little rent was paid for the first few years.[119]

A highly publicised major reclamation scheme described in the *Statistical Account* of 1799 as 'the most considerable and significant improvement in Scotland' also put much of the responsibility for the work on the shoulders of the tenant.[120] It was undertaken by Lord Kames on Flanders Moss, just outside Stirling (Figure 22).

It differed from the Sutherland example, not only in the scale of work involved, but also in the type of tenant sought. Rather than the large scale capitalist farmers which were required in Sutherland, Lord Kames recruited small holders. Until the end of the seventeenth century, the area of lowland west of Stirling along the Forth and Teith rivers was an almost continual peat bog, used mainly for peat digging and wildfowling with limited grazing in the summer months. There had been some piecemeal enclosure along the fringes of the moss, but it was not until after Robert Maxwell's publication in 1743 on 'how to farm mosslands profitably', that any efforts at cultivation were tried. His highly impractical ideas of ploughing and seeding the peat were soon abandoned and instead the heather and the peat were burnt, the ashes then being ploughed in. This again proved unsuccessful in the long term. In 1766, Lord Kames, who wrote to a friend in 1763 that he congratulated himself on having chosen 'the noblest plan for the conduct of life – that of the improver',[121] began a more ambitious scheme which involved the removal of between five and six feet of peat to reveal a rich clay soil. The main problem was how to get rid of the peat. The easiest method seemed to be to float it to the sea, but the problem was the poor gradient of the rivers. To overcome this Lord Kames installed a water wheel to speed the flow of water across the flat valley floor so that the peats could simply be tipped into ditches, floated to the river Forth and then to the sea. The flow created by the wheel was said to have been capable of carrying as much peat as 20 men stationed 100 yards apart could throw into it. However, it was still a very expensive business, estimated at a prohibitive £12-£15 an acre. Because of this, he decided to lease the land to small holders who would pay no rent for the first seven years in

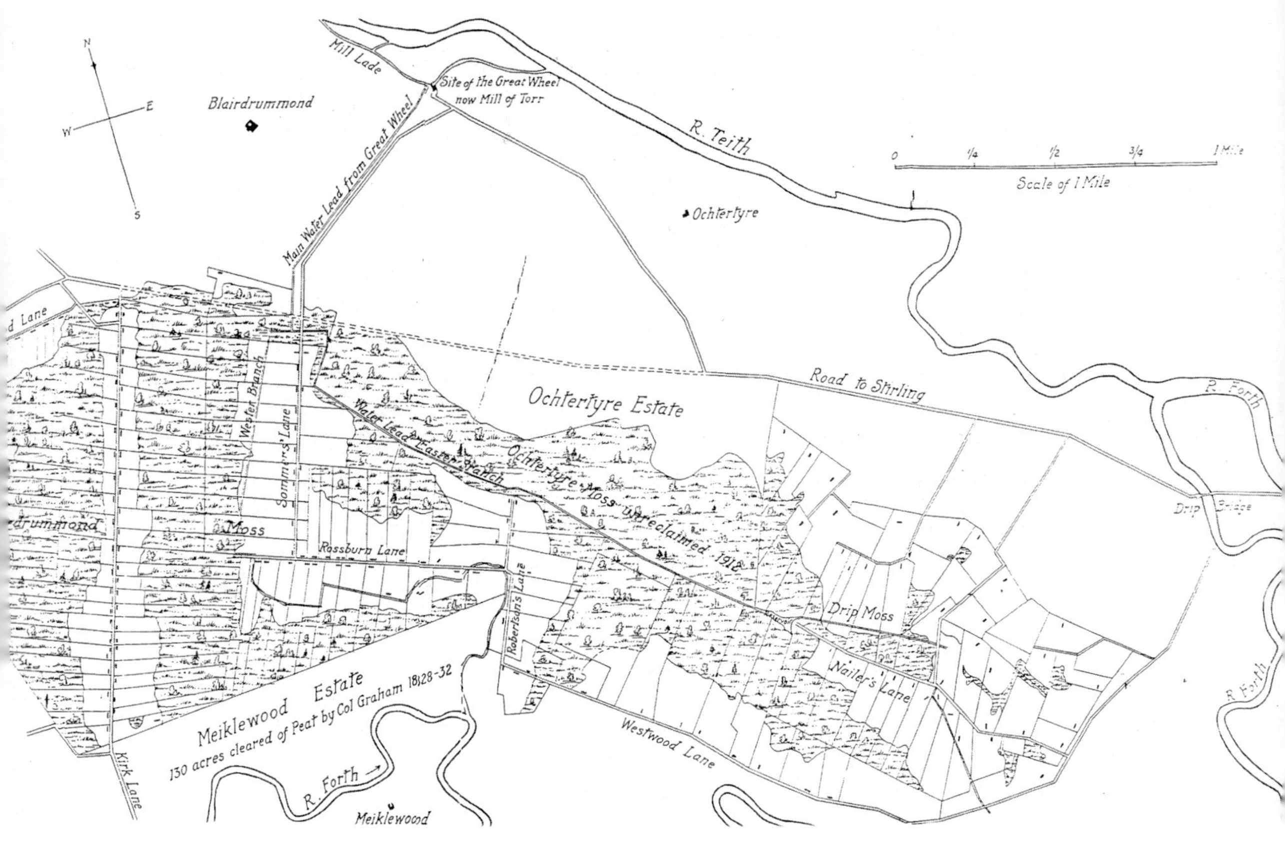

FIGURE 22.
The drainage of Flanders Moss. The map, reproduced in Cadell's *History of the Forth* shows the progress of reclamation by 1813. The small holders with their cottages along the roads were gradually nibbling back into the moss.

return for clearing the moss. Long narrow lots of ten acres at right angles to the channel were marked off. Leases were for 38 years. The landlord provided the timber for a house and enough food for the tenant while he was building it. By 1811, nearly 1500 acres had been reclaimed and 151 families supported.[122] The immediate result was not only the creation of an area of small mixed farms, but also the partial blocking and polluting of the mouth of the River Forth with rotting peat, destroying the salmon and oyster fisheries there.

Map evidence shows that in the early nineteenth century there were still striking contrasts to be found even across the fertile lowlands with crooked rigs lying next to a chequerboard of enclosed fields. By 1810, there had been considerable farm amalgamation and the reorganisation of most of the Scottish lowlands was complete by the time of the writing of the county *General Views* and the collecting of information for the *Statistical Accounts.* In Libberton (Lanarkshire), the minister described 'the ruins of demolished cottages ... in every corner because of the letting out of land in large farms'.[123] Galloway was an entirely enclosed county by 1813, although work had started much earlier with William Lord Daer enclosing land and building good farms from 1786. However, the state of improvement could vary greatly from estate to estate. On some there were still the 'same wretched plans of husbandry as had prevailed 40–50 years previously'.[124]

Some estimates suggest that over half of Scotland was in commonties (open land where the right to use them went with adjacent lands) in 1500 and they were crucial sources of peat, stone, turf and rough grazing for the neighbouring tenants. Legislation to allow their division had been passed in 1695, but it was not until the late eighteenth century that this really took place. In a sample of four lowland counties, 45 per cent of all recorded divisions between 1600 and 1914 took place between 1760 and 1815 and by 1870 virtually all had been formally brought into private ownership. This extraordinary level of activity is testimony to the rising profit levels of agriculture and the determination of landlords to secure sole ownership.[125]

The more regular the re-ordering of the landscape, the more pleasure it gave the powerful Whig landlords and as we have seen, it was in Scotland where the opportunities for the creation of extensive blocks of new landscapes were often greatest. The satisfaction which this gave is illustrated in a description of the newly drained Carse of Gowrie in Perthshire.

> The Carse is about 22 miles long and 3 miles wide along the banks of the Tay, almost a perfect level of the richest wheat lands ... the whole scenery an uninterrupted one of natural riches. Every quarter of a mile you meet a handsome farmhouse and farmyard ... twenty miles of the finest wheat, turnips, etc now growing ... this is a splendid, rich, happy and enlightened country. [126]

Within the boundaries of his new farm it was, as in England, up to the tenant to continue the work of reclamation and soil improvement. Many of the valley bottoms were very boggy and needed draining. Heaths were covered with peat which was simply burnt off. There was much discussion in the *General Views* about the efficacy of paring and burning and the general feeling was that the resulting arable needed careful farming if it were to remain fertile, although initially the crops might be good. In Berwickshire the ashes of the burnt peat were said to 'produce an extraordinary, but only temporary fertility'.[127] Fencing, dyking, liming, draining and clearing stones were all expensive and required men of capital to undertake the work. The main obstacle to improvement in Ross and Cromarty was said to be a lack of capital.[128]

The rise in prices that began in the 1760s and the gradual anglicisation of the Scottish nobility meant they needed to raise income from their estates to pay for increasing levels of conspicuous consumption. As a result we see a complete change in the farming system of most of the Scottish Lowlands within two generations. Almost nothing survives in the Scottish landscape to indicate the farming systems before the 'age of improvement' and during the Napoleonic War this drive for greater profits on the rising tide of agricultural prices accelerated in the Highland zone.

Change in the Highlands had begun with the work of the Commission for Annexed Estates, which ran 14 of the estates forfeited by their owners for supporting Charles Stuart and the Jacobite cause. By an act passed in 1752 the rents and profits of these estates were to be used solely for the 'purpose of civilising the inhabitants upon the said estates and other parts of the Highlands and Islands of Scotland'. In 1755 the first commissioners were appointed, many of them already active 'improvers' on their own estates. They began by commissioning surveys and thereafter there were annual reports on progress. Land was divided and enclosed and drained. New farming methods were encouraged with new crops, fertilisers and implements being introduced and livestock management improved. One of the largest estates taken over was that of Rannoch where a new village was built and farms laid out. Whilst this work of the commission was a brave and radical attempt at state control over land and social reform, much remained to be done when the estates were returned to their owners in the late 1760s.

Progress in the Highlands could be slow and expensive and the money for this activity often came from fortunes made in commerce, or down south. The activities of the Duke of Sutherland using wealth from his Staffordshire estates and the Duke of Bridgewater's canal has already been mentioned. By 1800 much of Kilmartin and Kilmichael Glassary in Argyll was the property of the Malcolms of Poltolloch. Neil Malcolm, who inherited in 1796, owned extensive plantations in Jamaica and spent much of his time in London where he was the main investor in the new West India Docks. On his estates he was responsible for the building of the Crinan Canal, draining the Crinan Moss and creating new farms. When this was complete much of the rest of the moss (3000 acres) was advertised to be let on 'long improving leases on liberal terms'. Applicants would have to bring 'satisfactory testaments of their being possessed of the skills and capital necessary to occupy the land'. The owner built a limekiln to provide fertiliser and also set up Experiment Farm, to provide an example for others to follow as well, as its name suggests, to carry out agricultural experiments. Careful records were kept of the farming activities.[129]

Some of the most famous northern improvements were made by the enthusiast for agricultural improvement, Sir John Sinclair, who was the initiator of the 21-volume *Statistical Account*, and responsible for the setting up of the Board of Agriculture during the Napoleonic Wars, becoming its first President. Sinclair owned much of the county of Caithness and he, along with his neighbours was responsible for ending the old communal farms and laying out large regular rectangular fields in which both turnips and artificial grasses were grown in rotation with cereals. Much of this was undertaken by the estate factor, Mr Henderson, mostly between the compiling of the *Statistical Accounts* in the 1780s and the *General View* of 1813. To achieve this, drainage of the flat land was often needed and much was expected of tenants who were given long leases to encourage them to invest. 'It is the judicious, diligent and persevering efforts of the husbandman which extends improvement and renders it beneficially lasting to the public at large.'[130]

It is important to remember that if it was large-scale and dramatic reclamations, mostly undertaken by the wealthier landowners and their capitalist tenants, that made their way into the pages of the books and journals, just as important were the gradual nibblings at the edge of hillsides and fens which went unreported, but which contributed to the great drop in the acreage of uncultivated land of Britain by the last quarter of the nineteenth century.

These landscape developments were dramatic, but how important were they really to increased output? Certainly much of the newly reclaimed common land was the poorest and so was only worth cultivating while prices were very high, as yields would never equal those on the more fertile soils. Some of the most ambitious enclosures were never even completed. However underdrainage and marling were significant improvements which were unlikely to have been carried out in open fields. We know that grain prices fell between 1690 and 1750 while population was already beginning to rise suggesting an increase in cereal production. We know that output doubled between 1750 and 1850.[131] While the new landscapes were not essential for these changes to take place, they certainly greatly assisted them.

The period of two generations up to 1830 saw an immense change in the landscape over many parts of Britain. Open fields and commons were enclosed, the newly reclaimed land was drained and the fields marled. Much of arable, open-field, midland England was enclosed for pastoral farming, while the light-land sheep walks and associated fields of the east became arable. New farming practices therefore resulted in a reversal in the agricultural regions of the country as heavy midland-clay wheatlands became cattle country and the light sheeplands grew cereals. Hedges and walls were laid out and roads created. However, there were other areas where little changed at all. The old pastoral counties of Devon and Cumbria and the claylands of Essex and Suffolk for instance retained into the twentieth century their small irregular fields which were laid out well before 1700. Underdrainage too had begun in East Anglia by the beginning of the eighteenth century. Elsewhere, the challenges of drainage and deep ploughing were simply too great for the Hanoverians. Here 'improvements' had to wait for the scientific knowledge and stronger machines of the Victorian age and it is these changes that will be considered in the next chapter.

CHAPTER THREE

Landscapes of 'Improvement' after 1830

Scientific improvement: high farming, 1830–1870

By the time agriculture was recovering from the post-Napoleonic War depression, advances in science and technology were allowing landowners and speculators to turn their attention to areas which previously would have been regarded as 'unimprovable'. Agriculture was entering the period described by contemporaries and historians alike as that of 'high farming'. The phrase was already widely understood by the late 1830s, when the reporters collecting information for the tithe files, compiled from 1837, were asked to note whether a parish 'was high or low farmed so as to affect materially the quantity of produce'.[1] With the founding of the Royal Agricultural Society of England, firstly as the English Agricultural Society, in 1838, the phrase came into common use and was used to describe a high input-high output system based on increased use of oilcake as an animal feed and imported and manufactured fertilisers to increase cereal and fodder yields.[2] The pages of the *Journal of the Royal Agricultural Society of England* (*JRASE*), first published in 1839, as well as of the much older *Transactions of the Highland and Agricultural Society of Scotland* (*THASS*) contained many articles on field trials and the relative merits of the various products on the market. David Low, professor of agriculture at Edinburgh University from 1831 to 1854, wrote several popular farming text books which emphasised the need for scientific understanding of soil chemistry and nutrition if the best use was to be made of these new products.[3] By 1860 modifications to the classic four-course rotation were being suggested. The need for more than a four-year gap between clover and turnip crops was recognised as land could become 'sick' of them. Sainfoin could replace clover and on heavy soils it could be alternated with peas and beans. Rape, tares and mangold wurzel could be substituted for turnips. A six-course of turnips, barley, clover (or other seeds), wheat, beans, wheat, was recommended as more suited to heavy land.[4] Elsewhere, tenants were asking permission to break the terms of their leases by growing two cereal crops in succession with the aid of artificial fertilisers.[5]

Machinery too began increasingly to appear on farms with steam engines taking over from water and horse power. Threshing machines began to be introduced in the 1780s in Scotland and by 1840 there was hardly a Scottish farm over 50 acres without one. Progress was slower in much of southern England and Wales, but after the 1830s uptake increased. Reaping machines began replacing hand mowing of the harvest from the 1850s and were one of the reasons for the removal of hedges in the second half of the nineteenth century. The Reverend Jessop in Norfolk remarked in 1887 on the 'small fields which were so picturesque and wasteful are gone or going'. The Cambridgeshire naturalist, Charles Babington wrote of south Cambridgeshire in 1860 that 'the modern agriculturalist' was ploughing up 'waste plots' and flattening tumuli and 'other interesting works of the ancient inhabitants' which he regarded as 'deformities'.[6] All these expensive developments were the farmers' responsibility and will be discussed further in chapter six. Suffice it to say that they accelerated the rate at which large-scale commercial operators came to dominate agricultural production. Alongside these high-profile innovations, the period of high farming saw the extension of earlier developments in farming practice to a far wider range of farms. What had previously been exceptional now became common-place.

Of more importance to the farming landscape was the development of improved systems of drainage and reclamation and Philip Pusey, the editor of the *JRASE* had no doubt that it was the duty of the land owner to undertake these and other land improvements. 'If the plain means of improvement and employment are still neglected, it will be impossible not to tax the owners of those needless deserts with supineness; and difficult to deny that they hold in their hands more of the country's surface than they are able to manage for their own good or that of the community.'[7]

As we have seen, the importance of field drainage was already appreciated. Some landowners such as the Duke of Portland attempted to improve on systems based on hollow drains filled with bush or stones, by setting up tile-drainage works on their estates. These early attempts produced hand-thrown flat or horse-shoe tiles which were very expensive and so were not widely used.

Of great significance was the publication in 1831 of the Stirlingshire mill-owner,

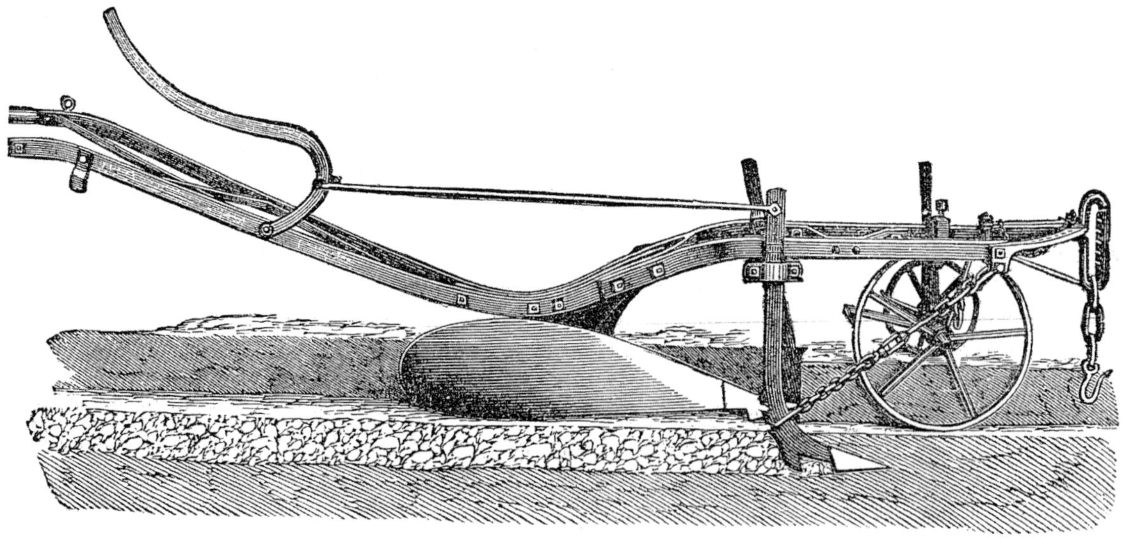

FIGURE 23.
A sub-soil plough. By the 1830s, the need to break up the subsoil to increase drainage was understood and there were several sub soil ploughs on the market.

John Smith of Deanston's book *Remarks on Thorough Draining and Deep Ploughing*, which had run through seven editions by 1844. It emphasised the importance of combining sub-soil ploughing (Figure 23) to break up the non-porous hard-pan layers, with tile drainage. Cylindrical pipes still had to be made by bending a sheet of clay over a wooden mandril but the 1840s saw the beginning of the manufacture of cylindrical tiles and by 1853 there were forty-five different pipe machines available. With a great reduction in the cost of pipes the laying of pipe drains became a far more viable economic proposition. The price could be halved to £3 an acre.[8] As well as being cheaper, the new drains lasted longer, it was estimated that they should last a good fifty years. Articles appeared in the *THASS* and between 1840 and 1855 about 10 per cent of the articles in the *JRASE* were on drainage.[9] Philip Pusey declared that 'Thorough draining is to the land as foundations are to a house.'[10] The 1850s and 1860s saw a rapid spread of drainage, encouraged by the availability of government-backed loans through loan companies, first set up in 1846 by the Public Moneys Drainage Act. Between 1847 and 1899 £5.499 million was borrowed for underdraining and altogether about £27.5 million was borrowed, half of which was probably spent on drainage and the other half on buildings. The result was the drainage of about 35 per cent of the land that could have benefited from it (although James Caird put the figure nearer 20 per cent[11]). The distribution of drainage activity was not evenly spread across the country with more being carried out in regions where little had taken place before, such as the west midlands and the north of England. Because of the expense, it was on the large estates where there was most activity and landlord enthusiasm was fired by suggestions that the profits to be made in the form of increased land values and rents could be between 10 and 25 per cent. These figures were based on the belief that output, particularly of wheat, could be increased by anything between 10 and 30 per cent.[12] A Norfolk farmer claimed that drainage was allowing turnips to be grown where none grew before and another wrote, 'I consider under-draining to be the very best piece of husbandry that can be done on cold, wet or springy ground, for without it you can grow neither quantity or quality of corn. You may grow straw, but not corn'. Increase in output could lift the farmer's return by about £1 an acre.[13] On some estates the landlord undertook the work and then charged 5 per cent interest to the tenants at the end of their leases.[14]

Elsewhere the tenants undertook the work themselves, especially in areas where tenant-right agreements were customary and so they could expect compensation for unexhausted improvements. As early as the 1820s, James Loch, agent to the Stafford estates was giving 'an allowance of drainage tiles wherever the exertions of tenants seems to merit such a reward'.[15] Tycho Wing on the Duke of Bedford's fenland estates found that tenants preferred to do the work themselves using their own men as it provided winter work. He was not convinced that inexperienced labourers would build drains satisfactorily. Instead the estate took the men on: 'If I want to drain 100 acres in the parish, I go to each farmer on whose land the work is to be done and inquire how many draining men he can spare me.' A gang of twelve men under a single superintendent was then put together to do the work with up to 100,000 drain pipes being laid in one fortnight in 1843.[16]

Much of this activity was concentrated in the thirty years following the invention of the first pipe-making machine. Between 1847 and 1878 the Duke of Northumberland spent nearly £1,000,000 on improvements, much of it on draining, resulting in the reclaiming of nearly all his wetlands. In County Durham tile drains were said to be being laid in 'every direction' and in Cumberland thirty tile works were operating in the Workington area. The Earl of Derby and Lord Sefton were busy draining in Lancashire. Elsewhere, as in East Lothian, it was the tenant who was responsible for the work, sometimes with the help of loans from the drainage companies. By 1853, the work which was said to have been going on for some 15 years was nearly completed.[17] Not only were drains being laid where none had been before, but land was being re-drained using the new tile drains and improved engineering skills. In 1868 Kerquarter farm in Roxburghshire was redrained at a cost of £1,200.[18] All the county reports published in both the Scottish and English journals of the period contain descriptions of the drainage being carried out. There were many local theories on how deep and how far apart drains should be laid and it is very likely that in some areas, much of the work was badly constructed. There is no doubt that many very wet fields remained in 1900, but land drainage was a major technical achievement which could boost dramatically agricultural output on some land. The early Victorian period saw an enormous input of labour, horse power and materials into major field drainage projects which transformed the landscape and agriculture on a scale that can be compared with the enclosures of the previous generation. It is a typical example of the combination of technical and scientific advance coupled with high capital expenditure in pursuit of increased productivity which was at the heart of the high farming movement.

Some of the landscapes where the technical achievements of the high farmers can be seen at their best are the areas of reclaimed marsh such as Sunk Island on the Humber Estuary (Figure 24). Here tree-lined straight roads cross an entirely flat chequer-board landscape on which farms are spaced at regular intervals. The only variety is provided by a mid-nineteenth century church and school. Like most other such areas, drainage had begun long before with embanking of some 13 acres (known as Old Island), in 1669. A further 200,000 acres was embanked in 1744 and by 1800 the main areas had been reclaimed and new farms laid out. Salt marsh on the east side of Sunk Island was increasing in height and extent and the major period of development was in the 1850s, by which time most of the final 2,250 acres had been added, with only Newlands left to be reclaimed in 1897.[19] Eight new farms were built in 1856 designed by the fashionable architect, S. S. Teulon, as well as a church and a school. As the area could be said to be new land emerging from the sea, it became the property of the Crown and was managed by the Crown Estate who were responsible for its development.

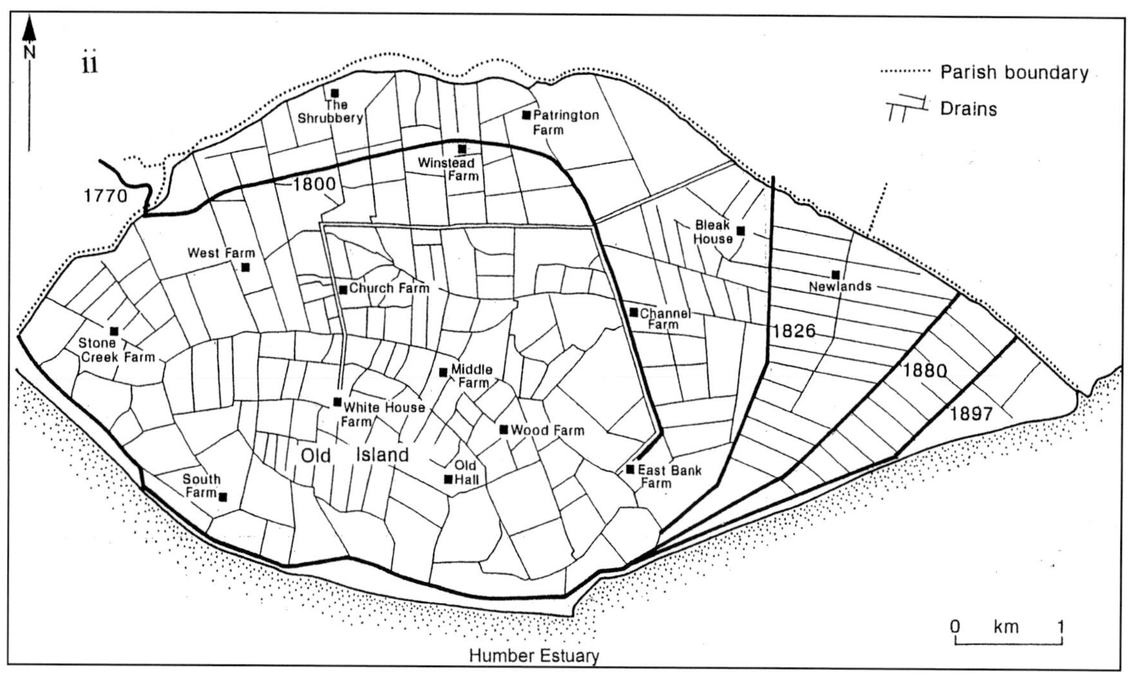

FIGURE 24.
Sunk Island, East Yorkshire.
This area was created by deposition in the Humber estuary and as such was owned by the Crown. It was finally laid out as farms in the 1850s.
PHILLIP JUDGE

Similarly, in most of the other areas of extensive marsh drainage, the Victorian period saw the finishing and stabilizing of work begun earlier, which had had to await the development of reliable steam pumping engines. This was particularly true of the Great Level of Fens stretching north across the marshlands of Norfolk, through Cambridgeshire nearly as far as the Lincolnshire Wolds. Wind pumps were being replaced by steam power while remaining wetlands such as Whittlesey Mere were drained in the 1840s. Ramsey Mere, between Huntingdon and March, 'which used to grow long reed now comprises three farms of beautiful land. There are now farm buildings built upon its bed and a good gravel road running through the middle, the whole producing good crops of wheat and oats.'[20] The North Level covered much of the area north of the River Nene of which the Duke of Bedford owned 18,500 acres around the village of Thorney in Cambridgeshire (Figure 25). Efforts at drainage were hampered by the silting up of the Nene downstream at Wisbech and finally, following acts of Parliament in 1826 and 1827, the outfall was dredged and lowered by ten feet. This allowed the water to flow through the drains in Thorney. The North Level main drain was built between 1831 and 1834 and a steam engine installed. The Duke of Bedford's agent, Tycho Wing, was so confident in the success of the project that he was offering his windmills for sale to his neighbour; 'it is impossible that they will ever be required again for drainage'. Immediately land values rose from £5 an acre to £60 or £70.[21] With some certainty of land clear of water in the spring, grain could be sown earlier, wheat crops would not be lost or grass seed washed away. Once the external drains were complete, it was up to the Bedford estate to complete work on its own farms and the Duke's lands were noted for 'neat

FIGURE 25.
Thorney Level, Cambridgeshire.
The Duke of Bedford's Thorney estates were not finally drained until the 1830s. The regular fields and roads contrast with the small area of irregular fields of the 'highland' around Thorney Abbey.
PHILLIP JUDGE

farmsteads and good management'.[22] Expenditure rose through the 1840s, reaching a peak in 1861 when £19,326 was spent on 'new works and improvements'. By 1875, £188,991 had been spent since 1839 at Thorney. Eighty farms were rebuilt as well as Thorney village, created by S. S. Teulon, with its elaborate estate workshops. A Victorian estate landscape had been created which makes Thorney a very distinctive area within the fens.[23]

An even more ambitious scheme for which an act of Parliament was obtained involved the drainage of much of the Wash. This would create 150,000 acres of new land to be called the Victoria Level. However, this project defeated even the optimistic mid-century high farmers and it came to nothing.[24]

Problems plagued the drainage of the Somerset Levels. Although steam engines had been installed in the area of the Parrett valley below Langport, the constricted and winding course of the river meant that it was unable take away the surplus water. The invention of the centrifugal pump in 1851 to supersede the water wheel, meant that steam engines could be more efficient, and several were installed along the Parrett in the 1860s. The main problems along the river remained and in spite of various efforts to improve sections of the main channel, no solution was found by the end of Victoria's reign.[25] The result is a landscape very different from that at Thorney. The lack of a dominant and very wealthy landowner meant that the finance for the major works needed on the rivers was not available and the land was always going to be improved pasture rather than arable. Because of the large number of people who had rights to what had been common grazing, the landscape remained a complex one of small meadows and individual new brick farms. Such problems were swept away as insignificant by the enthusiasts. 'Surely, in this age of enlightenment, and especially in this time of necessity [the scarcities of the years of the potato famine were uppermost in the writer's mind], prejudice for old customs and circumstances-which proverbially appertains to the character of a farmer, and notoriously to that of a fenman – will not be permitted to impede so important an improvement.'[26] The work of reclamation through drainage continued, often with the aid of steam power, and the work that had been started, often several centuries before reached as effective a conclusion as was possible before the introduction of powerful modern pumps.

Alongside these large-scale examples, there are many smaller ones to be found on individual farms and estates. Often they were part of a project of reclamation which not only involved drainage, but also ploughing and clearing heath. The era of high farming represented the final phase of land improvement. As we have seen, Arthur Young reckoned there were about 8,000,000 acres of waste remaining in England and Wales in 1795, much of which was 'capable of improvement'. The area of waste in England alone had dropped by a third by 1873. The area of cultivated land in the United Kingdom reached a peak in 1893, after which it declined until the ploughing-up campaign of the Second World War. More difficult to ascertain is how much of this reclamation took place during the Napoleonic Wars and how much during the period of high farming. Isolated examples are described in the contemporary journals. Two thousand eight hundred acres were brought into profitable cultivation around Wigton (Cumbria) in the thirty years after the Napoleonic Wars and a price of £8 an acre was the estimated cost of further reclamation around Kendal.[27] The General Enclosure Act of 1845 reduced the legal costs and resulted in the enclosure of a further 600,000 acres in England and Wales before 1870. To this must be added the many areas where recourse to a Parliamentary act was not needed.[28]

In Scotland particularly, ever more expensive schemes were being embarked upon, the only limitations being the strength of the available steam power and the depth of the owner's pocket. In the ten years after 1843 over a dozen articles appeared in the *THASS* describing individual projects. These all involved peaty upland and the methods of reclamation were similar. First the boundaries of the area to be reclaimed were marked out, often in the form of deep ditches to start the draining process. A main drain might be dug through the area and which could be as much as 12 feet deep. Fields would be laid out, usually with a road running through so that there was easy access to all the fields. Then stones would be removed and this could involve blasting. These stones would often then be broken for use in the drains. The field drains were about three feet deep and either tiled or filled with stones. The land would also have to be 'trenched' or deep ploughed to a depth of about 18 inches enabling the farmer to take up an inch or two of the subsoil for mixing with the upper soil. Stones would be removed and the sods turned down to the bottom of the trench. A second method involved paring off the top layer of peat and then burning it. The ash could then be spread back on the land. If the ploughing was not deep enough to turn up a layer of clay, then this would have to be brought in and spread on the surface to a depth of about six inches before the land was ploughed again and limed. Costs could be in the region of £20 to £30 an acre. The contributors to the *THASS* claimed to be well satisfied with the results, with profits in increased rents or returns on in-hand land of about six per cent. Some projects were simply adding land to existing farms, but where completely new farms were created, well-planned steadings might also be erected.[29]

The *nouveaux riches* such as James Fletcher who, with wealth made in Peru, took on the Rosehaugh estate (Moray) in 1867 might undertake extensive reclamation such as the drainage of the six-acre Loch Scadden.[30] A similarly expensive scheme was undertaken by John Fowler, the traction engine manufacturer when he bought the Inverbroom (Ross and Cromarty) estate in 1866. Land along the River Broom was drained and large square fields laid out. The old-established landowners were also responsible for projects with the Earl of Galloway reclaiming on Wigton Sands and the Earl of Stair draining Auchrorar Moss and Loch Dowlatan (Wigtonshire).[31] In Caithness the work begun by Sinclair and his contemporaries was continued by their heirs. Drainage and reclamation continued stimulated by the increased profits for livestock which were possible after the opening of regular steam ship routes to the south in 1830. By 1875 much of Caithness had been turned from a 'wild desolate plain into a highly cultivated country'. However, much to the chagrin of the improvers, 50,000 acres of peat (much of it in what is now the Flow Country) still remained.[32] The amount of arable in Selkirkshire increased from 14,441 acres in 1857 to 23,302 acres in 1885.[33] One of the most dramatic landscapes of improvement to be created in this period is that on the island of Shapinsay (Orkney) where in 1843 Lord Balfour took the home farm in hand and drained 700 acres. (Figure 26). In 1846 £6,000 was borrowed from a land improvement company and used for drainage and building. Roads were laid out and regular ten-acre fields created. New farmsteads were built along the roads for farms ranging from 30 to 200 acres.[34]

Elsewhere it was the tenants who were responsible for reclamation. Work on the Earl of Fife's estates around Elgin was undertaken by tenants on a

FIGURE 26.
The island of Shapinsay (Orkney). The first edition six-inch Ordnance Survey map shows the island of Shapinsay as laid out by the Duke of Balfour in the 1850s. The regular grid created both large and small farms and a new village and model farm were also built.

nineteen-year lease.[35] Aberdeenshire was characterised by its large number of small farms, and although some of its landowners were lavish spenders the small tenants too were expected to become colonisers of new land. Small farms were often created on the margins of old cultivated land when the communal township farms were broken up.[36] They were let on low rents and long leases, obliging the new tenants to bring new lands into cultivation. At Banchory, near Aberdeen, 170 acres were let to 21 tenants who were expected to 'improve the land'. The owner, Alexander Thompson was scathing about the advantages of this method of improvement. Although cheap, the work might be poorly done. It only worked where, as in this case, the small tenants could find a good local market for their produce and work to supplement their meagre incomes. There was also the danger of 'getting a pauper population' upon the estate who would then have to be supported through the local poor rates.[37] In Gairloch the tenants of the crofts created in 1848 were encouraged to improve their plots by draining and to put up buildings erected to a plan approved of by the estate.[38]

Of all the reclamation projects in Scotland, the most extravagant must surely have been that of the third Duke of Sutherland in the north of Sutherland and around Loch Shin.[39] The third Duke inherited in 1867 and immediately began a programme of estate drainage and reclamation on his own behalf as well as advancing loans to the larger tenants to encourage then to undertake improvements themselves. One of the main problems of the great sheep farms created as a result of the clearances was that of providing enough winter fodder for the stock. In many cases this was overcome by these holdings being let alongside a lowland coastal farm and the sheep would be driven down for the winter. The fertility in many of the inland strathes, which had been carefully manured prior to the clearances, was declining and so the amount of grazing available, even in the summer, was decreasing. This was resulting in more deaths and fewer lambs being raised and thus the danger of a decline in the value of the estate. The Duke therefore decided to reverse this trend by creating arable on the sheep farms to produce winter feed for the sheep. Between 1866 and 1882 100 acres near the farmhouse of the 70,000-acre Melness Farm was reclaimed at a cost of £1,800, interest of 2.5 per cent being charged to the tenant. At the equally remote Ribigill farm there was said to be land suitable for turnips. Two eight horse-power ploughing engines were imported through the northern harbour at Tongue to break up the soil and pull out fir roots. At Forsinain, on the edge of the Flow Country, dynamite had to be used to clear stones. Between 1876 and 1879 £3,676 was spent on deep-ploughing and clearing 147 acres. However the crops frequently failed and in 1888, the tenant gave up and the farm had to be taken in hand. Attempts to create more mixed farming in these remote upland areas were mostly a failure.

A second area of activity was around Loch Shin. Between 1872 and 1877 four new farms were created on what had previously been peat bog. Specially adapted steam ploughs were used to break up the soil and dig drains, costs rocketed to as much as £66 an acre, but still cultivation was difficult and was soon abandoned. The farms were difficult to let and when taken in hand usually ran at a loss. By 1914 all the reclaimed land had reverted to rough pasture and two of the farms disappeared. A more innovative scheme was adopted a few miles away at Kinbrace (Figure 27) where the aim was to create small family farms of 80 to 100 acres. However, this social experiment was also a failure and the Duke saw little in the way of return on the expenditure of the enormous sum of £148,556.[40] For each of these well-publicised examples, there were many more that went unrecorded with lochs, bogs and morasses being drained to extend both arable and pasture.

By the 1830s most of the Welsh lowland open fields had been enclosed and it was the upland moors that remained open sheep and pony grazing. Enthusiasm for enclosure of these commons continued through to 1870 with 128,128

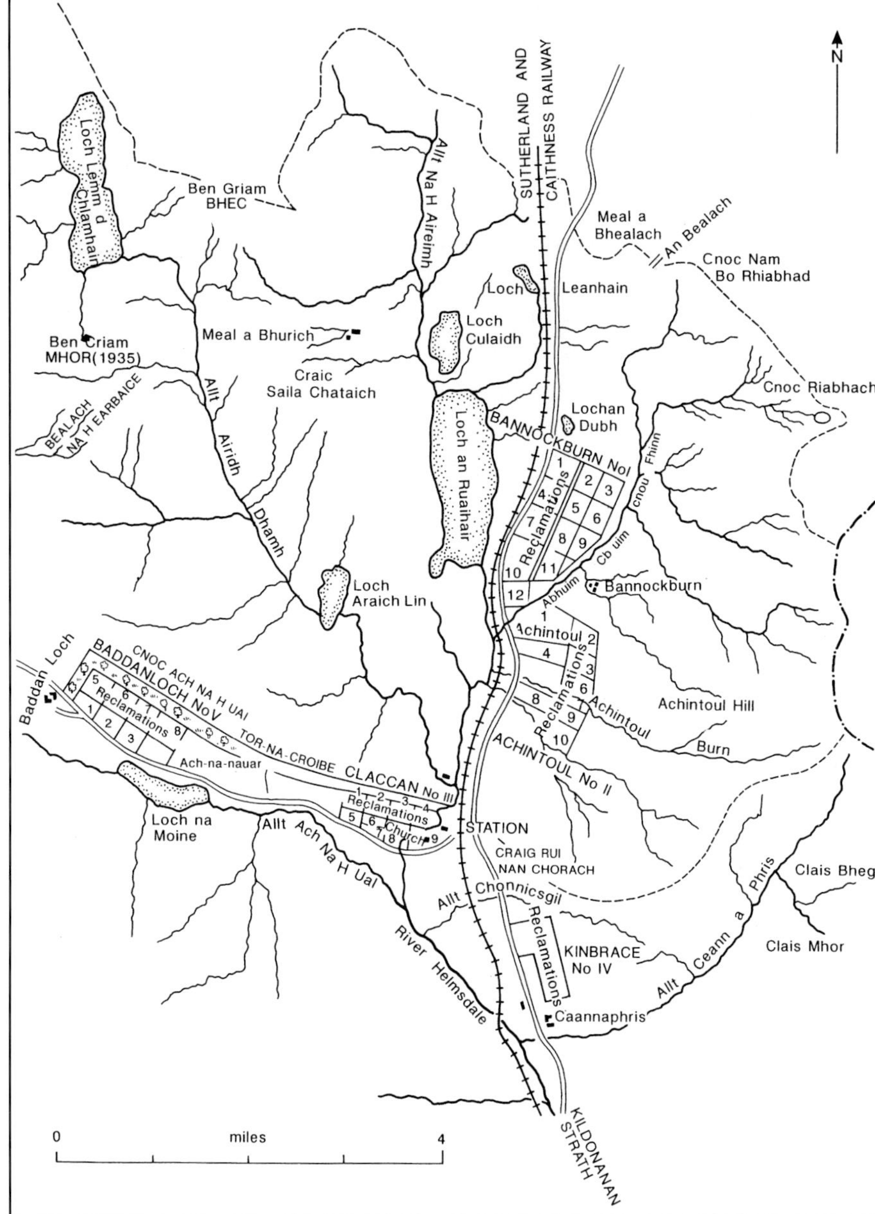

FIGURE 27.
The Kinbrace reclamations (Sutherland). These reclamations of the 1870s differ from most others in that they were designed to create small family farms and restore population to an area that had earlier been depopulated.
PHILLIP JUDGE

acres being enclosed by parliamentary act in the thirty years after 1840. On much of this land little improvement in the form of tree planting or drainage took place, but the Act did define ownership and prevented encroachments. On larger estates where the capital was available, such as 5,000 acres purchased by the wealthy Liverpool merchant Henry Sandbach on Hiraethog Moors, land was fenced and improved pasture was created. The fact that sheep were contained within fixed areas and undisturbed by other flocks was bound to lead to some improvements in sheep breeds and general livestock husbandry.[41]

In few areas of England did large areas of open upland similar to that in Scotland and Wales await reclamation. However, the 20,000 acres of Exmoor forest, sold by the crown in 1820 to the Worcestershire landowner and iron-master, John Knight, did seem a likely candidate (Figure 28).[42] Although this area of open heath and moor was all over 800 ft (240 m) he did hope to enclose and cultivate much of it. The first plan was to farm it all as one huge enterprise, cultivating as much as possible and buying in lowland sheep to graze the rest during the summer. Much of the moorland is covered with peat on a layer of clay and iron-pan impervious to water. Reclamation involved firstly paring off two or three inches of the top layer of peat which was heaped up and burnt, the ash being spread back on the land. This was followed by a heavy dose of lime, probably up to three tons an acre. The land was then deep ploughed into the clayey subsoil and breaking up the iron-pan using first oxen and later steam power.[43] This proved highly successful in draining the soil with contrasts between reclaimed and unreclaimed soils still obvious today. In 1841 John Knight handed control to his son Frederick who changed the farming policy to one of creating tenant farms. Between 1844 and 1852 11 farms were established, all of which had to be fenced with hedges in the form of earth banks faced with stones planted with a double row of beech. Wind breaks of beech were also planted behind each farmstead as a protection against the severe weather. Much of the responsibility for the fences within the farm and the reclamation was passed on to the tenants, who were granted allowances for improvements. The cost of reclamation was calculated at about £4 5*s*. an acre.[44] However, deep ploughing, followed by massive doses of lime failed to make this land, all of it over 800 ft (240 m), suitable for growing wheat and barley. By the 1860s a cattle and sheep rearing system based on pasture, alternating with crops of turnips and meadow grasses, had been established and proved to be economically viable. An enclosed landscape with some improved pasture, capable of supporting livestock farming, had been created on what had been rough grazing on open moor.

An area of reclamation in Lincolnshire impressed contemporaries. It was begun during the Napoleonic Wars but was not completed until the 1840s. In 1843 Philip Pusey travelled north from Sleaford to Lincoln and then on to Brigg across forty miles of what had been heathland, but which was now some of the 'best farming on very moderate land'. In the Wolds too, Lord Yarborough and Mr Chaplin had been enclosing in the 1820s. Near Blankney Mr Chaplin had replaced gorse by farmland and Lord Yarborough's lands near Brocklesby which had only been suitable for rabbits and fox hunting were now good arable. '230,000 acres (nearly the extent of Bedfordshire)', Pusey exclaimed, 'has been added in our own times to the cornland of England'.[45]

Elsewhere, individual owners were grubbing up hedges, felling woodland and removing the stumps with the help of steam ploughs, whilst at the same time creating plantations for game preservation. There was a need for the flattening of fields and removal of hedges, to allow the use of new machines for surface cultivation such as grubbers, scarifiers, clod crushers and rollers.

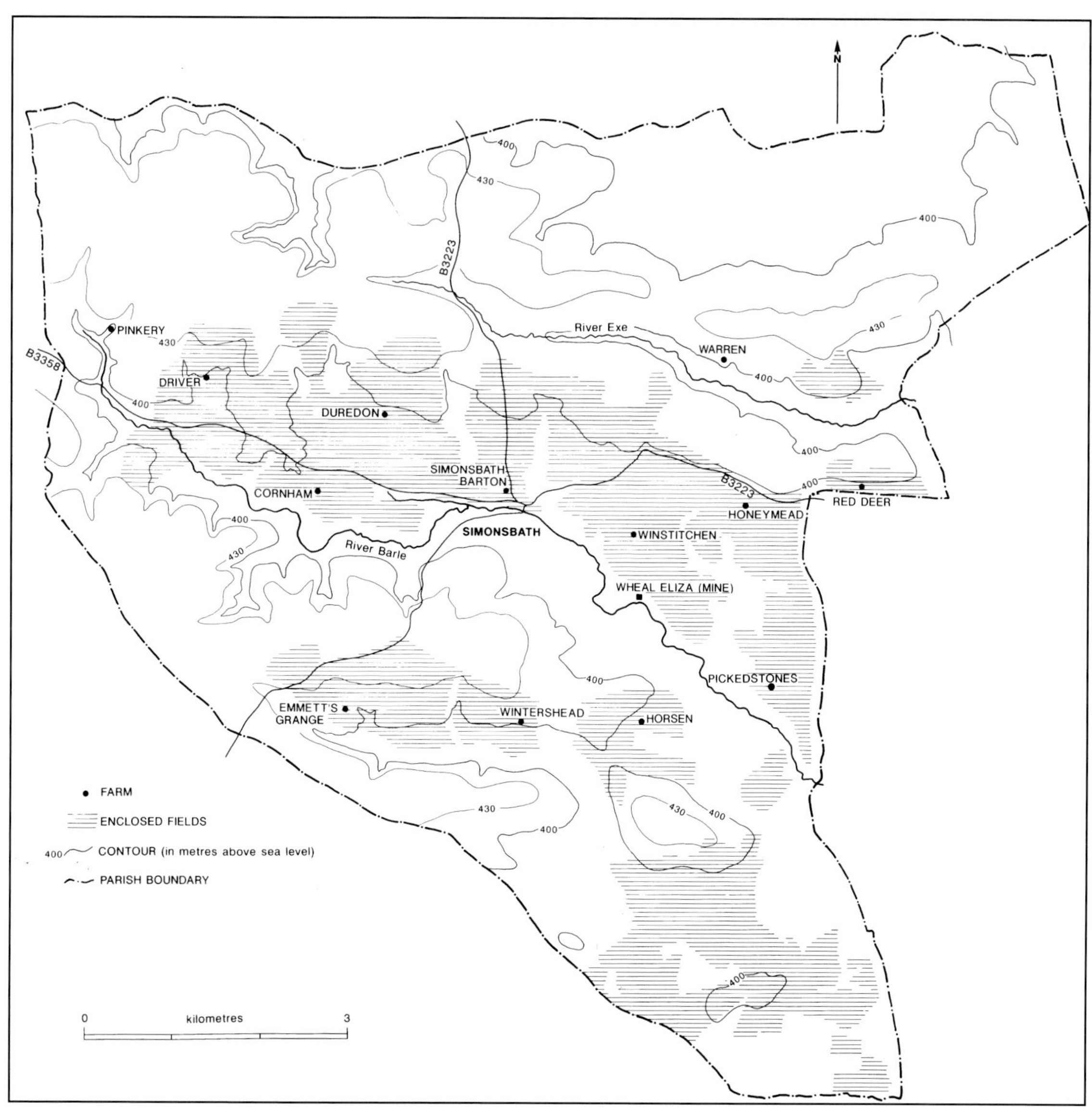

FIGURE 28.
Exmoor Forest (Somerset and Devon). The parish of Exmoor was created from the old royal forest in 1856. The lower land was enclosed and divided into farms with the farmsteads placed in the centre of their holdings.
PHILLIP JUDGE

These activities completed the transformation of much of the British landscape that had been begun over a century before.

One improvement that had been pioneered at an earlier date continued to excite interest during the high farming era: water meadows. The early volumes of the *JRASE* contained much discussion on their value, but Philip Pusey for one was convinced of their worth. He described them as 'the triumph of agricultural art: changing as it does, the very seasons … a slight film of water trickling over the surface rouses the sleeping grass, tinges it with living green amidst snows or frosts, and brings forth a luxuriant crop in early spring, just when it is most wanted while other meadows are bare and brown.'[46] Pusey himself built a system on his own downland estate, claiming that one 20-acre meadow kept 400 sheep in feed for five months. Altogether, he claimed to be able to keep 550 ewes where previously he had kept 170. One of the largest and most ambitious schemes was the Duke of Portland's meadows, covering 400 acres in Nottinghamshire and costing the huge sum of £130 per acre to construct.[47] However, a major difference between the earlier and these later projects was that many were to be found in the uplands of Britain and it was here that Pusey thought they would be of most importance. These were 'catch work' and much cheaper to construct. Here a main 'carriage' or watercourse was dug across the slope above the dam in the stream, with gutters leading from it, allowing the water to trickle down the slope. At the bottom of the slope a further main drain took the water back to the main watercourse or stream. Ideally this flowed through the farmyard to gather urine or dung before going out onto the hill. The profits of underdraining old arable were very little compared with those claimed for John Roal's water meadows high up in the Brendon Hills.[48] The Knight's land agent on Exmoor, Robert Smith, built a complex system and was regarded as something of an expert on the subject. His meadows were laid out in five or six-acre sections and proved invaluable in producing early grass for ewes and lambs and an abundance of hay for the winter. As a result of his enthusiasm 'new meadows were being laid out on nearly every [Exmoor] farm'.[49] Indeed water meadows were seen by Pusey as 'the talisman by which a mantle of luxuriant verdure might be spread over the mountain moors of Wales and Scotland, of Kerry and Connemara'. Devon was regarded as the classic land of catch meadows and their remains are to be seen on hillsides on Exmoor and Dartmoor. Accounts of their construction are to be found in county reports and the *THASS*, showing that they were being tried further north. However, in many of these areas their use was very short-lived. Although nineteenth-century agricultural encyclopaedias continued to enthuse about them, Copland admitted in 1866 that the practice of irrigation had spread very little outside the core area of the southern chalklands.[50] The problem undoubtedly was that the system only worked in mild climates; regions where frost was likely to ice up the system were not good candidates for water meadows. A few mild winters might encourage their creation, but a few cold ones would soon dishearten even the most enthusiastic advocate. As Pusey himself wrote 'There is one test often applied by farmers when a person adopts or recommends some improvement – has he gone on with it?'[51] As with other types of land improvement, even the optimistic Victorian high farmer, with capital at his disposal, could not beat the weather.

It is clear from these few examples that in many cases the optimism of the improvers rushed ahead of what was economically possible. The expenditure of between £2 and £5 per acre on drainage in the 1840s had probably paid for itself by the onset of depression. Indeed, tenants believed that an investment of £3 an acre on drainage paid for itself in higher yields within a year. However, by the 1870s investments were returning losses.[52] Pusey advised against 'the adoption of entirely new principles or contrivances, but instead the cautious, yet courageous development of existing practice'.[53] In Sutherland much of the reclaimed land rapidly reverted to rough pasture, while on Exmoor viable farms for livestock rather than the hoped-for cereals were created. These examples illustrate yet another aspect of high farming – the belief that with the help of science and the strength of steam power all types of terrain could be made productive. This confidence was based on the conviction that food prices would always remain high enough to make these very expensive schemes economically viable. However when prices fell after 1870, many certainly were not, and interest in reclamation came to an end. Work in Sutherland stopped abruptly in 1882 with one new farmstead half completed, and articles on the subject ceased to appear in the agricultural press. Instead, as grain prices fell relative to livestock, interest in creating good grass land rose. Some, such as James Caird, criticised the recent enthusiasm for increasing the arable acreage. 'There is no doubt that vast areas of poor down and heath land in the south of England, were converted to arable at the beginning of the century – land that cannot be tilled profitably now, and that cannot be restored to its former condition within any reasonable limit of time, if ever.'[54] This view was echoed by another eminent commentator on the farming scene, Clare Sewell Read, who wrote, 'It is a thousand pities that so many of our sheep walks, heaths and warrens were broken up years ago. The soil is so sandy and poor, that no sort of grass will grow upon it for more than a year or two. It dies off and the soil is left as bare as the sand on the sea shore.'[55]

It is clear that enormous sums of money were invested in improvement during these middle years of the nineteenth century for which a return was never seen. Some schemes were clearly unsuited in the long term to the terrains in which they were executed, and much of this land has, under the regime of international competition which began to take effect after 1870, reverted to rough pasture, if not 'waste'. It is the spectacularly expensive schemes which received publicity. However, there would have been few farms in the clays where underdrainage did not take place and where both the productivity of the farm and the appearance of the countryside would not have been altered as a result. The great majority of reclamation was small-scale nibbling at the edges of uplands and has gone unrecorded. The agricultural statistics are difficult to interpret as definitions of waste, commons and rough pasture change from year to year, but the recorded acreage of agricultural land was rising until 1890. From then on there seems to have a retreat from less hospitable land with an increase in waste until 1941. It is likely therefore that while in the long run much of the effort at underdrainage did have a significant affect on agricultural productivity, the reclamation of wasteland, although it may have helped to boost food supplies for a few years before American grain reached the British market, was of less long-term importance. Landowners would have been better off financially investing in the stock market than their estates, but throughout the period 1800–1870 they recognised the social value of land and the moral duty of improvement.

CHAPTER FOUR

The New Farms

The classical ideal, 1720 to 1820

The contrast between evolved and planned landscapes is as obvious in the buildings as in the fields themselves. As we move from the heavy cheese land of north Wiltshire with its small, often owner-occupied, farms and scattered hamlets to the huge arable farms on the newly enclosed chalk of the great landowners, the contrast could not be more clear. In the north Wiltshire village of Hilmarton, there were 19 farms in the 1840s and the average size of the nine largest was only 167 acres. The lifestyle of many of these small farmers was said to be 'barely distinguishable from the labourers with whom they lived shoulder to shoulder'. Little capital was needed to set up as a dairy farmer and mobility from the paid labourer to independent farmer class was not uncommon.[1] Such farmers were unlikely to have the capital to replace their farm buildings. To the south, on the Marlborough Downs and Salisbury Plain, the large estates were enclosing land into some of the largest arable farms in the country and erecting great courtyard and E-plan steadings suited to the new generation of commercial farmers. There were 40 Wiltshire landowners of more than 3,000 acres in 1883, and these were mostly concentrated in the light-land arable areas. The Earl of Pembroke owned 39,000 acres around Wilton where farms, mostly well over 500 acres, were created covering both low-lying meadow and high chalk. Sets of well-planned buildings were erected around a yard and designed for mixed farming; the keeping of cattle in yards was essential to produce the manure to keep the land fertile.

Similarly the buildings on the sandy Brecklands and light soils of western East Anglia (Figure 29) contrast with the scatter of free-standing timber-framed buildings of the claylands to the south and east. On the Culford and Grafton estates, well-planned groups of brick-built buildings stand in the centre of their newly enclosed farmland and set back from the main roads between Thetford and Bury St Edmunds. The reasons for the dispersal of new farms with their fashionable houses to attract 'men of capital' as tenants may not simply have been for the convenience of a central position for conducting farming operations. The social standing of these new farmers may well have meant they wished to be separated from the village and several of their houses have park-like home pastures spreading out to the front. The enclosed landscapes involved a 'radical reshaping of social geography'.[2] In England, cottages, where they were needed, were placed at a short distance from the

FIGURE 29. Barnham in Breckland (Suffolk) and plans of farm building layout, 1840 and 1900. a) (*opposite, top*) The First Edition Six-inch Ordnance Survey sheet Suffolk 22NE shows part of the parish of Barnham to the south of Thetford Heath. Much land is still unenclosed but East, West and North Farm have been created and huge fields laid out. The farm buildings themselves are extensive and the farms covered over 1,000 acres each. b) The farm plans, redrawn from the tithe map and the First Edition 25-inch Ordnance Survey show that the planned farms of the enclosures were only slightly modified in the second half of the nineteenth century. PHILLIP JUDGE

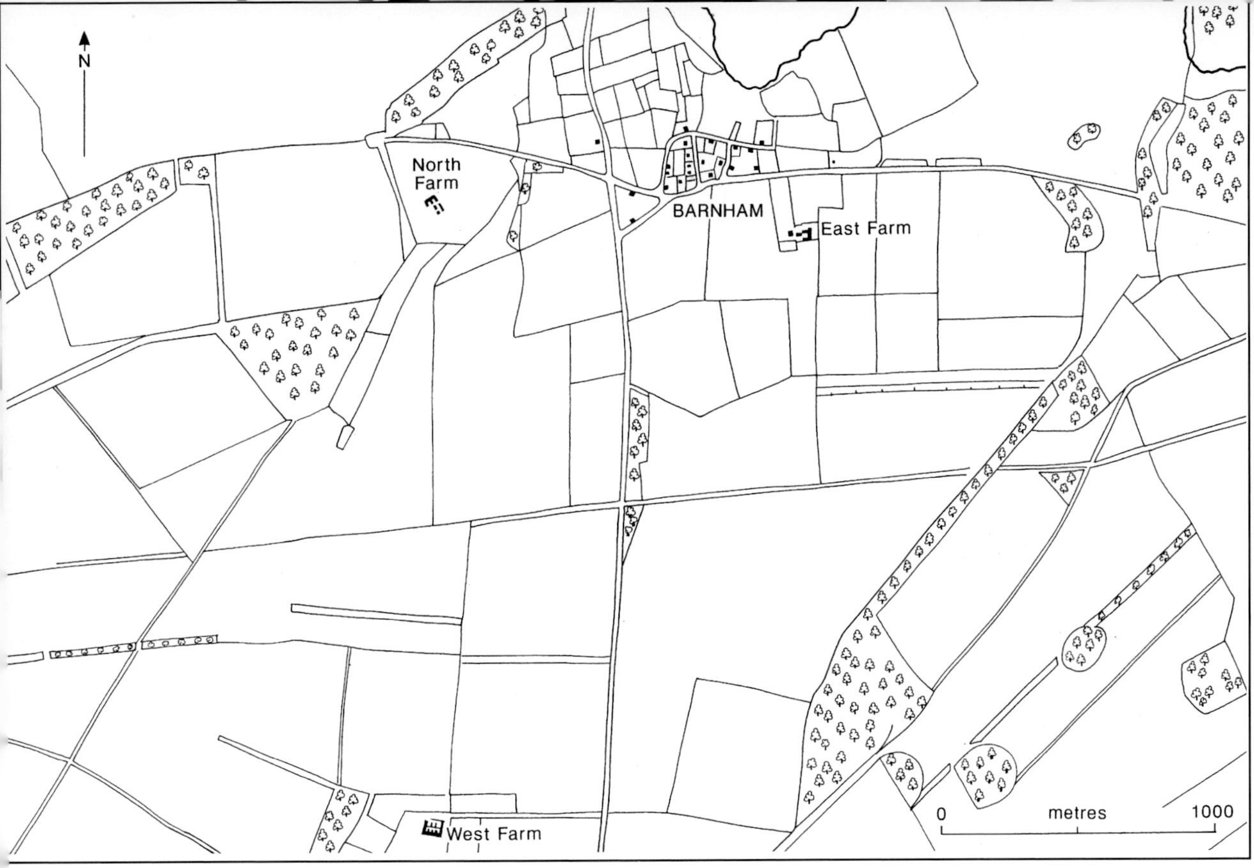

N
North
Farm
BARNHAM
East Farm
West Farm
0
metres
1000

Barnham, Suffolk
Farm Layouts c.1840 & c.1900
c.1840
c.1900
1646 acres
North Farm
976 acres
East Farm
1591 acres
West Farm
0
feet
300
0
metres
100

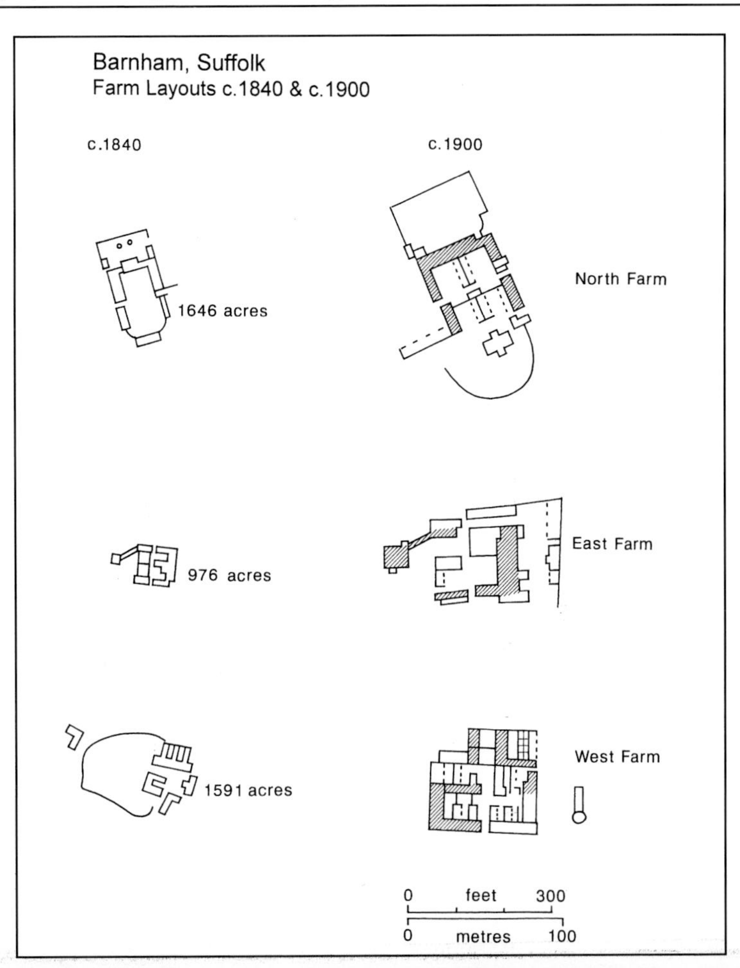

farmhouse, while in Scotland a row of bothies might take up one side of the farmstead.

However, the connection between new farmsteads built out in the fields to serve newly enclosed land is not always a simple one and rationalisation of land holdings did not always eliminate village farmsteads. The owner-occupier farmer Frederick Barnwell, in Mileham (Norfolk) rebuilt his house and buildings on the main street between 1816 and 1821 – a time of field re-organisation in the parish – and declared on a plaque above the side door to the house that because 'the previous buildings were falling down through old age' they were replaced by 'these which are both more convenient and (being square-shaped) more beautiful'. Conversely, dispersed farmsteads in several moorland dales predate enclosure. Some are of monastic or pre-Domesday origin.[3]

It is in the farmsteads built by the 'improving' landlords that the philosophy of 'beauty, utility and profit' central to the Enlightenment as discussed in the first chapter of this book can most clearly be seen. An interest in farm building can be traced back to the early eighteenth century, in the areas of new enclosure in the north of England. By 1777 a visitor to Harewood in West Yorkshire could write 'the whole countryside forms a theatre of ornamented farms'.[4] One of the first books written on the subject was that of Daniel Garrett, published in 1747 and entitled *Designs of Farm Houses etc for the Counties of Yorkshire, Northumberland, Cumberland, Westmorland and the Bishoprick of Durham* (Figure 30). Garrett was an established country house architect and his designs for farmsteads are simple courtyard layouts with a house on one side of the yard and a barn on the other. Designs range from small, single-yard layouts to larger double yards. There is little cattle accommodation against the yard walls, but it is possible that this would have been of a temporary nature and the responsibility of the tenant. All the layouts are symmetrical and of a functional classical design, demonstrating the all-pervading influence that neo-classical architects such as Palladio had on every branch of architecture. Garrett's designs were primarily for the new farms being created by enclosure to be built in 'as regular, cheap and convenient manner as possible', rather than elaborate home farms. As we have seen, the 'improved' farming techniques being advocated required that stock should be kept in yards where manure gathered to be spread on the fields, and so without suitable buildings such farming systems could not be practiced. The providing of yards was therefore an important element in the encouragement of the new agriculture on enclosed fields. The straw for bedding in these yards was the by-product of threshing in the large barns and therefore it made sense for the barn to be next to the yard. Some of the straw would be chopped into chaff for feeding to horses, so again it was best for the stable also to be near at hand. The typical planned farm therefore would be around a yard with the barn and house at either end, and stables and cow houses linking the two sides. Hay was frequently stored over the stable and threshed grain above cartsheds facing out away from the yard. Feed stores for turnips might also form part of the layout.

Courtyard designs such as those of Garrett did not owe their origins purely to classical architectural traditions. Some are to be found associated with manorial farmsteads developed within a moat or around a bas-court. Gervase Markham in 1635 recommended a courtyard layout to the west of the house. On the north side should be the stables, an ox house, cow house and 'swine coates' (pig sties), all with doors facing south. On the south were the hay and corn barns, poultry houses and malting kilns and 'over betwixt both sides your bound hovels to carie your Pease ... under which you shall place, when they are not in use your Carts, Waynes, Tumbrells, Ploughes, Harrowes'.[5] His book and much of the farming literature that followed it was aimed at the practicing farmer. However, by the 1700s the control of much of the countryside – which was to become the planned landscapes of the following two centuries – had fallen into the hands of the great landowners, whose fashionable interests pulled them towards the classical architects. Their financial concerns encouraged them to build farmsteads suited to the new farming techniques which would encourage the men of capital needed to realise the land's potential. The courtyard plan fulfilled both of these criteria (Figure 31).

As early as 1699, Lord Belhaven had recommended that all entrances to the yard should be such that they could be seen from the house[6] and a feature that was common to even the grandest of the eighteenth century planned farmsteads was that the house was an integral part of the layout. The new race of tenant farmers was intimately involved in the everyday affairs (and smells) of their farms. They were also probably, as we shall see, involved in the initial financing of the buildings themselves.

No planned farmsteads from the first half of the eighteenth century survive in their entirety as most estate farms have been re-modelled many times to suit them to later farming practices. However we know that several north-country estates were active at this time. New farmsteads, possibly designed by Garrett, formed part of the improvements on the Wallington estates of Sir William Blackett in the 1740s and several un-named farm plans survive amongst his drawings for the remodelling of the front of the house.

Much more activity can be dated to the period when cereal prices began to rise after 1750. The farms that survive tend to be those designed by architects near owners' houses and parks, but these are only the finest examples of a far more general trend coinciding with the great increase in enclosure activity at the time. The names of famous architects such as James Paine, Robert Adam and John Carr are associated with much mid-century farm building on the great estates in the north of England and nearly all architects with a country-house practice designed farms as part of their work. For others, an increasing number of pattern books were becoming available. Many farms were erected to the designs of agents and landowners, possibly in consultation with the farmers themselves working in numerous estate offices across the region. The Duke of Northumberland instructed his estate architect, David Stephenson in 1806 to consult with him on all plans for new buildings. He also wrote, 'When it becomes necessary to build a wholly new farmstead, the architect, the bailiff and the tenant of the farm shall have consultation whether the

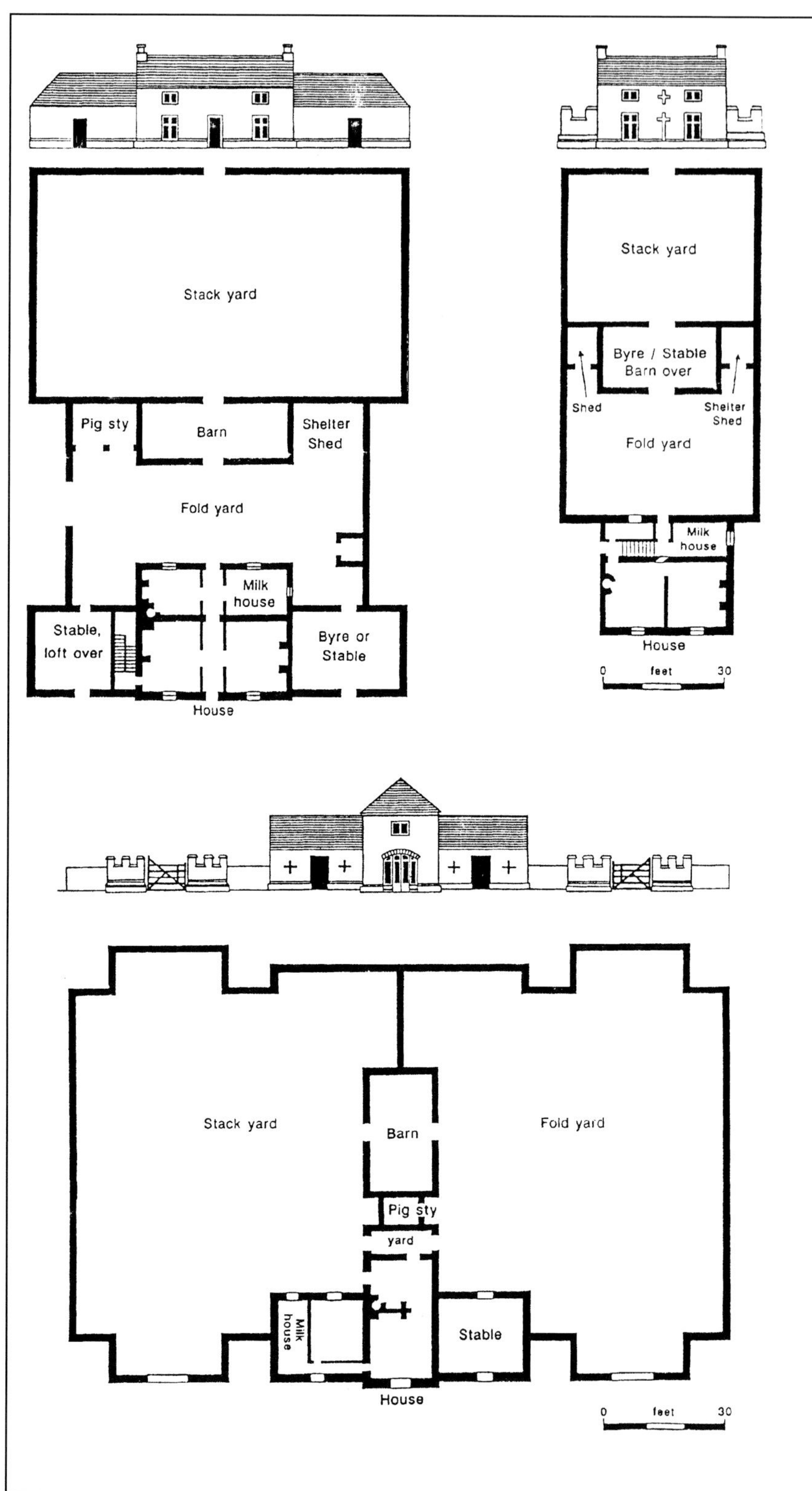

FIGURE 30.
A selection of Daniel Garrett's farm plans (*this page and opposite*). Garrett published ten plans in his book of 1747. Although the yards enclose large areas there are very few buildings other than a barn, around them. A small enclosure, often between the house and the barn, is labelled 'yard', possibly for milking.

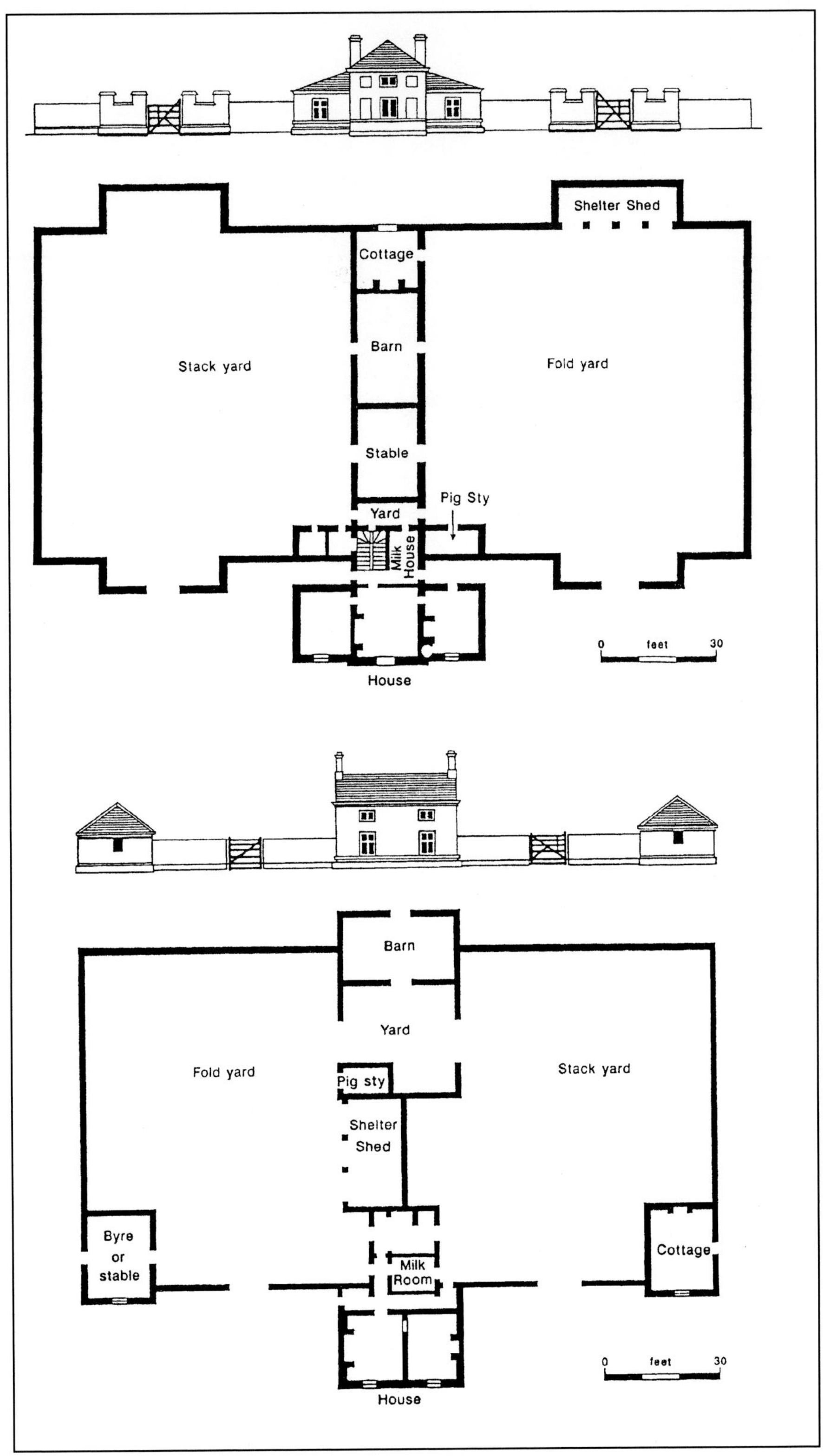
Shelter Shed
Cottage
Barn
Stack yard
Fold yard
Stable
Pig Sty
Yard
Milk House
House
0 feet 30
Barn
Yard
Fold yard
Stack yard
Pig sty
Shelter Shed
Byre or stable
Milk Room
Cottage
House
0 feet 30

FIGURE 31.
Park Farm, Fornham St Genevieve (Suffolk). This very large house and farmyard was designed for the Duke of Norfolk's Suffolk estate in 1819. Although the farmhouse is a large classical building suited to a gentleman farmer, it opens straight into the farmyard.

JACKSON-STOPS

whole site is in the properist place for its renewal or whether the general and material interests of my estate may not be benefited by its building on a more proper site.'[7] The question of how far new building was the result of tenant initiative and how much the landlord is an interesting one. When Robert Adam was commissioned to work on designs for farms at Kedleston by Nathaniel Curzon in 1760, his tenant, John Sherwin helped in the drafting of design specifications.[8] The evidence from Holkham suggests that pressure for new buildings came from the tenants. When Francis Blaikie arrived at Holkham in 1816 he was highly critical of the influence the tenants had had on the estate's building programme. He wrote, 'Mr Cokes' tenantry generally are much in the habit of erecting unnecessary buildings and frequently do so without due consideration; such buildings are not only attended with uncalled for expense to the landlord in the first instance, but entail a lasting encumbrance on the estate. For every particle of building not absolutely wanted is an encumbrance on the estate and a deterioration to the property. These remarks apply more immediately to Mr Coke's estate than any other in the kingdom'. It would be greatly to the advantage of the tenant as well as to landlord and much to the credit of the former if they would condescend to be guided by the sound advise I give them in regard to the buildings on their farms.'[9] The fact that in the years up to about 1820 entries shown in the Holkham audit books for new building show regular payments over several years suggests that the tenant was originally responsible for undertaking projects for which he then received regular payments from the estate. Certainly on the newly-created farms of the Sutherland estate, the tenant was responsible for the buildings, for which he was to have 'reasonable and proper encouragement' and which had to be on a plan approved by the estate.[10] In 1810, the tenant of Culmaily was allowed £1,500 for building in advance and this was considered unusual. In 1812, he was granted a lease by which he was required to build to an approved plan, but would be paid the full value at the end of his lease. The similarity of farm plans along the east Sutherland coast suggest that the estate kept a tight control on what was built.[11] Certainly the survival of books of 'Ameliorations' in many Scottish estate archives suggests that such a system of repayment for improvements was typical.

Those farms built as home farms or within newly created parks were likely to be more architecturally showy than those built further afield. John Carr designed a group of farms within Hornby Park for the 6th Duke of Holderness in 1766, one of which (Street House Farm) was clearly visible from the Great North Road. All contained architecturally striking houses with symmetrical buildings behind and of Street House farm, Cobbett was to write 'Against a road, things are made for show.'[12] Such buildings demonstrated to visitors and passers-by the patriotic concern for improvement as well as the architectural good taste of the owner.

However, many farm buildings were not designed by professional architects. George III himself left it to the land agent, Nathaniel Kent to design the new buildings in Windsor Great Park. Kent had always been critical of expensive buildings and he intended, where possible, to re-use building materials. In 1791 he wrote in his journal, 'Examined several of the buildings standing near the Lodge to inform myself which of them would answer removal to the intended Norfolk farm.' A week later he staked out all the proposed buildings ready for inspection by the king.[13] The fifth Duke of Bedford inherited the Woburn estate in 1787 and under the guidance of the clerk of the works, Robert Salmon, promoted to 'architect and mechanist' in 1794 many new farms were built (Figure 32). Only at Park Farm, Woburn do examples of his work survive.[14] On the Marquis of Stafford's estates, the agent, James Loch, took a personal interest in the design of buildings which he said should be of 'common country style, uniting as many advantages and as few faults as many buildings of the sort, and will supply useful hints to others'. Although an estate architect, John Smith was employed from 1805, Loch sent him long letters, often criticising unnecessary expenditure.[15]

By the time Arthur Young embarked on his tour of the north of England in 1771 farm buildings had been erected on many a newly-enclosed estate. Fine courtyard farms had been built around Kirkleatham and Redcar as well as further west at Wombwell, by Charles Turner 'with convenient barns, stables and cowhouses etc in the strongest manner'.[16] The Earl of Darlington had enclosed and rebuilt many farms on the estate, possibly with the help of Daniel Garret and John Carr. Young visited the grand home farm at Raby Castle (County Durham) designed by James Paine and built for the Earl of Darlington behind an ornate gothic screen. He was impressed by the systems for handling manure. 'I cannot but admire the ingenuity of the contrivance (in which) his lordship ... has so well adapted each part to its respective use and so well connected those that mutually depend upon each other'. Young illustrated the Gothic screen built about 1755 to illustrate 'how much beauty and utility can be united'.[17]

Of the many Yorkshire landowners who embarked on building programmes on their estates, the work of Sir Christopher Sykes at Sledmere must stand as an example. The new steadings, of which he was the architect were built

FIGURE 32. Home Farm, Woburn (Bedfordshire). These elegant buildings, designed by Robert Salmon were built as a back cloth to the annual sheep shearings, held from 1797 to 1813.

PHILLIP JUDGE

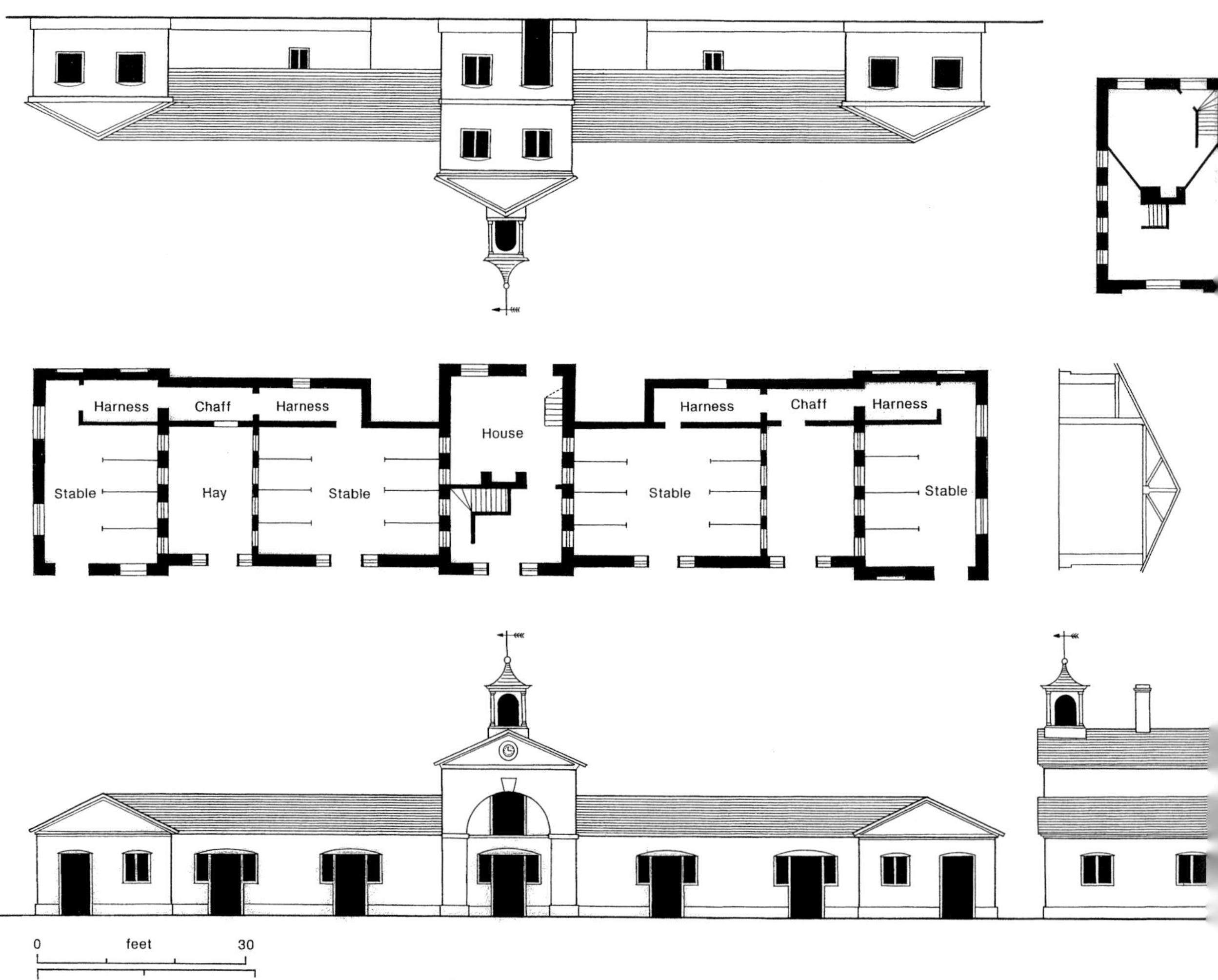

as the new landscape of enclosure was created from the 1770s. Houses formed part of south-facing classical facades and were linked by yard walls to corner pavilions containing stores above and loose boxes below. Behind, the barn was to the north of the yard with open shelter sheds and stables on the east and west sides. The houses backed right onto the cattle yards and so were firmly in the centre of the farming system intended for working rather than gentlemen farmers.

From the 1780s and particularly during the Napoleonic Wars, enthusiasm for farm building and improvement reached a peak as grain prices and rents rose. The number of pattern books available to landowners increased dramatically. Architects such as Samuel Wyatt and John Soane were active in their design. The basic principle of a symmetrical courtyard layout providing shelter for cattle and the accumulation of manure, adjacent to the barn and buildings for storage, did not change although the ever-innovative Wyatt experimented with new layouts at Holkham (Norfolk), Donnington (Cheshire) and Hatch Farm, Thorndon (Essex) where the barn was at the centre of the complex. Curved and circular layouts were also tried by both Robert Adam at Wonersh (Surrey), and Samuel Wyatt at Leicester Square Farm, South Creake (Figure 33), and Wheycurd Field Barn, Wighton, both in Norfolk. Perhaps the most elaborate layout is Robert Adam's plan for the Home Farm at Culzean Castle (Ayr) with buildings within an octagon.[18] Also in Scotland are a few semi-circular layouts. Several farmsteads were built for the fifth Duke of Argyll in Glenshira between 1771 and 1790 (Figure 34). Maam steading, designed by Robert Mylne was originally designed as a circular steading but was only half completed.[19] A similar semi-circle stands at Aden Home Farm (Grampian) and on the Isle of Islay at Kilchiaran. William Marshall claimed that curves or angles less acute than right angles were preferable in farmyard boundary walls and recommended curved or polygonal layouts as they were easier to get into and clean out. However he admitted that 'a complete set of buildings has not yet been erected (in England) on such a plan'.[20] The first volume of *Communications to the Board of Agriculture* published in 1797, is devoted to plans for farm buildings and contains many based on curves and semi-circles, sometimes with the buildings linked and in others free-standing behind the house. However, in spite of these many experimental designs, the courtyard remained the basis of farm layout on most newly enclosed farms.

A change which did begin to appear during the last years of the eighteenth century was the separation of the house from the farm buildings. As farming prosperity increased, so did the social standing of the large commercial farmers. No longer did they wish to overlook their farmyard, but rather this was left to a bailiff. At the tenanted Leicester Square Farm, Norfolk we see this distancing of the farmer from his place of work beginning to take place. The gentrified farmhouse designed by Samuel Wyatt is separated from the yard by curved office ranges and a low wall (Figure 33).

A second change was brought about by the invention of the threshing machine and by the 1790s farm plans began to be modified to accommodate

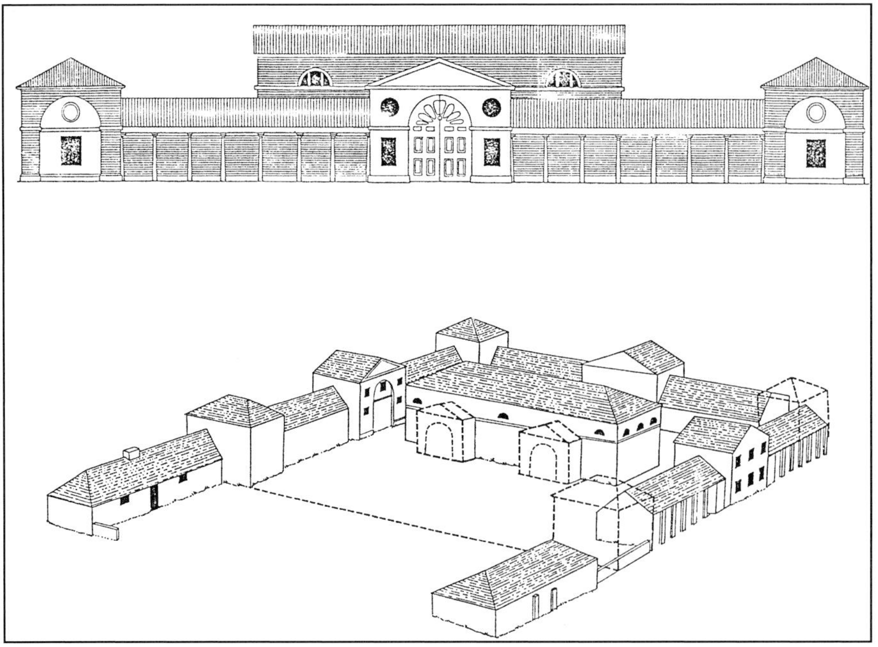

FIGURE 33.
The original approach of Samuel Wyatt to farm design:

a) (*above*) Leicester Square Farm, South Creake (Norfolk): the house is at a short distance from the yard, but linked to it by the original curved outbuildings.

DEREK EDWARDS, NORFOLK MUSEUM AND ARCHAEOLOGY SERVICE

b) (*left*) Hatch Farm, Thorndon (Essex): the barn is in a central position within the yard.

PHILLIP JUDGE

it. The adoption of mechanical threshing was a slow process, especially in regions where there was a surplus of labour, but in the industrialising and coal mining districts take-up was swifter. One of the earliest barns to use water-power to drive a threshing machine was at the Home Farm, Shugborough, Shropshire, designed by Samuel Wyatt in 1795[21] while the earliest threshing machine in Argyll was also water-powered and installed on Neil Malcolm's Experiment Farm near Poltolloch in 1798.[22] At the developing coal port of Workington on the Cumbrian coast John Curwen had installed a wind-powered threshing

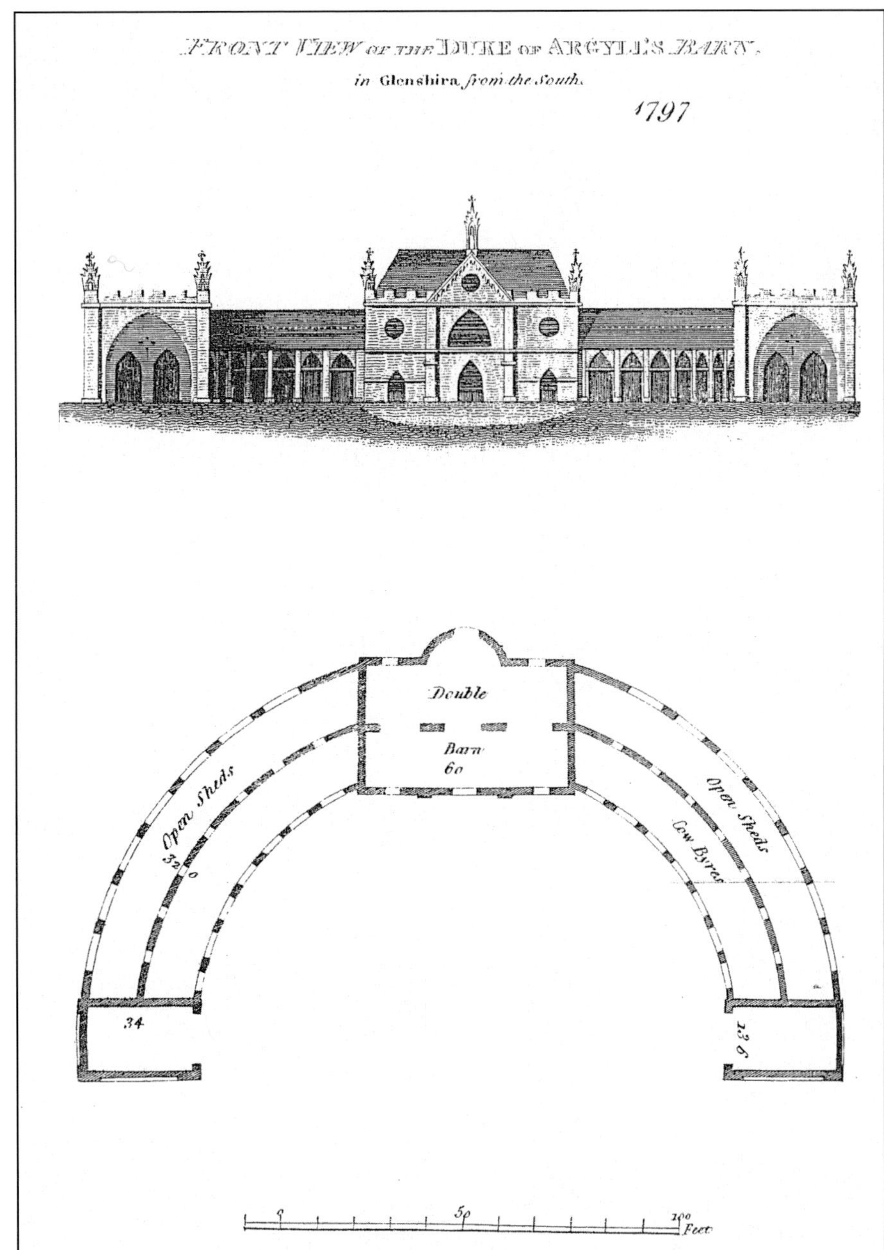

FIGURE 34.
Barn at Glenshira (Argyll).
This highly ornate example of a semi-circular farm layout was built shortly before 1797 and contained an innovative system of hay drying racks in the central barn.

machine by 1807. Many of the plans for the new farms built by the Marquis of Stafford during the Napoleonic Wars include round houses to accommodate a horse engine. The earliest steam engine for agricultural purposes was designed by Richard Trevithick and installed for Sir Christopher Hawkins at Trewithen Farm, Probus in Cornwall in 1811.[23] The great barn with its opposing doors for winnowing out the threshed grain in the draft between them was becoming obsolete. Instead on new planned farms the barn frequently abutted the long range of the main courtyard at right angles, allowing the power source to be alongside it (Figure 35).

The re-arrangement of almost the entire Scottish lowland landscape in the hundred years after 1750 meant the creation of new farms. Generally change started in the south and worked its way northwards as areas were pulled into the spheres of the southern markets. A map of the area around Roxburghe of 1769 shows courtyard and U-plan steadings alongside the earlier linear layouts.[24] Tenants of the estate were submitting estimates for new buildings and the lease granted to John Douglas for his farm at Berrikirk Quarter of Swinside (Roxburghshire) stated both the amount to be enclosed and put a limit on the amount to be spent on buildings.[25] Nearly every volume of the county *General Views* commented on the contrast between the old and new-style farm buildings. The comments of the Rev Smith writing in 1810 contrasting the farm building of Galloway are typical of many. The older-style farmhouses and buildings he described as 'paltry hovels' often owned by wealthy landlords who, 'though possessed of large fortunes are unwilling to lay out a single shilling'. Alongside these were the two-storey four to six-roomed houses with barns, stables, cow houses and sheds served by threshing machines powered by water or horses and suited to the size of the farm which were gradually replacing them.[26] As in England the reasons for these changes were the need to attract good tenants. 'Proprietors of land are now sensible that, in order to induce men of capital and respectability to live on their farms, it is necessary to accommodate them with good farmhouses and convenient offices. Few good farms can be stocked and improved unless the farmer can raise a considerable sum of capital: and men of capital are not willing to live in hovels when they pay handsome rents.'[27] Everywhere the home, or mains farms were being built with fine stone steadings where the often conflicting styles of baronial gothic and picturesque, through to classical and utilitarian are all to be found. Spires, clock towers and dovecotes often formed decorative features. Similar, if less flamboyant buildings were frequently erected on the newly enclosed tenant farms as well. East Lothian was the most advanced of the Scottish counties with, if Lord Belhaven is to be believed, many farm buildings already arranged around courts by 1700. Robert Somerville described the typical East Lothian planned farms in 1805. The houses were on two stories with attics and behind was a square of farm buildings. The open central yard was either used for animals, or, if they were kept in byres, for the dung hill. All farms had barns, a stack yard, stables, cow houses, feeding houses, hog houses, a poultry house, granary and implement store. Threshing machines were

FIGURE 35. Newton Fell Farm (Northumberland). This farm was built with a horse engine house abutting the barn which is itself at right angles to the farmyard.

already widely used. As more fodder crops were grown, livestock accommodation was expanded and barns altered to suit them to mechanical threshing. However, even in this progressive region some steadings were still 'totally in the style of the last century'.[28]

New building further north was limited to a few influential estates. At Blair Atholl, Blairuachdar Farm (Perthshire) was built on a courtyard plan in 1790 and St Columba in 1802 while in the far north, Sir John Sinclair in Caithness and the Marquis of Stafford in Sutherland were, as we have seen, the most influential of 'improvers' and this involved new buildings as well as landscape change. Of Sinclair's estates it could be said in 1812 'There is hardly an estate in northern part of Scotland where there are so many good farmhouses and offices'.[29] However in fact Sinclair's neighbours such as Sir John Anstruther and John Traill were also advocates of new building. As on most Scottish estates it was not the landowner, but the tenant who financed the new buildings initially. They could then claim 'meliorations' at the end of their leases.

Improvements in Sutherland had begun by the 1780s with squares of buildings being shown on maps drawn in 1788.[30] However, the main period of building began with the appointment of James Loch as factor for the Duke of Sutherland in 1816 and the creation as we have seen of 36 lowland mixed farms along the west coast, all with new sets of steadings (Figure 36). Seven were illustrated in Loch's book, published in 1820. It was the tenant who was responsible for the new buildings. All the new steadings were on a conventional U- or E-plan, with stables and cattle shelters, often with a granary above, sometimes separated from the central fold yard by a paved way. The

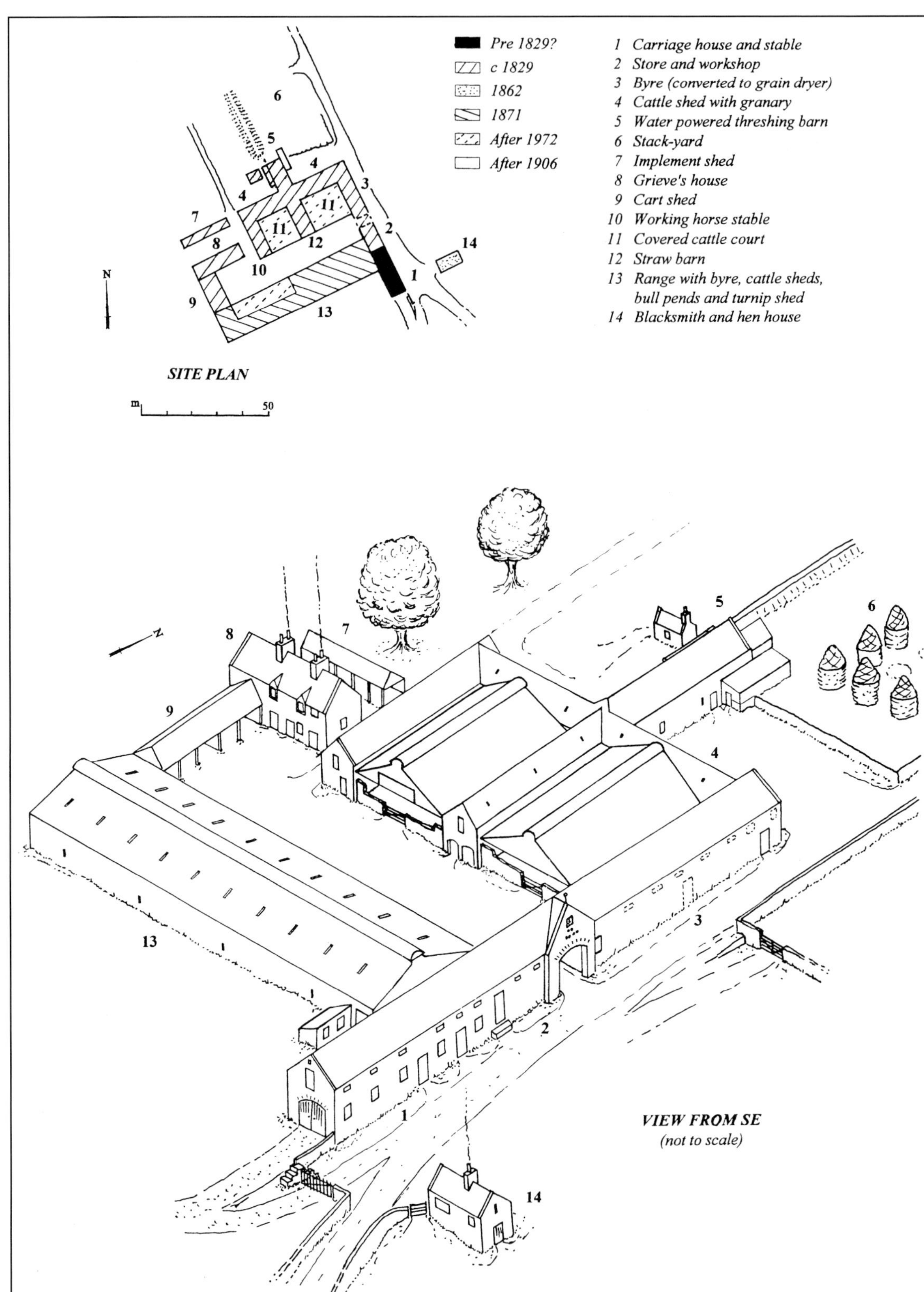
Pre 1829?
c 1829
1862
1871
After 1972
After 1906
1 Carriage house and stable
2 Store and workshop
3 Byre (converted to grain dryer)
4 Cattle shed with granary
5 Water powered threshing barn
6 Stack-yard
7 Implement shed
8 Grieve's house
9 Cart shed
10 Working horse stable
11 Covered cattle court
12 Straw barn
13 Range with byre, cattle sheds, bull pends and turnip shed
14 Blacksmith and hen house
N
SITE PLAN
m
50
VIEW FROM SE
(not to scale)

barn with its threshing machine was on a third side. Turnip houses, cart lodges and a few loose boxes were also included in the plan. As nearly all the farms were on streams, the threshing machines were mostly water-powered. In a few cases an ornamental gateway was surmounted by a dovecot, but most of the farms were simple, functional buildings with little ornamentation except for the Sutherland/Stafford coat of arms.

There is a certain sameness about these planned farms north and south of the border with few of the regional differences which are obvious on the evolved farms within their more traditional landscapes. However a few local characteristics are obvious. For instance bank barns are typical of the planned farms of the Lake District and other western counties. Dovecots over entrance-ways are found in Scotland and south into Northumberland. Local building materials also help give local distinctiveness. It was the spread of mixed farming based on the 'Norfolk' four-course system, which was seen as the basis of all 'improvement' which demanded similar farmsteads for its efficient implementation. Land agents, concerned for the financial viability of any capital investment constantly advised against extravagant building. As Nathaniel Kent wrote, owners should not 'build anything that was not really useful'.[31] It was the work of architects, often with a national clientele, as well as the use of the widely read pattern books which ensured that the fashionable symmetrical, classical building styles of the country houses spread good quality functional buildings across the newly planned countryside.

The landowners' home farms were more likely to be architect-designed than the buildings for tenants. They could be classical, or fronted with mock gothic facades. Sometimes, as at John Curwen's home farm at Workington, they could be crenellated. Some were built as show-pieces. Both Thomas William Coke at Holkham and the Duke of Bedford opened their farms and estates to inspection at their annual sheepshearings and Curwen's Schoose Farm was the venue for the annual meetings of the Workington Agricultural Society. They form an important element in many parkland landscapes that survive today as an indication of the influence and fashionable status agriculture had by the eighteenth century.[32]

FIGURE 36. Craikaig Farm (Sutherland). Craikaig Farm is an example of one of those rebuilt by the Marquis of Stafford at the beginning of the nineteenth century. It was a conventional U-plan with a barn abutting at right-angles powered by water. The Sutherland-Stafford coat of arms are above the dovecot on the main façade.

GRAHAM DOUGLAS, CROWN COPYRIGHT ROYAL COMMISSION ON THE ANCIENT AND HISTORICAL MONUMENTS OF SCOTLAND

The factory ideal, 1820–1870

The 1820s and 1830s generally saw a pause in estate farm building as rents stagnated after the heady days of the Napoleonic Wars. When interest re-emerged in the mid-1830s there were many changes on the agricultural scene to be taken into account with, as we have seen, the beginning of the Victorian age marking the start of a new scientific farming era. The practical skills passed from father to son now had to be supplemented by a scientific education. In many ways the initial phases of industrialisation and urbanisation in Britain had only been made possible by the increased output of farming. Now however, it was the turn of farming to benefit from industry. Every market town had its iron foundry producing ever-more sophisticated implements, and feed and

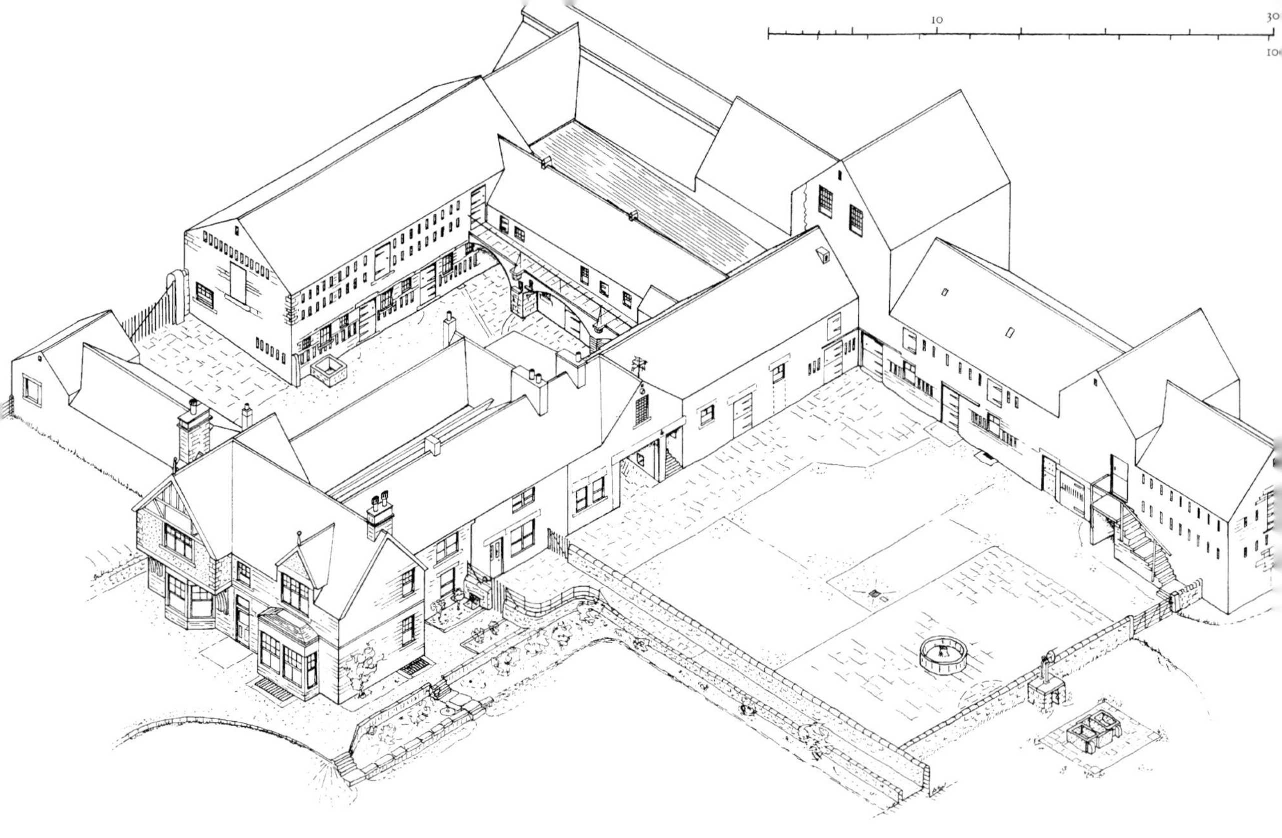

FIGURE 37.
Dalley Farm.
This Derbyshire farm, built by the Strutt family of industrialists in the 1830s, is one of the most unusual of the period, incorporating ideas and building materials such as cast-iron first introduced in factory building.
GRAHAM DOUGLAS

fertiliser mills were preparing the raw materials for farming. Some larger iron works, such as Musgroves and Sons with works in London and Belfast, were operating on a national level, providing fittings for livestock sheds and stables, thus taking the place of local carpenters. Steam engines, which had initially been developed to work pumps in mines and machines in factories could now power threshing and feed preparation machinery on the farm. Industrial money was also finding its way back into the countryside as successful manufacturers bought landed estates. Coal money was responsible for much of the building that was undertaken in Northumberland and by John Curwen of Workington on the Cumbrian coast.

As well as this agriculturalists were learning from the buildings and methods of industry. As J. B. Denton wrote in 1864, 'To farm successfully with defective and ill-arranged buildings is no more practical than to manufacture profitably in scattered inconvenient workshops in place of one harmoniously contrived, completely fitted mill.'[33] One of the earliest and best examples of this attitude is the work of the Strutts in Derbyshire (Figure 37). The Strutt family built and ran cotton spinning mills in the Derwent valley, one of the heartlands of the 'Industrial Revolution' and were pioneers in factory design. Their buildings were iron-framed with floors tiled for fire protection. Ventilation to the different floors was provided through hollow earthenware pipes and vents set within the walls and the factories were so designed as to aid the passage of the raw materials through the building and their processing into a finished product. As estates were purchased in the parishes of Milford and Belper, farms were built which conformed to these principles. There was little regard for classical symmetry. and their layout owed less to the conventional pattern books than to an understanding of the work-flow in factories. By taking advantage of the lie of the land, raw materials could be transferred from one stage of the agricultural process to the next. Ventilation ducts ran from the cow sheds up and out onto the roof of the hay stores above. The buildings were iron-framed with stone floors and vaulted brick ceilings. The dates of these extraordinary buildings are unclear, but they were complete by the 1840s.[34]

This enthusiasm for all things scientific from steam engines to plant breeding can be followed through the pages of the *JRASE*. While the understanding of science was becoming crucial to advanced farming practice, the development of systems in farm building design was also seen as essential to agricultural progress. Interest in farm buildings reached a new height with the Society's farm prize competition of 1850 (Figure 38). This allowed architects and some practical farmers alike to indulge their fantasies and produce drawings for an ideal farmstead. Very few of those published were in fact built, but they did provide a show case for architects and a new profession who described themselves as 'agricultural engineers'. The judges were impressed by the high standard of many of the entries which illustrated the view expressed by the *Journal*'s editor, Philip Pusey, that 'farm buildings, like certain countries, are

FIGURE 38. Thomas Sturgess' design for farm buildings. This design by a Bedale surveyor was submitted to the *JRASE* farm building competition of 1850. Its sturdy stone and slate construction which includes a steam engine house and four separate fold yards is typical of a North Yorkshire farm.

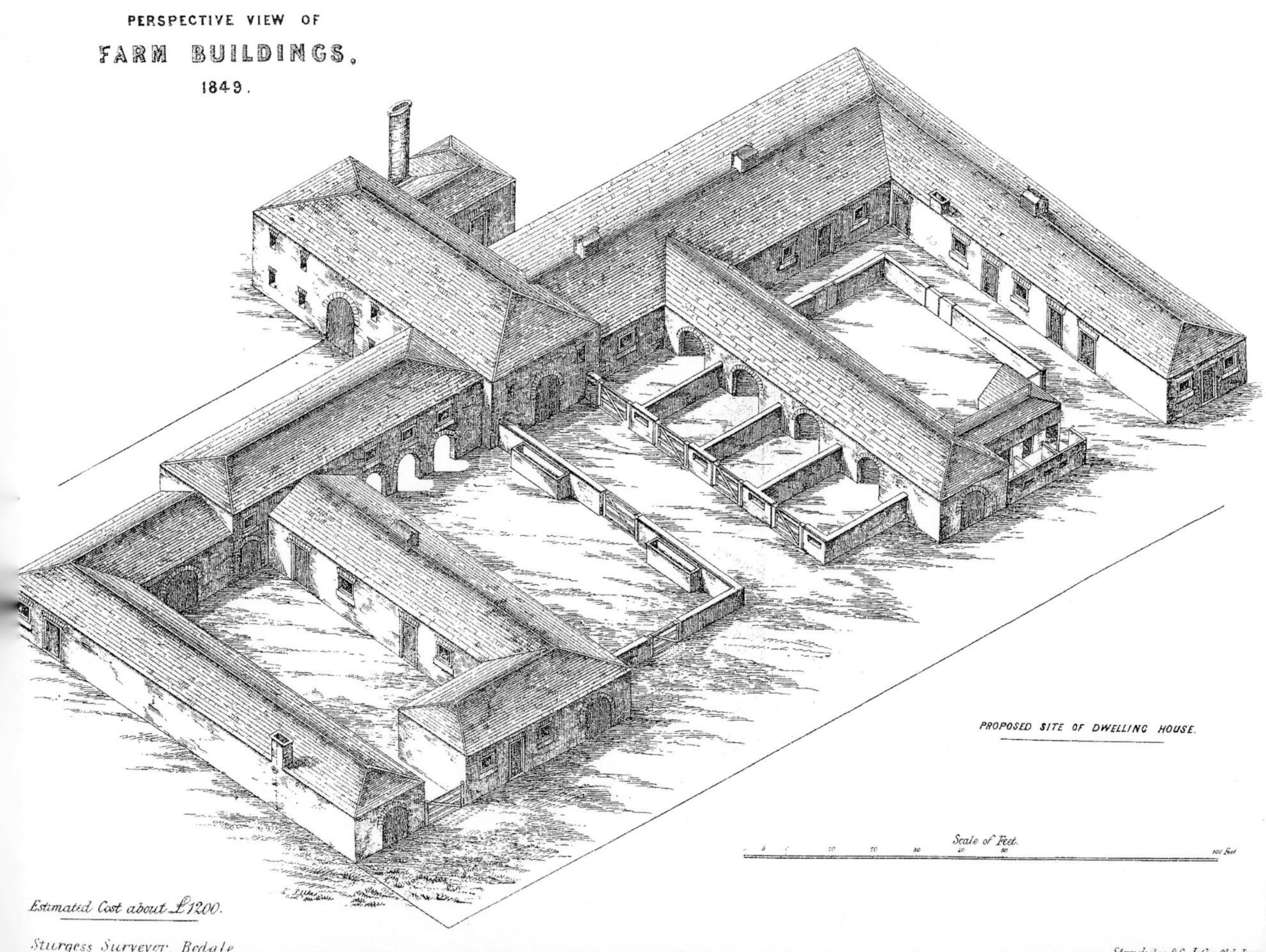

in a state of revolution'.[35] As one of the judges wrote 'There are no doubt many that are not convinced of the advantage of thrashing by steam, box feeding or other modern practices, ... but there are probably very few who would be satisfied with any plan that was not capable of being adapted to such a system whenever it might be desirable to commence it'.[36]

The resulting plans are similar to the planned farms that preceded them in that they are mostly of a symmetrical layout around open cattle yards. However, the yards are usually divided up to allow for the selective feeding of different groups of animals. As well as open yards there would also be loose boxes for fattening up stock ready for sale. As markets were opened up by the spread of the railway, interest in efficient methods of meat production increased. The barn often takes up part of the rear range, but it may also be a separate wing out to the back allowing for a steam or horse engine to be placed beside it to work machinery. Tram lines were also often included for the pushing of trucks of feed from the preparation rooms to the livestock and of manure out to the manure house. Lines might also run out to the stack yards to aid the transport of corn stacks to the threshing machine. 'When the cattle are to be fed, the trucks take up their load of roots, cut or boiled in the root boiling or cutting store, or the chaff and linseed compound for another meal, obtained each from their respective store houses adjoining the rail, and proceed on their way through the cattle boxes giving out to each animal its accepted allowance. The trucks are again available for littering the animals, procuring the supply from the straw barn; and when the accumulation of the manure in the boxes has reached its limited height of increase the trucks convey this mass of dung direct to the dung pit. One man could thus easily by means of the rail and truck manage all these operations in a short time.'[37] Here we have a description of what is essentially an industrial operation working its way through a factory. The links between industry and farming were becoming increasingly close. A further development indicates the changing social status of the farmer. He too was becoming a manager in charge of an increasingly remote workforce. The new farmhouse was often at a distance from the farm, emphasising the increasing social status of the farmer during the prosperous mid-century years of high farming.

Interest, particularly in the development of cattle accommodation continued to dominate the pages of the agricultural press throughout the middle years of the century and it was in the 1850s that the first covered yards began to appear (Figure 39). The sheltering of stock in covered yards had two advantages. Firstly protected stock did not need to use so much energy keeping warm and thus fattened more quickly. Secondly, the manure would not lose its value through being constantly soaked with rain. However, covered yards were expensive and there was always the problem of providing enough ventilation. Many estates were not convinced they were worth the expense. Although some that remain date from this period, more were built after 1870 as part of the desperate measures needed to extend livestock farming as the main branch of agriculture that remained profitable during the depression.

FIGURE 39.
An 'industrial' farm. These buildings at Nutfield (Surrey), were designed by the Essex architect, Frederick Chancellor in 1857. They incorporate the latest thinking in animal husbandry in the form of covered yards, but also have architectural detailing in the gothic façade.
ESSEX RECORD OFFICE

'High' farming as a system was only suited to farms over 200 acres and demanded substantial investment from the tenant; he in turn demanded similar investment from his landlord. The increased use of bought-in feed allowed more animals to be kept and these in turn needed housing. Although there was much interest and enthusiasm for these factory farms in the pages of the agricultural and architectural press it was only on the largest and most expensively managed estates that they were likely to be built. These were likely to be those with wealth being generated outside agriculture. This is particularly obvious in the Northumberland countryside where the coal mines provided the wealth and also ensured that there was a shortage of cheap labour for farm work which encouraged mechanisation. In 1913 'The most striking feature of Northumberland farming … [was] the magnitude and excellence of the farm buildings – great blocks of well-built stone structures, dominated by a very factory-like chimney.'[38] This situation extended across the border into Berwickshire and the Lothians where equally impressive farmsteads remain.

As the final phases of land reclamation were completed across Scotland grandiose steadings were erected to process the increased produce and house the stock that could now be fed. In Fife new farmsteads were being erected of 'the greatest magnificence and magnitude'.[39] In Moray the Earl of Moray's factor, Mr Brown, designed new buildings including a 'magnificent steading at Westermanbeen which covers about an acre'. Eight new farms were created and 712 acres reclaimed between 1850 and 1877.[40]

Although it was on the large cereal-growing estates of eastern Scotland that this wholesale estate remodelling was most obvious, some western landlords helped their tenants adapt to the growing demand for milk from the industrial centre of Glasgow. Almost every farm on the Logan estates of Col. MacDouall's Wigtonshire lands was provided with good dairy accommodation.[41]

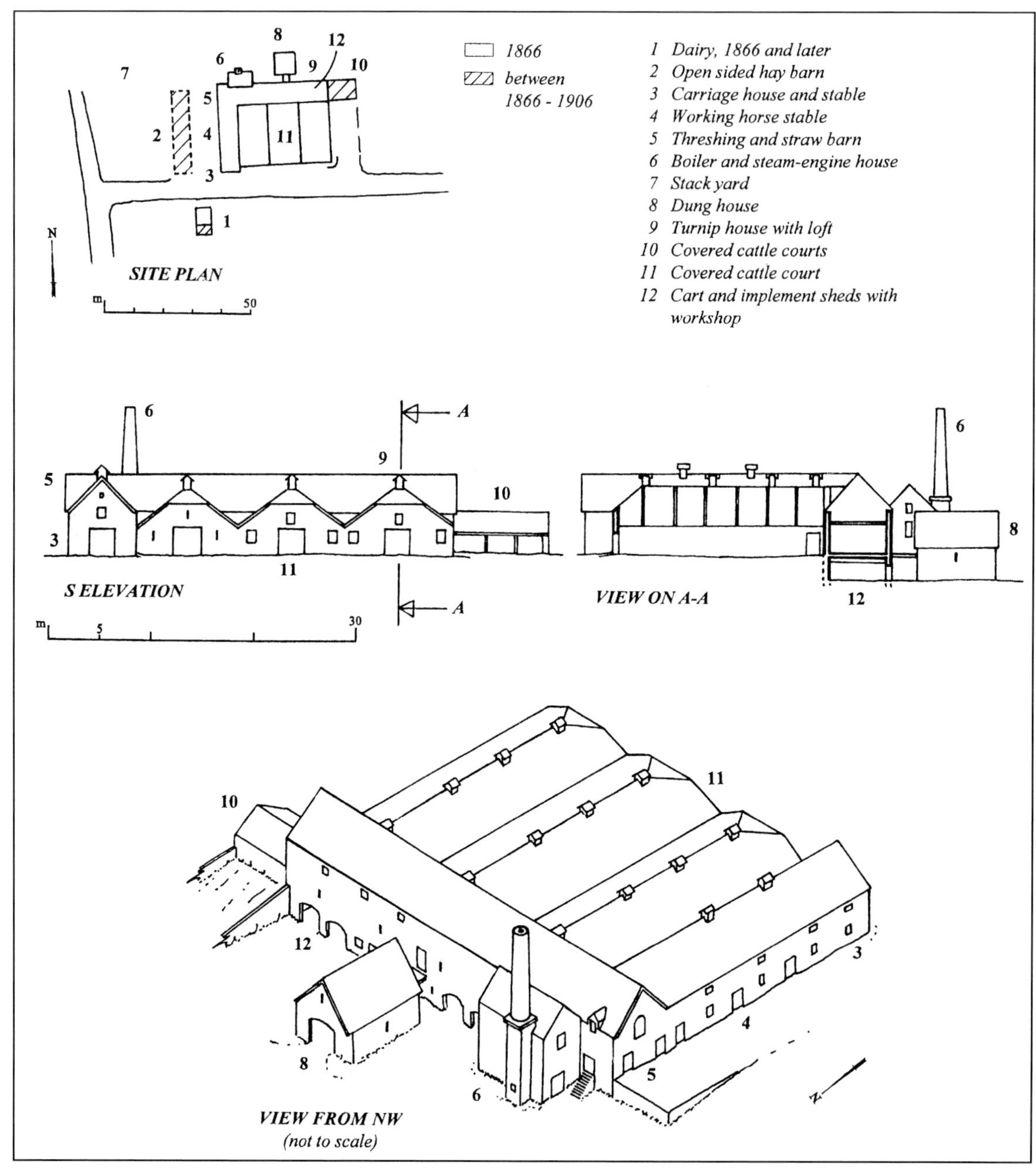

Amongst the wealthiest British landowners were the Marquis of Stafford who was also Duke of Sutherland, and the Duke of Bedford and both these men continued their family's earlier interest in farm building, rebuilding or adding to the work of their predecessors. In Sutherland, the Duke entirely replaced the steading at Clynleish in 1866, creating a state-of-the-art steading with a steam engine, covered yards and a covered manure house reached directly from the yards (Figure 40). The fact that the farm was built into the slope meant that the rear wing behind the cattle courts could have three levels with a lower cart shed accessed from the rear side. Above was the cattle court level with a walkway to the manure house, and the granary/feed store was above. The work of reclamation undertaken by the Duke of Sutherland in the 1870s has already been described. Four new farms were created at Shinness and provided with 'well-built steadings' with large cattle courts.[42] Further buildings were added in 1882 and some of the cattle courts roofed in 1887. A silage pit was also built in an innovative effort to solve the problem of winter fodder for stock in an inclement climate and with soil conditions unsuited to turnips.[43]

All the tenanted farms built by Robert Salmon on the Woburn estate of the Duke of Bedford were replaced in the 1850s and 1860s. Huge buildings with several cattle yards and wide stock sheds were erected. Many had steam engine houses with tall chimneys dominating the Bedfordshire countryside. Unlike many such buildings which are placed in a regular, newly laid-out landscape, many of the forty Bedfordshire farms are in areas of old enclosures. The reason for all this expense was said to be to 'satisfy the requirements and take advantage of the recent improvements in agriculture and to enable tenants to meet the competition to which free trade in corn and other agricultural produce has given rise, and through building in brick to protect against incendiarism and so ensure the durability of the buildings'.[44] Much of the Duke of Bedford's wealth came from his copper mines in and around Tavistock and here too he rebuilt farms in the middle years of the century. The old small farms and fields were amalgamated and the new farms were intended to be more commercial enterprises than the small dairy farms they replaced. Before anything was built, the estate surveyor was sent to investigate other farms in the region and the result was a monumental farmstead just outside Tavistock at Kilworthy, built in 1851 'upon a new plan, which, if it should be found to answer, may become a model for the other farm buildings ... the main feature ... being the great compactness, having the farm buildings nearly all under one roof, keeping the manure under cover, free from the influence of rain, wind and sun, economising labour by means of tramways and providing extensive housing for cattle'.[45] The result is a farmstead with extensive covered yards and stone floors with the stones set somewhat apart to allow the liquid to drip through into a manure shed underneath which could be approached from outside by carts down the slope. Barn machinery was water-powered by a huge water wheel fed from a reservoir in the field above.[46]

Although there are many other estates across the country where building schemes were embarked upon on a grand scale, 'model' farms were often

FIGURE 40
Clynleish Farm (Sutherland). This is an example of an industrial farmstead, built by the Duke of Sutherland in 1867. The machinery was worked by steam, the cattle yards were covered and the manure was toppled from the cattle sheds into a manure house from where it could taken to the fields.

GRAHAM DOUGLAS, CROWN COPYRIGHT THE ROYAL COMMISSION ON THE ANCIENT AND HISTORIC MONUMENTS OF SCOTLAND confined to the home farm. The value of these showpieces was doubted by many writers of the day. Mr Browick, the agent at Stoneleigh (Warwickshire), wrote in 1862 that model farmsteads, 'although to be met with in most counties, are not essential to the system. They are all very well in their own way, but ... rather let the estate bear a quiet unassuming aspect, its buildings being plain but sufficient ... neatness and order should alike prevail.'[47] The agricultural engineer and writer, George Andrews commented that farmers associated home farms with 'the practices of those gentlemen who, having pockets which overflow with wealth derived from other sources, erect the most costly places imaginable, and carry on their agricultural operations regardless of the great question as to whether they pay or not'.[48] Certainly when some of the more elaborate structures erected at the time are considered there would seem to be much truth in these statements. However behind their architectural facades many such buildings are very practical and as showpieces would be visited by both fellow landlords and tenantry. Some of the techniques demonstrated in their design might well have been copied, if in a simpler style, by others. One of the most ostentatious, with its Italianate clock tower and facades, was the Dairy Farm in Windsor Home Park. The architect, George Dean wrote, 'I have always viewed these works in the light of a national undertaking. No greater benefit in my opinion could be conferred on agriculturalists or the agricultural labourer than the erection of such buildings as many Noblemen and landed proprietors of this and other countries will doubtless inspect them when built and go and do likewise.'[49] Elsewhere in the Park, Flemish Farm, with its facade of polychrome brickwork, is a typical farmstead adapted for high farming. The barn wing contains a steam engine with an impressive chimney, in front of which are three covered yards.[50]

Some model farmer designers experimented with new building materials. At Eastwood Manor Farm, East Harptree, near Bristol, built between 1858 and 1860, there are two huge covered yards each about 100 feet wide, and roofed with corrugated iron. A 27-foot diameter water wheel worked barn machinery and tramways delivered the stacks to the barn. A fountain played in the centre of one of the yards and the water was then pumped through cast-iron pipes around the water troughs in the buildings. Iron fittings were all mass-produced by either a Bristol or a London foundry.[51] Concrete was first used for the buildings of a home farm in 1870 by Robert Campbell who had returned from Australia with a fortune and bought the Buscot estate in Berkshire. Whilst it was used on a few other estates over the next twenty years, the idea was not widely taken up.

Another splendid example of the optimism and confidence of the period is the Home Farm at Apley (Shropshire). Again built using money made outside agriculture by the Foster family of iron masters, it was completed in 1875. It is of red brick with black detailing and a highly decorative chimney. Its basic layout is traditional, if on a large scale, on an E-plan with two covered yards. The most impressive features are the wide yards spanned by huge curved laminated timber trusses, a technique known from the 1820s, but rarely used for farm buildings. The resulting building is one of the finest examples of the industrial mid-nineteenth century architecture of farm buildings.

Historians have always tended to look at 'agriculture' and 'industry' separately, to the extent that they have both been ascribed their own 'revolutions'. Only in the last 50 years or so has the division broken down so that we now talk of the 'agricultural industry'. However, as these grandest of buildings show, by the late nineteenth century contemporaries saw agriculture as part of the general trend towards mechanisation and industrialisation. In reality there was a complex web of inter-relationships between farm and factory. As we have seen agriculture had relied on better transport and marketing structures to develop from a self-sufficient to a commercial activity. Transport allowed for regional specialisation which in itself required specific types of building. The replacing of wooden by iron implements relied on the development of the iron industry and in the industry's early days, agriculture was its main market. Engines, belting and gearing as well as trucks and tramways found their way onto these factory-like farms. Trevithick's early steam engines quickly reached not only the Cornish tin mines, but also Cornish farms where they were working threshing machines[52] and the water wheel technology developed for the Tavistock copper mines was used on nearby farms. Similarly, new building materials such as corrugated iron, concrete and laminated timber were also replacing, albeit in a small way, locally produced products and cast iron fittings were taking work from village carpenters.

The blurring of the distinction between agriculture and industry as far as methods and philosophies are concerned is most clearly seen in the factory farms of the second half of the nineteenth century and the new farm buildings clearly reflect the improved farming practice being promoted at the time. The erection of these farmsteads is an indication of the degree to which the ideas being put forward in the farming literature were being taken up. Whilst these farms are mostly confined to the great estates, their influence can be seen in many of the adaptations made on the more typical evolved farms across Britain.

CHAPTER FIVE

Evolved Landscapes

The landscapes

Oliver Rackham divided the British landscape into two types which he called 'ancient' and 'planned'. The previous chapters have considered Rackham's planned landscapes, the farming they supported and the buildings this farming required. His 'ancient' landscapes are the subject of this chapter. However the term 'evolved' rather than 'ancient' will be used because 'ancient' suggests a static environment, whereas, in agricultural terms, change was taking place. In contrast to the planned landscapes of improvement, however, change in these ancient landscapes built on what was there before.

Rackham defined the ancient landscape as one of hamlets, medieval farms in the hollows of hills, lonely moats, great barns in the clay lands, pollards and ancient trees, holloways, foot paths and thick hedges. It was one that appeared to have altered little since 1700.[1] Indeed, many of the changes that took place in the planned landscapes after 1750 had already taken place here. Firstly and most importantly, the fields were already enclosed. This was often because the fields were created by colonisation away from an old established settlement. Moor and forest was taken into cultivation during the medieval period by individuals clearing land and taking it over, usually building an isolated farmstead in the middle of their newly assarted land. This was happening everywhere that there was forest left to fell or hillsides to cultivate, including the moor edges of the west country, the forest of Arden and parts of Hampshire. There are very few other cultivated regions of the United Kingdom where open fields never existed, although in some, such as Zennor in West Cornwall, Bronze Age fields seem to have been continuously farmed since their creation (Figure 41).[2] The area of West Penwith, of which Zennor is part, is divided into small fields by massive banks of granite boulders that zig-zag to take in immovably large stones in their foundations. Deep lanes, used as drove roads meander between the banks and cross streams by clapper bridges, converging on the settlements.[3] The remarkable survival of this ancient farming landscape as a functioning farming system is due to the fact that these tiny fields were ideally suited to the small-scale pastoral farming practiced in the area into the twentieth century. Secondly of course they would have been very difficult to remove. The existence of enclosed fields did not necessarily ensure that a farm's fields were grouped as a unit. In fact in Zennor the fields of a single holding were scattered across the township, and in this they differed

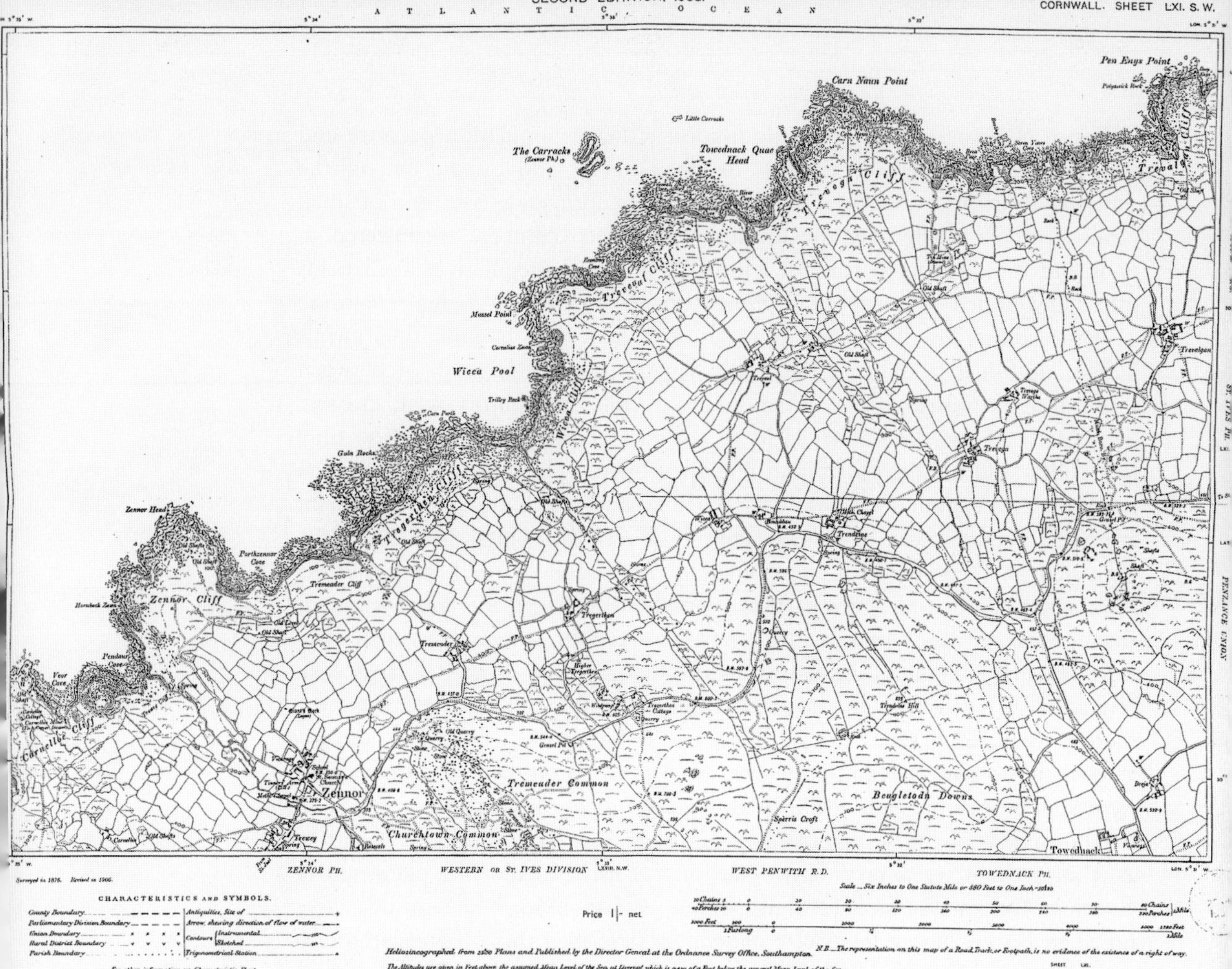

FIGURE 41.
West Penwith in 1860. The First Edition six-inch Ordnance Survey map shows a landscape of small fields little changed since the Bronze Age (Cornwall 61 SW).

from the tightly ring-fenced fields of an assarted farm in the wood-pasture areas. This situation was probably the result of a partible inheritance system which resulted in the creation of small hamlets of between two and eight holdings and scattered buildings, where even single houses were sometimes divided between two families in the eighteenth century. Farms were small throughout the nineteenth century, averaging 40–60 acres with field sizes of about two acres. The rearing of cattle was the main activity until dairying took over in the late nineteenth century. The main crop was oats which was grown on an in-field, out-field system, with the fields nearest the farm being manured and planted and those further way being used for grazing.[4] These small farmers survived because many found secondary employment in the local tin mines which were expanding production during the nineteenth century. Anciently enclosed fields, consisting either of prehistoric enclosures and amalgamations of them, or medieval enclosures, make up about 57 per cent of the land area of Cornwall.[5]

In neighbouring Devon, piecemeal enclosure had begun by the late fourteenth century and it is recognised as one of the earliest counties to be enclosed. The existence of wasteland ripe for colonisation reduced population pressure and therefore tension over the end of the open fields[6] and by the end of the sixteenth century few survived. By this date the countryside consisted of small farms scattered singly over the hillsides or in deep combes, or clustered in twos and threes to form hamlets within their small, irregularly-shaped fields often surrounded by waste. The years 1500 to 1800 saw a gradual enclosure of waste adding anything from 15 to 20 acres at a time to individual farms. These additional fields were frequently larger than the original, of between three and four acres each. Occasionally entirely new farms were created, particularly in the Blackdown Hills to the east of the county. By 1800 only the wildest and most exposed land remained open.[7] The eighty enclosure acts for Devon date from 1804–1923 and cover upland waste or low-lying marsh. Except, therefore for a few new farms built on these intakes, most farms remained on their medieval sites, often in the middle of their lands.[8] Fields were small (about four acres in 1848) with hedges 'larger and more frequent than necessary'[9] and were farmed on a 'convertible' system by which they were left in grass for a long period before being ploughed and planted with cereals for a few years and then reverting to grass. Arable and pasture were therefore transitory states. Farms were small, averaging between 20 and 40 acres with few over 200 and none over 300 acres.[10] Both dairy and store cattle were kept and turnips and artificial grasses were being grown on a small scale by the middle of the seventeenth century, not so much as part of rotations as a supplementary animal feed. One of the earliest recorded plantings of clover in Devon was at Payembury in the east in 1666, while turnips were noted in Bovey Tracey in 1686.[11] Vancouver described this progressive group of yeomanry as 'respectable'. Above them on the social scale were the 'resident gentry',[12] but there were few influential large landowners. The resulting landscape was one of small farms, scattered farmsteads and hamlets, small enclosed fields, winding lanes and high hedgerows, much of which remains today.

Devon agriculture was not static during the eighteenth and nineteenth centuries. With the introduction of fodder crops in the seventeenth century, the area of pasture as a percentage of farmland was declining by the 1790s. The tithe maps show 23 per cent of the county's titheable area as arable and 51 per cent as pasture and crop yields in this area, climatically more suited to pasture, were below the national average.[13] Arable reached a peak of 67,000 acres compared with 400,000 acres of grass in 1872. This allowed for the increased production of fodder crops for an intensifying livestock sector and the development of distinct high-quality Devon breeds. Although most Devon farms were mixed, with a greater emphasis on grain in the better soils, the county was best known for its fine cattle and pastures and many of the county's farmers excelled as breeders of pedigree livestock.

The area most famous for its independent farmers was the Lake District. Here as in the previous examples there had been a considerable degree of piecemeal enclosure by 1700. The eighteenth century saw further enclosure by private agreement, fossilising common field strips within the evolved landscape. Parliamentary enclosure was mostly confined to the wastes with 29 per cent of Cumberland and 24 per cent of Westmorland being affected.[14]

The weakness of baronial control and the lack of powerful gentry had allowed a class of tenant farmers to emerge in the more isolated parts of the region who were able to exert a considerable control over their lands. The end of the border wars with Scotland resulted in the emergence of independent 'statesman' farmers operating small-scale farms which were the basis of farming life from the seventeenth into the nineteenth century. As late as 1790 two-thirds of Cumberland was held by small customary tenants whose security was virtually that of a freeholder. Many of these farms were under 50 acres.[15] This pattern of development was in contrast to that other border county, Northumberland, where the union of the crowns had led to the strengthening of the power of the already powerful landowners and the development of landlord controlled enclosures rather than the gradual changes of the Lake District.[16] This can be partly explained by the rugged terrain and remoteness of many farms and settlements. Farming prosperity was based on cattle both as store and dairy animals. Its position on the major droving routes between Scotland and the expanding markets of the south allowed the Cumbrian farms along these routes to develop beyond a subsistence economy. Unlike elsewhere, Cumbrian

FIGURE 42. Langdale (Cumbria). This map shows the three medieval farms and irregular in-bye fields with surrounding ring-garth dividing off the open pasture. The sheep folds are mostly along the ring garth. Some of this was enclosed during the Napoleonic Wars into large, regular fields.

PHILLIP JUDGE, DRAWING ON NATIONAL TRUST RESEARCH

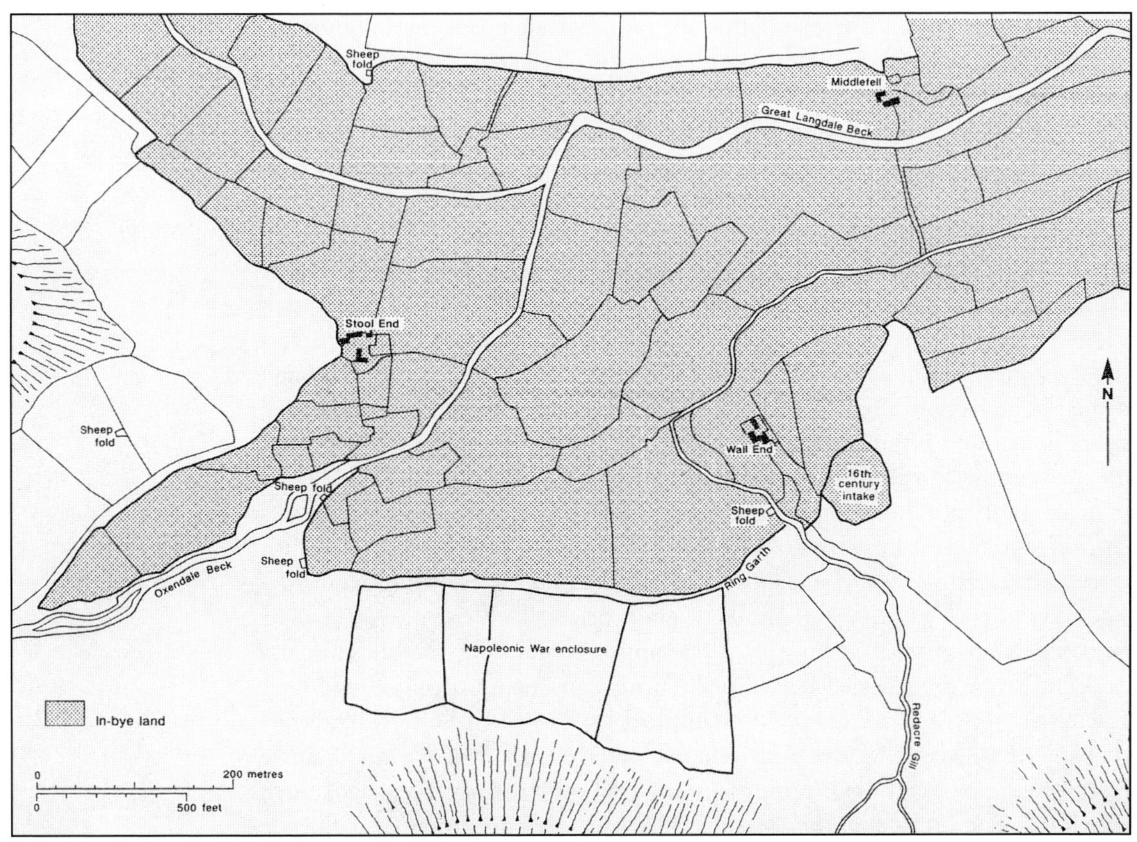

agriculture thrived when the price of corn and therefore animal feed was low. The Lake District valleys were cultivated on an in-field-out-field system and a stock-proof wall (the ring garth) divided these fields from the open fells beyond which were used mainly for sheep grazing (Figure 42).[17] By the eighteenth century, many of the statesmen farmers were prospering and there had been much recent rebuilding. Long, low stone farmhouses stretched far up the fertile vales into the fells, replacing the clay and timber buildings of which no trace remains. Alongside the houses was an increased provision for cattle shelter, which facilitated the wintering of cattle and sheep.[18] However, although well-off in their own terms, these small farmers did not have the capital for improvements, such as the drainage of the heavy clays that was a necessary pre-condition for fodder crops such as turnips. Only a third of the land in Cumberland that could have benefited from drainage had been tackled by 1850.[19] Farm amalgamations began in the 1750s. Whilst most farms were still under 50 acres in 1833, by 1852 smallholders were described as farming between 40 and 100 acres.[20] The statesmen remained influential with 37 per cent of farmers in the lakeland counties described as 'yeomen' in 1829.[21]

The claylands of south Norfolk and Suffolk are another example of Rackham's 'ancient landscape'. A piecemeal process of enclosure by agreement had largely been completed by around 1700. Like the open fields elsewhere in East Anglia, those of these claylands were irregular and the pattern of settlement dispersed consisting of farms and hamlets often on the edges of greens and commons. With the late medieval decline in population, the region had come to specialise in livestock and few farms ploughed more than a quarter of their land regularly. Not surprisingly this shift was accompanied by gradual piecemeal enclosure into often very small fields divided by thick hedges, often with large-scale trees allowed to grow up within them.[22] Small fields surrounded by thick hedges and wide borders often cut for hay if the field was being cultivated, were typical of the region by 1800. Outside manorial control, a class of independent yeoman farmers prospered. Young described the Suffolk farmers as a rich yeomanry who were 'a most valuable set of men who, having the means and the most powerful inducements to good husbandry, carry agriculture to a high degree of perfection'.[23] Parliamentary enclosure was almost entirely concerned with the removal of greens and commons and the regular fields created stand out in contrast to the adjacent small irregular enclosures.

In contrast to the claylands of the midlands, where open field arable was converted to enclosed pasture in the eighteenth through to the early nineteenth century, the early-enclosed dairy lands of north Suffolk were being converted to arable to take advantage of the high grain prices. Here we see an evolved landscape able to take advantage of the improved farming methods usually associated with the planned landscapes. Turnips are mentioned as a field crop as early as 1624 and were widely established by the end of the seventeenth century.[24] It appears that the shift to arable here began before the marked rise in cereal prices after 1760. Young wrote in 1786 'about forty years ago, there was little under tillage' and this is supported by the documentary evidence that survives.[25] Initially, this ploughing up was to grow more fodder crops, both turnips and cabbages, in an intensification of the existing cattle-based economy. Indeed, farms with a quarter of their land ploughed up were able to keep more cows as a result.[26] By the end of the century, the arable was being expanded far more rapidly and the high grain prices of the Napoleonic Wars saw the end of dairy farming. 'Pasture farming, with its herds of milch cows and butter at 9*d.* a pint could not stand before the temptation of £3 a coomb of wheat.'[27] How was it possible for the farmers on these evolved landscapes to take advantage of the grain bonanza when those on the newly-enclosed midland clays did not? The answer must surely lie in the tradition of draining that existed in East Anglia. Underdrainage was first developed in the region, spreading from Essex in the early eighteenth century, when it was referred to as the 'Essex' method. A variety of sources point to the digging of drains which were then filled with various types of bush and faggots and then back filled. This method, known as 'bush drainage', was introduced into the East Anglian clays after about 1760 and was widely established by 1790. It would certainly have been necessary before turnips and cabbages were grown. The comment in the tithe files of the 1830s for the long-enclosed Suffolk parishes of South Elmham All Saints and St Nicholas, stating that 'There is a great spirit of improvement pervading this part of the county and that by means of underdraining which is now in very general practice the produce of these heavy lands is very much increased' shows the importance of the practice.[28] However, this type of drainage was not open to the farmers in the open fields, where ridge and furrow was the only system possible. Once the expense of enclosure had been met, they were unlikely to wish for more outlay and so a pastoral system was more profitable.

In Cornwall, prehistoric fields appear to have remained in continuous use while elsewhere, Roman field patterns can be identified. Here it is likely that open fields did for a time overlay the Roman boundaries which were preserved delimiting the furlongs, to re-emerge as field boundaries at a later date.[29] Whatever the life-span of the open fields, in evolved landscapes they had all but disappeared by 1700. How this enclosure took place is not recorded, but that it must have been a piecemeal process is suggested by the irregular fields in the surviving landscapes. There are several possible explanations as to why this enclosure took place. As population began to decline in the later middle ages, cereal growing was no longer necessary on such a large scale and soils that were more suitable for livestock could be converted to pasture. Hedged fields were by far the most practical way of keeping animals. However, this change was only possible where the manorial system was weak and so whilst the claylands of Suffolk and Devon were enclosed, those of the midlands, as we have seen, were not.

Though the examples of evolved landscape discussed here are obviously limited in number, it is clear that they share certain features. They developed in areas with weak manorial influence where individual farmers were independent enough to control their land. They were also in areas where small farms and pastoral activities dominated. Some cereals, for both subsistence and animal fodder, were grown, but this was either under traditional systems of convertible husbandry (land cultivated for a few years before laying down for pasture) or in-field-out-field. Both these systems were very much frowned upon by the agricultural commentators, committed as they were to the advantages of rotational systems including turnips and artificial grasses, and for whom the increasing of cereal output was the *raison d'etre* of improved husbandry. Of Devon W. Marshall wrote 'The spirit of improvement was deeply buried under an accumulation of custom and prejudice.'[30] However, much of Cornwall and the Lake District was unsuited to arable production, and the farmers of Devon and Suffolk had been some of the first innovators in livestock management, growing small acreages of turnips for fodder from the seventeenth century and developing the much prized cattle of Devon and the dun and red poll of Suffolk.

A feature of these evolved landscapes is that change was a continuous process which did not end with the final enclosure of the last open fields by the eighteenth century. As farming systems changed from pasture to arable, then larger fields were required. In Suffolk we find tenants taking out hedges with the permission, but without the financial support of their landlords. Comparison of the tithe maps in several south-Norfolk parishes with the First Edition Six-inch Ordnance Survey shows the changes that took place in field patterns in the 40 years from 1840 to 1880. It is clear that the scale of change in this period was considerable and greater than that between the 1880s and the two-and-a-half inch maps of the 1950s.[31] This is supported by Augustus Jessop, vicar of Scarning in the Norfolk clays, who wrote in the 1870s,

> The small fields that used to be so picturesque and wasteful are gone or are going; the tall hedges, the high banks, the scrub or the bottoms where a fox or weasel might hope to find a night's lodging ... all these things have vanished.[32]

The increasing introduction of machinery encouraged the removal of hedges around small irregular fields. Caird visited an 160-acre Devon farm in 1850 where, to allow for the use of machinery, the average field size had been increased to ten acres by the removal of seven miles of hedge.[33] The tenant farmer of Park Farm, Wrotham in Kent was asked by a Select Committee in 1845 whether there were large hedgerows in his neighbourhood to which he replied, 'Not much now – we had a good many, I have grubbed a good number up on my farm.' He went on to say that it was not possible to farm profitably on land that was 'wood-bound'.[34]

Woodland too continued to be felled. Pressure from the shooting fraternity could not prevent the intensive farmers of the mid-nineteenth century grubbing up woods with the help of the newly-available powerful steam ploughs. Hitcham Wood, Suffolk and much of Rockingham Forest, Northamptonshire, disappeared at this time.[35] It was only an Act of Parliament of 1878 that prevented Epping Forest following other Essex woodlands into arable cultivation.

The farmsteads of the evolved landscapes

The difference between the evolved and planned countryside is nowhere more evident than in the farm buildings. The clusters of buildings of local materials which appear almost to have grown out of the landscape surrounding them is one of the most enduring images of the British countryside. The elements within a single farmstead can date from the medieval to the nineteenth century and they reflect the slowly changing patterns of farming over the period. The influences on their building will have been local rather than the pattern books of the improving landlords and so they demonstrate uniquely regional vernacular traditions developed to provide for specific local agricultural requirements. Lack of capital resulted in a need to adapt rather than rebuild which again is evidence for farming changes over the period. However, the ideas to be found on the planned farms might well be adapted and incorporated into existing farmsteads and it is in the deviation from best practice that much of the historical significance of evolved farmsteads lies. They tend to have dispersed rather than regular plans, or, as is the case in west Berkshire and south Lincolnshire, the plan can be more compact, but with individual buildings not always standing in the best relationship to each other in terms of the flow of processes through the steading.[36] Typically a late medieval barn was extended or a porch added in the eighteenth century as grain yields began to rise. Where the importance of arable increased, a second barn might be built, or, as frequently happened in Suffolk, a stable originally forming part of the old barn was removed, thus allowing for the opening up of the barn, and rebuilt elsewhere on the farmstead site. Similarly separate cowsheds, cart sheds and granaries appeared. Eighteenth-century yards for inwintering of cattle were often temporary enclosures. The journal of Randall Burroughes, farming near Wymondham in the 1790s records how in the autumn he 'divided up the parr yards', while leases on the north-east Norfolk Heydon estate from the mid-eighteenth century often gave tenants the right to take rough timber for the construction of racks and stalls for cattle, implying rather impermanent structures. As the management of stock and manure became more specialised new cattle sheds or dairies might be built and cattle yards enclosed.

The layout is evidence for this gradual accretion of buildings and could vary greatly across the country according to local conditions. At Old Manor Farm, Braceby (Lincolnshire) the oldest surviving building is the dovecote, dated 1707 with the nearby barn also eighteenth century. All that existed in 1839 was the dovecote and a linear range of barn, stable and trap house. A further stable and two cattle yards were built between 1840 and 1880, and the map evidence showed that they were not replacing earlier buildings, the enlarged stabling indicating an increase in arable and the cattle provision an intensification of livestock husbandry within a mixed system. Village Farm, Swaton also in Lincolnshire, presents a similar picture.[37]

We know little of the form of farmstead layout before 1600, but excavations suggest that while a linear arrangement, derived from the longhouse was usual in the north and west, a courtyard was always more common in the east and certainly pre-dated the agricultural changes of the eighteenth century. In Devon smaller farms in hilly terrain often consisted of a single range including barn, cowhouse and stable, sometimes with the house as part of the range. The buildings could often be of different dates, being added as required. Buildings on a dispersed plan are also typical with scattered and evolved courtyard layouts found across Devon as a whole. Tanner, in his survey of Devon farming, written in 1848, was highly critical of the farm buildings he found there. 'The homesteads appear to have been built without any regard for uniformity of convenience ... when additional buildings were necessary they were raised on the nearest point that happened to be free.'[38] The gradual development of a farmyard can be followed at Bury Barton (Figure 43) where the farmstead evolved from the sixteenth century although the house may well be medieval. It is made up of an inner court and and an outer yard of nineteenth-century linhays (a form of open cattle housing). In the inner court there are several sixteenth-century buildings including two barns, a granary, and a seventeenth-century domestic building, possibly for farm servants. It was not until the eighteenth century that the yard was finally enclosed with the building of linhays, making it suitable for the inwintering of livestock. In the nineteenth century a further linhay was built and after 1840, the second court was built to the north. Although many of these buildings may well be replacements and the yard may have been enclosed by hurdles at an early date, the building evidence would suggest that the farm had been largely arable in the sixteenth

FIGURE 43.
Bury Barton (Devon). This group of buildings has gradually evolved, with more livestock accommodation being provided over the centuries.
N. ALCOCK (1966), REDRAWN BY PHILLIP JUDGE

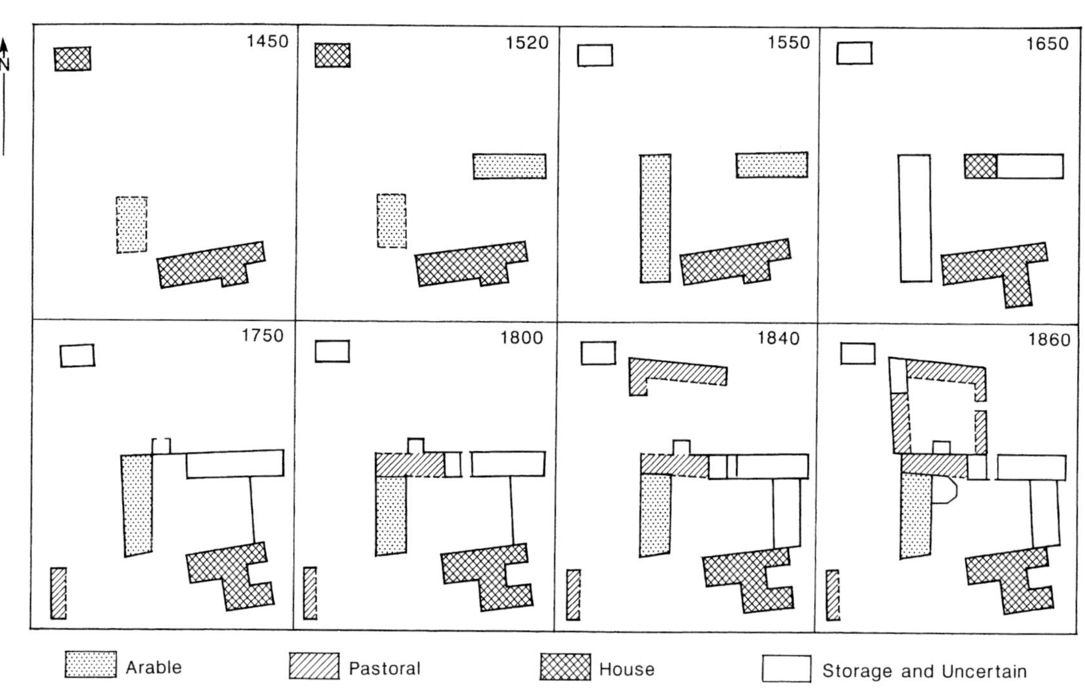

and seventeenth century with an increase in the importance of livestock in the eighteenth and nineteenth century.[39] This farm, like so many others in Devon was not small and poor but a 'barton' or manorial farm, indicating that both high- and low-status farms could evolve rather than be completely rebuilt. It is typical of many in the county which did not develop a courtyard or U-plan until after 1840.

A similar picture emerges in Suffolk where both scattered and courtyard layouts are usual. A map of Cranley Hall (Figure 44), drawn in 1626, shows a barn, stables and granary arranged around a courtyard. In Suffolk a barn and stable near the house and a 'neat house' or cattle shed in a near-by meadow are usual. The name 'carthouse meadow' is also frequently found near the farmhouse. The reason for this scatter is unclear. Possibly it is because the timber-framed tradition is more suited to the construction of individual buildings than long linked ranges which are usually of brick. As in Devon many high-status farms, such as the manorial complex at Badley Hall (Figure 45) could be evolved groups. The oldest building (a barn) is fifteenth-century and

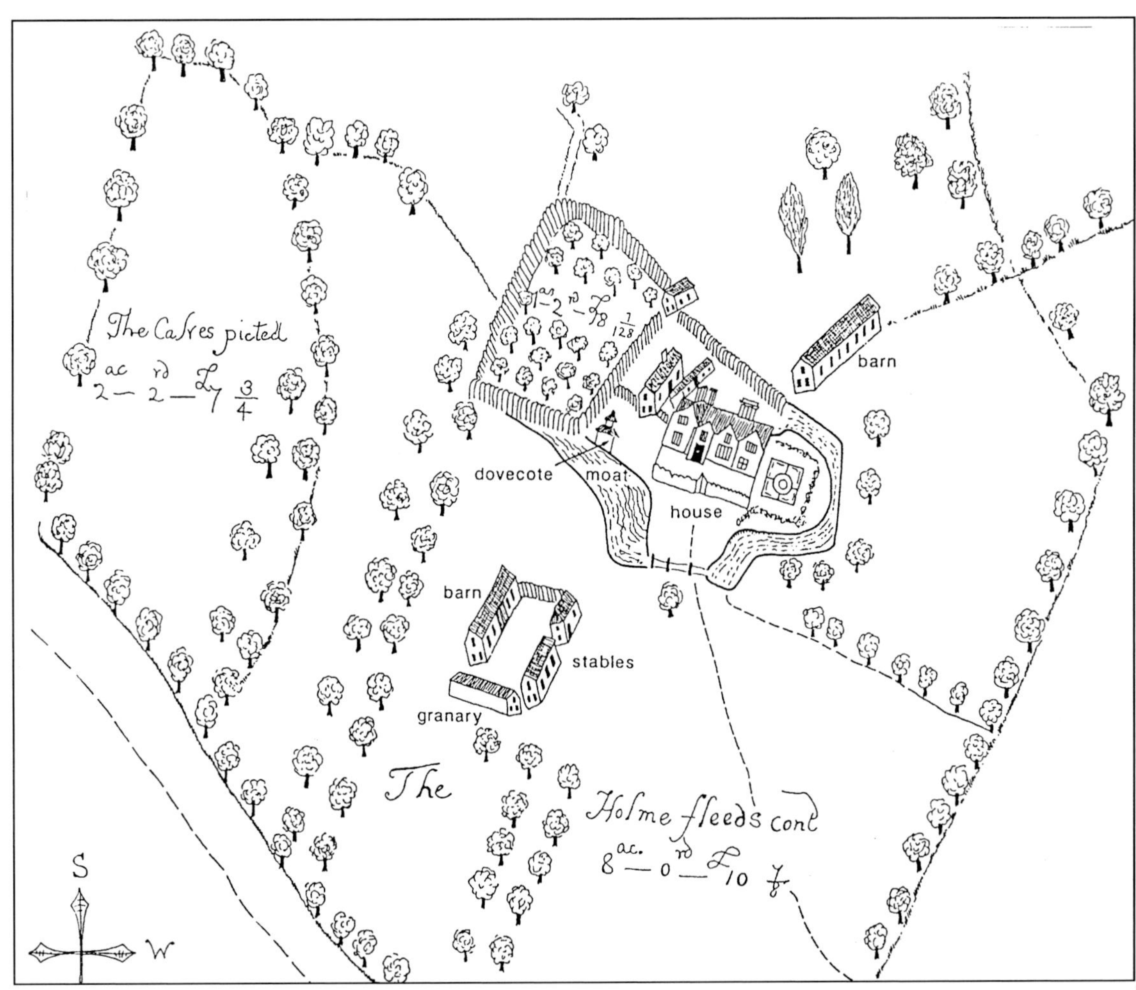

FIGURE 44.
Plan of Cranley Hall (Suffolk) in 1626. This early example of a courtyard farm is set within a largely evolved landscape (Suffolk Record Office IHD78).
PHILLIP JUDGE

a sixteenth-century barn was later converted to a stable while an eighteenth-century cowhouse (described in 1830 as for 12 cows with loft over)[40] became a work shop with saw pit. In the nineteenth century a cattle yard was created in front of the barn. Although, by the end of the 1800s, additions and alterations meant that many such farms had achieved a roughly courtyard arrangement, others certainly had not. Comparisons between plans on tithe and First Edition 25-inch Ordnance Survey maps in south Norfolk (Figure 46) show this change taking place. Regular layouts were rare outside estates until the 1840s whilst by 1880 E and U-shaped plans together made up the largest group.[41] In Suffolk however, E and U-plan steadings remained the exception throughout the period. Farm plan can also often be linked to farm size, with L and U-plans unusual on farms of under 70–100 acres and linear layouts being more usual on smaller farms (Figure 47).

On the North York Moors, while farmsteads serving smaller acreages retained a linear layout, on larger farms a few blocks of two or three units each were more common (Figure 48). Sometimes they were small blocks placed irregularly without any sense of a formal relationship to each other, or placed more closely together to create a sense of enclosure which could be completed by walls or fences to form a fold yard. At Stormy Hall, Danby (North Yorkshire) seven different dates are evidence for the gradual evolution or rebuilding of the farmstead.[42]

FIGURE 45.
Badley Hall Farm (Suffolk).
This fine manorial complex is an example of an evolved farmstead. It stands near an isolated church and consists of a late-medieval house, barns and dovecote with later buildings added in the eighteenth and nineteenth centuries.

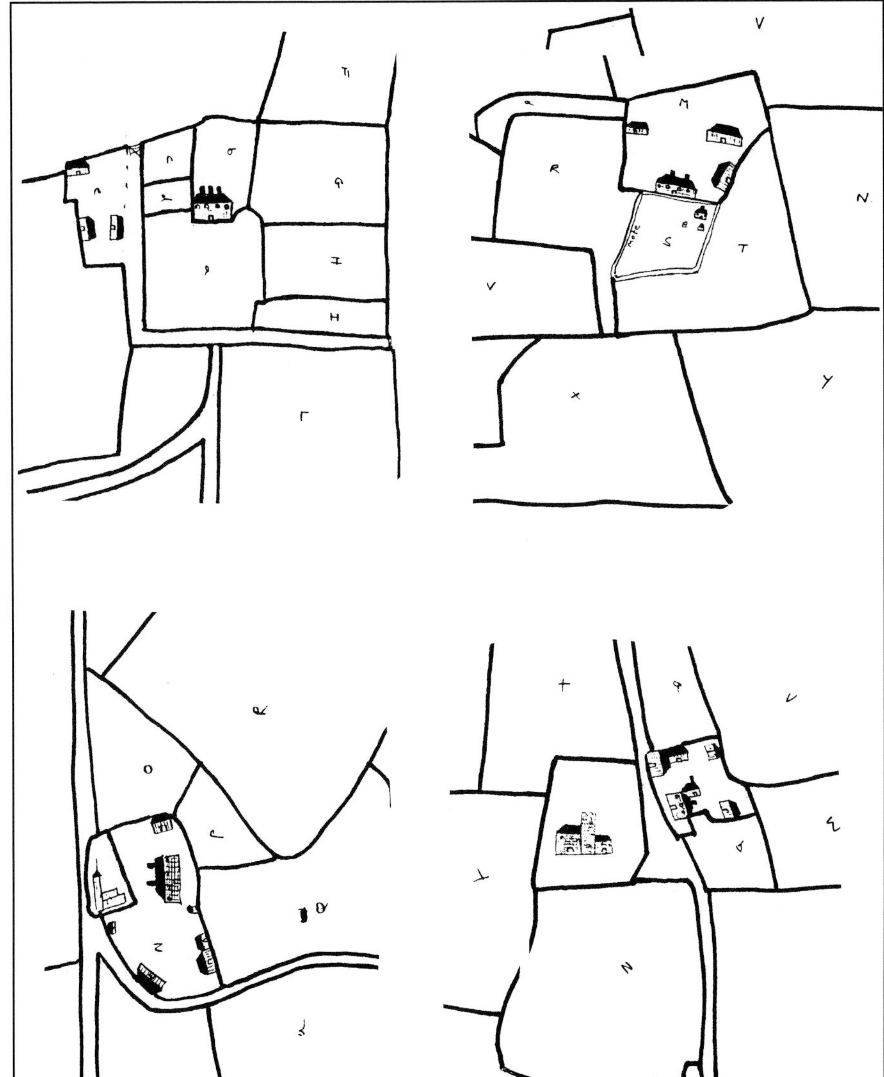

FIGURE 46.
Farms of the Duke of Norfolk's Norfolk estates in the 1720s. These redrawings from maps by John Miller of the Duke of Norfolk's Kenninghall estates in south Norfolk show scattered groups of buildings beside a farmhouse.

In Wales, longhouses had become confined to the southern part of the principality by 1800, but linear and scattered layouts were to be found across the region (Figure 49). The layout was governed by farm size with the smallest farms being linear as at Hendre Ifsan Prosser at Pontypridd (Glamorgan). The eighteenth-century house is abutted by a nineteenth-century stable, barn and cowhouse. Nearby is a circular pigsty, typical of many Welsh farms.[43] As farm size grew during the nineteenth century, so the buildings were extended and L- and U-plan layouts were created.

Evolved farmsteads were almost always built of local materials which affected their plan and layout. Timber-framed barns were often well-built and so are frequently the oldest surviving building on a farmstead in the wood-pasture regions. The other buildings were less substantial and so were frequently

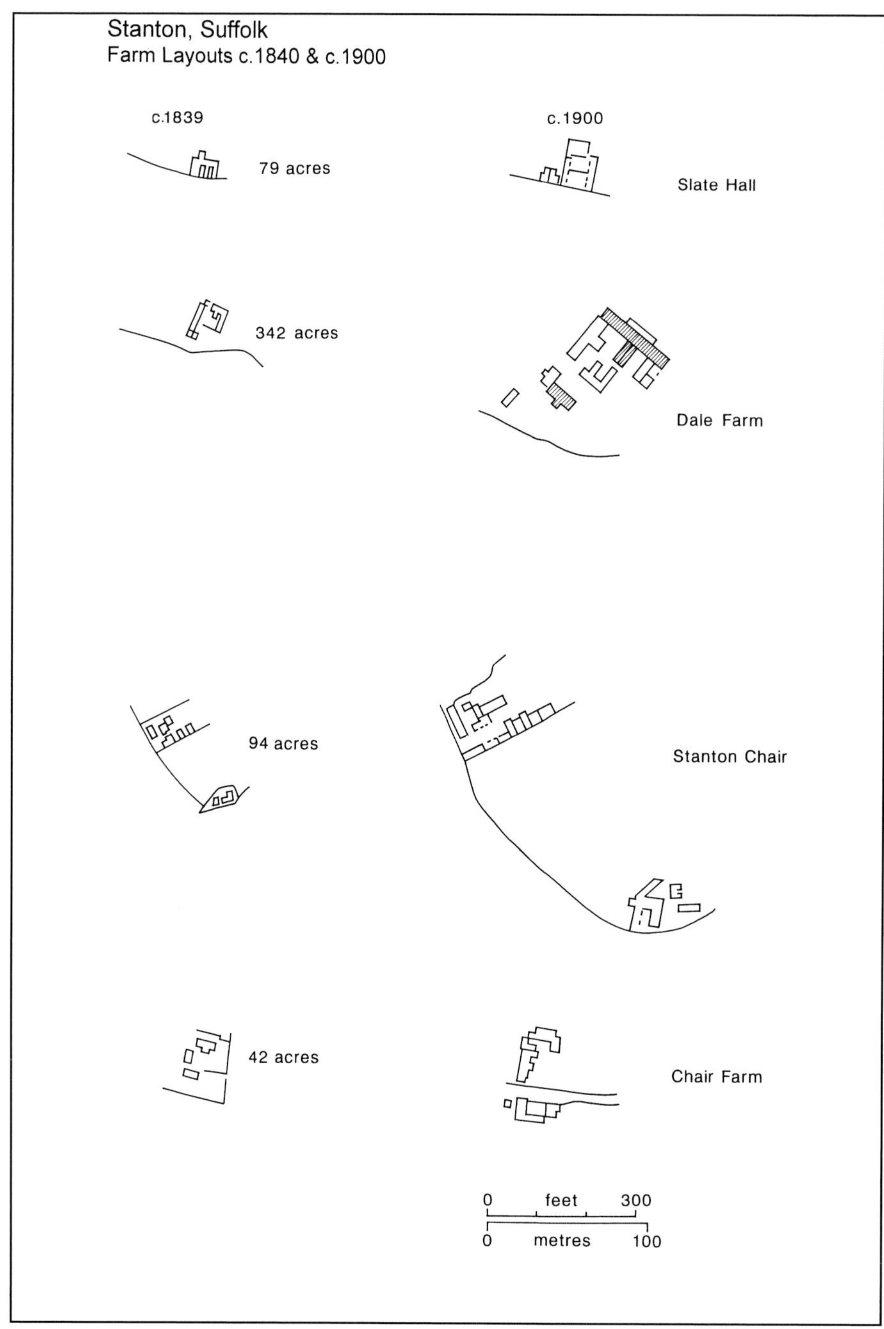

FIGURE 47.
(*left and opposite*)
The developing layout of farm buildings in two evolved Suffolk parishes, between 1840 and 1900. These drawings show the layout of buildings as shown on the tithe and the First Edition 25-inch Ordnance Survey maps. They show a gradual accumulation of buildings, sometimes, but not always resulting in an irregular courtyard layout.
PHILLIP JUDGE

replaced. A terrier of 1830 describing 25 farms in Needham Market (Suffolk) lists stables and cowhouses on all the farms, but those of timber was described as in poor repair while a new stable of brick for ten horses with a granary over was said to be 'capital'.[44]

The limitations of the terrain and the existence of small farms could lead to specific solutions to the problems of farm layout. The steep valley sides of the

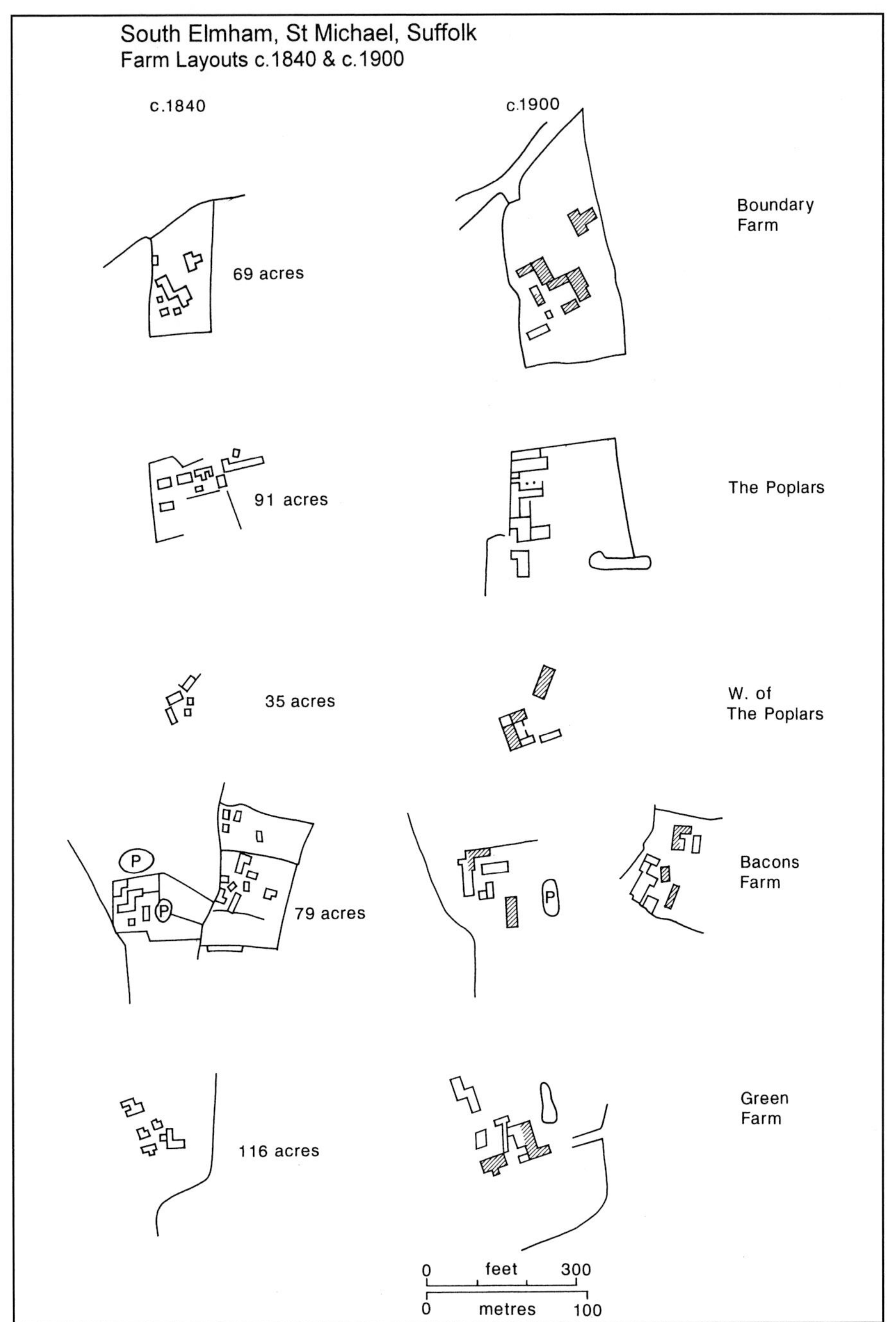

Lake District resulted in the development of a linear arrangement (Figure 50). Bailey and Culley wrote in 1794, 'Where farms are so very small, no great extent of offices is wanted; a barn, a byre for housing cattle in winter and a small stable are in general, all that is necessary ... they are mostly at each end of the farmhouse.'[45] As farm size and the importance of cattle increased, a second row of buildings, might be built parallel to the original building, or a

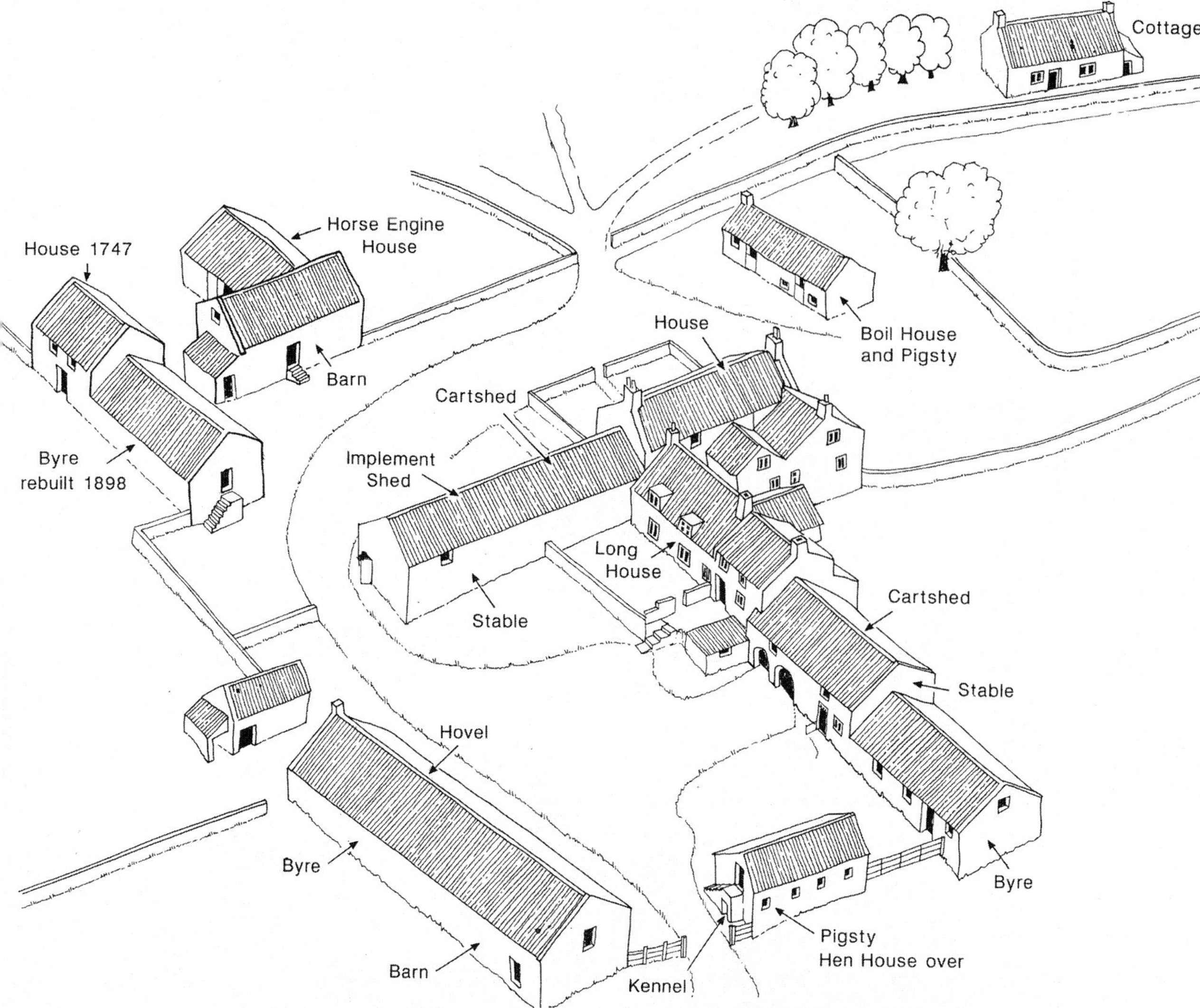

FIGURE 48.
Farm at Orterley, Bilsdale, Midcable (North Yorkshire). This farm is an example of an evolved farmstead. A longhouse, extended in line with farm buildings forms the core of a much more extensive complex including a second farmhouse of the eighteenth century.
PHILLIP JUDGE, REDRAWN FROM RCHME (1987)

building could be added to one end at right angles, creating an L-plan. Also typical of the area were isolated bank barns up the valley sides in the fields, mostly built in the nineteenth century. They provided housing for cattle within the pastures and storage for winter feed in the form of hay produced from the nearby fields. Come the spring the manure could also be spread on the surrounding fields, reducing the amount of cartage necessary. Where the site for the buildings was not so constricted, scattered farmsteads were also found. Plans of the Lowther estate, near Penrith, show that many farms in this relatively open landscape consisted of scattered groups. The farm of Crosby Hall at Crosby Ravensworth consisted of a barn with oxhouse beside it, and a free-standing cowhouse with a stable nearby.[46]

Also important is the the type of farming practiced. Most evolved landscapes were primarily areas of mixed farming with an emphasis on cattle. While cattle and dairying were significant in the farming systems of Devon, Suffolk and Cumbria, the buildings provided for them are entirely different in each region. Although, as we have seen, isolated 'neat houses' were a feature of the Suffolk

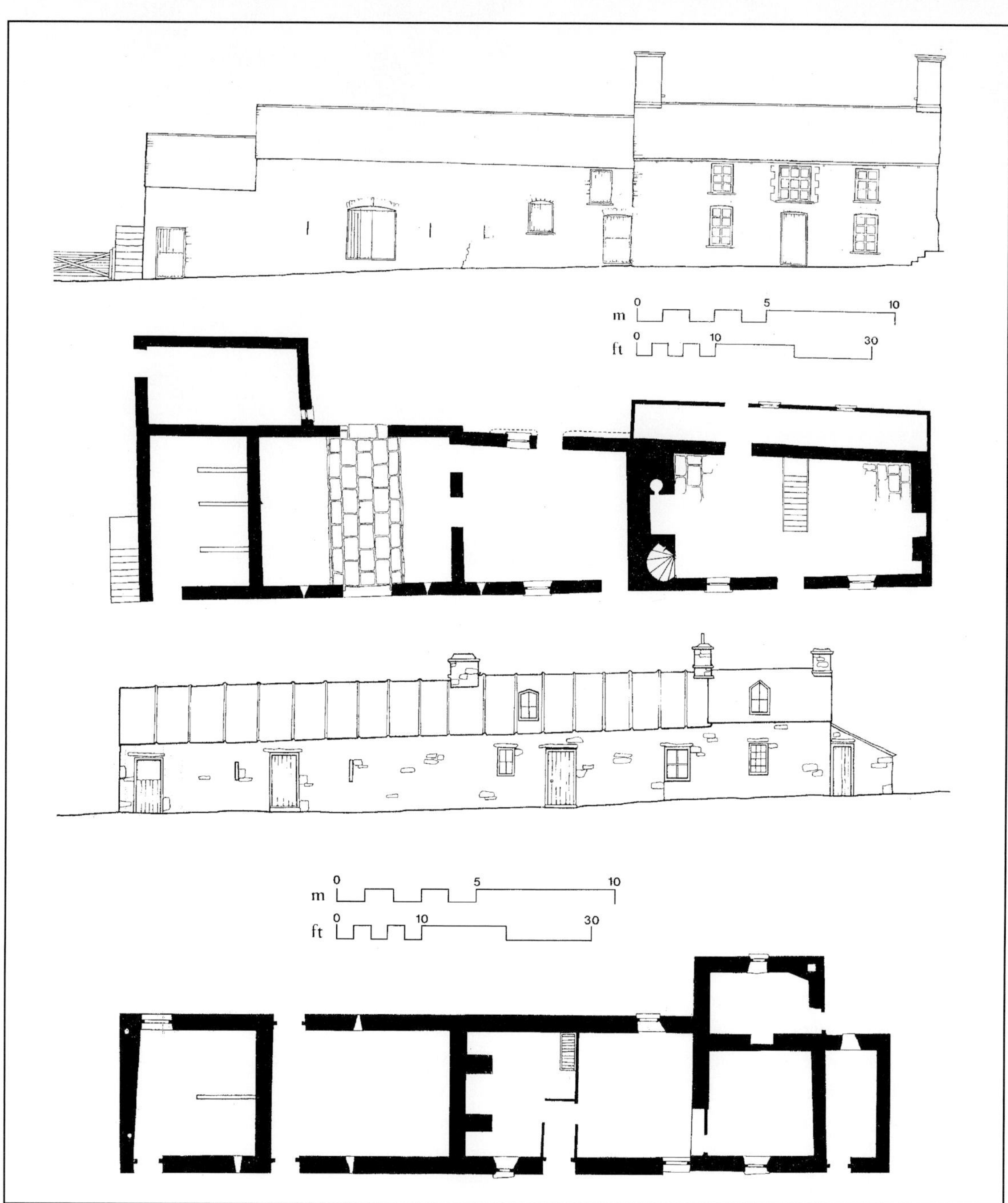

FIGURE 49. Linear Welsh farmsteads (Hendre Ifan, Prosser, Pontypridd, Glamorgan and Tresais, Caerfarchell, Pembrokeshire).

E. WILLIAM

farmstead by the eighteenth century, many dairy cows were still kept outside all winter at this date, often tethered in the fields in the winter, and only being brought indoors for calving.[47] One of the reasons given for tethering rather than letting them run free was that the dung could be collected for manure. This growing appreciation of the importance of manure led to the creation of yards between free-standing buildings roughly grouped around a yard linked by walls or temporary hurdles. Frequently there is evidence that timber-framed barns were originally divided to provide cattle and stable

accommodation in the end bays. A survey of the property of Pembroke College in Wyverstone described 'a large barn with a stable at the northern end of the same barn' while a map of 1740 shows a small four-bay barn Cookley Green Farm, Cookley with both a barn and stable door.[48] The architectural evidence shows that half the building was lofted and thus for stock. However as the farm was 70 acres with only 15 acres ploughed it is likely that cattle as well as horses would have been kept in the livestock half.

FIGURE 50.
A linear farmstead in Troutbeck (Cumbria). The bankbarn is to the left.
A LOWE

In the Lake District, a very distinctive form of combined barn and cattle accommodation was to be found from the late seventeenth century – a design suited to the terrain. Here the barn was built into a slope and cattle were stalled below. Hay as well as corn were stored in the barn above. A hay drop in the barn floor enabled the hay to be pushed down into hay racks below. This type of bank barn was ideally suited to hilly areas where cattle were an important element of the farming system and stone was available for these substantial buildings. However, they were expensive to build and so were only found on the larger farms of northern and western Britain, often as part of a nineteenth century re-build. In Cornwall a similar type of building was called locally a chall barn while in Devon, as well as bank barns, yet another type of building for cattle is found. This is the linhay (Figure 51) where an open-fronted hay loft is placed over an open shelter shed. A linhay usually had solid gable and rear walls with the front consisting of piers of cob, stone or wood. These either rise to the eaves or are broken at first floor level and

FIGURE 51. The thatched linhay at Cheldon Barton (Devon). The Devon linhay provided a very practical solution to storing hay in a well ventilated environment convenient for feeding to stock.

P. CHILD

the various types can be classified both regionally and chronologically. As a building type it dates back at least to the seventeenth century and continued to be built until the 1920s. The open loft allowed for hay to continue to dry once it had been stored which was obviously an advantage in a damp climate and its position over the cattle sheds meant it could easily be pushed down into the hay racks. It is somewhat surprising that this very convenient building is only to be found in Devon, and neighbouring districts of Somerset and Cornwall, with isolated examples elsewhere such as Herefordshire.[49]

A fourth type of cattle accommodation is the longhouse. The longhouse tradition was to be found throughout the southern half of Wales to the Welsh Marches as well as south-west England, Cumbria and north-east Yorkshire. This ancient layout has been identified in medieval excavations such as those at West Whelpington, Northumberland and Houndtor, Hutholes and Okehampton Park in Devon.[50] The longhouse consists of a dwelling house reached by way of a cross passage which provided the main access to both the house and the cowhouse. Sometimes there is a separate door into the cowhouse but there is always a direct link with the house. A Scottish variant combined a cowhouse and dwelling under one roof and entered through a single door, but without the cross passage. In Wales cowhouses were added to farmhouses with the aid of a cross passage to give a longhouse-like building until quite late in the nineteenth century.[51]

In Devon, the distribution of longhouses is remarkably restricted to the area around Dartmoor and the edge of Exmoor, and most date from the fifteenth to the eighteenth centuries. Only rarely did the longhouse provide all the shelter needed for the farming enterprise, as most farms were mixed with both sheep and corn as well as cattle. In value the cattle were worth more than the corn and sheep and so it is not surprising that they were housed next to the dwelling. Typically cattle accommodation within a longhouse was 25 feet long and 15 feet wide, large enough to house about a dozen beasts tethered down either side.[52] Beside the longhouse would be a small barn and buildings for other stock or fodder, creating a scattered layout typical of the moorland fringe and surviving at Lettaford (Figure 52) where a scattered settlement on the edge of Dartmoor consisted of three farms, each with a farmyard containing a barn, linhay and stable as well as the longhouse.[53] At Beetor Farm, North Bovey as well as the multi-phase longhouse, there was a separate cowhouse, threshing barn, pigstyes, cartshed, bankbarn, stables and beeboles.[54]

A linear arrangement of house and cowhouse is also typical of small farms in the Lake District. The dwelling and byre were divided by a cross passage with a chimney stack against it, but few examples are known where the byre and dwelling appear to be contemporary. Many date from the great period of rebuilding in the Lakes during the eighteenth century, but one example at Lamonby Farm, Burgh-by-Sands may be fourteenth century in origin. The byre end is of cruck construction and the walls clay-built.[55] From the beginning of the eighteenth century second floors were added with a staircase in a projecting wing to the rear. Here larger barns are often attached to the house

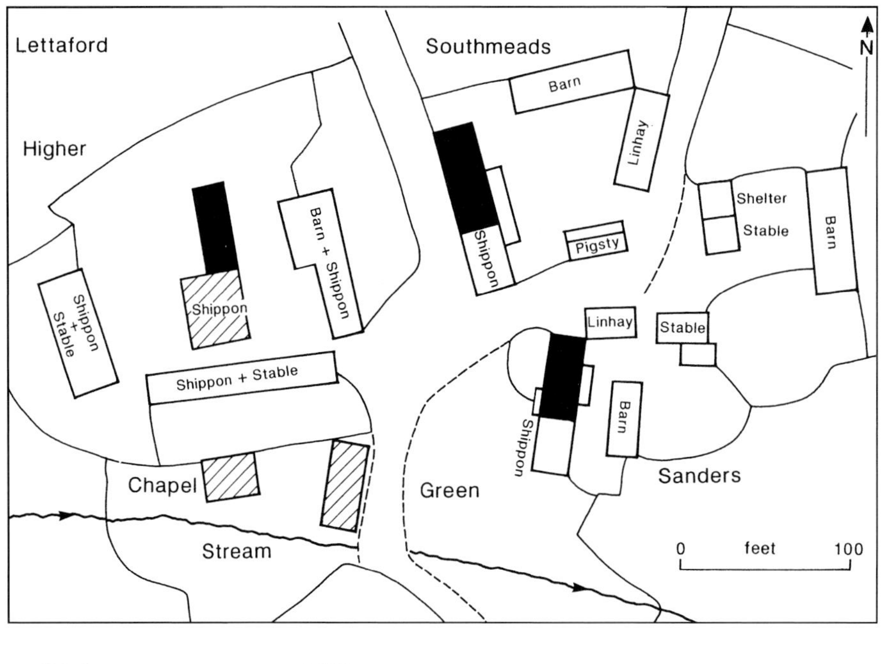

FIGURE 52.
The hamlet of Lettaford (Devon). This irregular hamlet consists of three small farmsteads based on longhouses but with separate barns and livestock buildings as well. The high architectural status of one of the longhouses suggests that these farms were prosperous establishments.

PHILLIP JUDGE, REDRAWN FROM ALCOCK, CHILD & LAITHWAITE (1972)

under the same roof line with cattle housed below and grain and hay storage lofts above. This arrangement is particularly common in the Hawkshead area.[56] Increase in farm size and farm yields resulted in the building of separate ranges of usually multi-purpose farm buildings.

Before the eighteenth century the longhouse was the most common type of farm building arrangement in the North York Moors. By 1800 the byre had mostly been incorporated into the house but the linear arrangement remained with byre, barn and stable being added to the original building, often under the same roof line, and frequently representing several phases of building. This development is evident at Raw Farm, Fylingdale where the original byre was rebuilt as a barn, with a new byre and subsequently a cart shed added beyond. At Bog House Bransdale the original byre was rebuilt as a kitchen and two byres, a byre and livestock boxes were built in separate phases at the other end.[57] The fact that these linear steadings were well suited to the limited flat land available along the valley sides meant that a gradual development on the original site, rather than the building of a complete new farmstead, was more practical. The fact that longhouses continued to be built for so long and also that they were of high social status, shows that they were not regarded as a primitive building type but rather as a sensible solution to an upland environment.

On the farms along the edge of the Norfolk broadland marshes a distinctive building was identified by William Marshall in the late eighteenth century (Figure 53). Here, where many farmers had limited amounts of arable but grazing rights on considerable areas of marshland, cattle were of major importance, but straw could be in short supply. 'Large expensive buildings' were used to fatten cattle for market. Up to 20 cattle were housed in aisles separated by arches from a central turnip store which was entered by double doors at each end. Above was a loft which could have been used as a hay or straw store. A few such buildings have been identified and they represent a very specific building designed to serve a special set of circumstances.[58]

It is clear therefore that the single problem of housing cattle could be tackled in a great variety of ways across the traditional farms of Britain. Some of these designs such as the linhay and the bank barn which were ideally suited to both the climate and the terrain of their respective areas, were taken on by the improvers and are to be found on both evolved and planned farms within their regions.

Barn and stable design shows less variety. However regional characteristics in the detailed construction of barns often have a functional origin. Stables, even when they are free-standing tend to stand near the barn, where the straw for bedding was produced. They are often the second oldest building after the barn on the farmstead, surviving perhaps because they were well-built. On the health of the horses depended the efficiency of the farm and so solid weather-proof buildings were provided, often with a hay loft above. Later additions include carthouses and granaries. Many Cumbrian and Devon farms could only be reached by packhorse until well into the nineteenth century

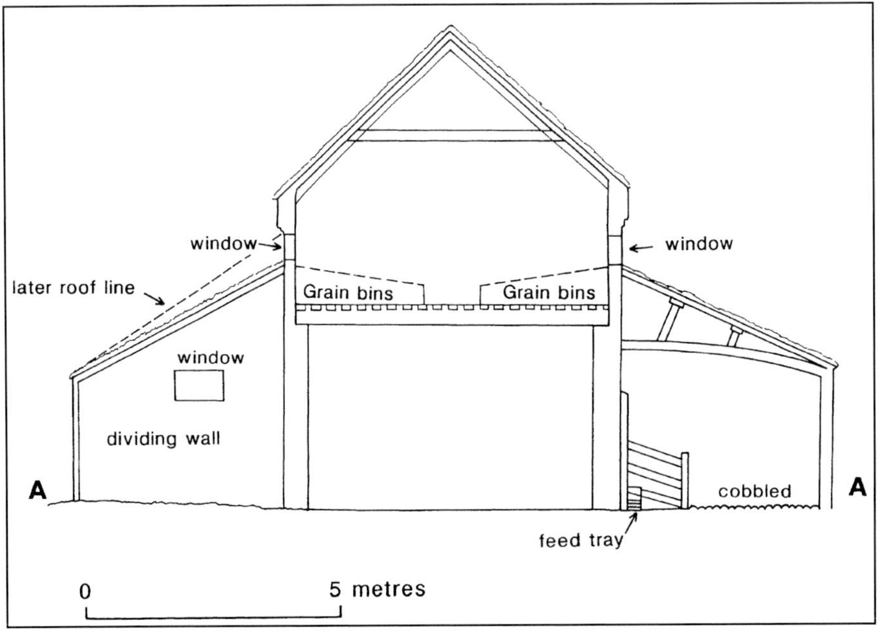

FIGURE 53.
Cattle houses at Manor Farm, Freethorpe (Norfolk). This unusual survival with some internal fittings intact is of a type described by William Marshall in the 1780s.

ENGLISH HERITAGE (photograph) and PHILLIP JUDGE (line-drawing)

and so carthouses were not needed. Grain was frequently stored in the house as the crop was only thrashed out as required. All this changed with mechanical threshers which threshed most of the crop at once, and so granaries are also mostly nineteenth century. Regional traditions have produced two distinctive designs. Over much of the south and west granaries are typically placed on stone 'mushrooms' or staddle stones to keep the contents secure from rats. Elsewhere they were frequently placed above cartsheds.

Conclusion

Map evidence shows that evolved farming landscapes have been continually developing since the seventeenth century. Field boundaries were changed and small-scale drainage undertaken. Buildings were replaced and new ones added and rebuilt. As a result few, other than barns, survive from before 1700. Evolved farmsteads are not confined to smaller establishments; many manorial farms did not rebuild their steadings as a whole and fine agglomerations of buildings survive across England and Wales.

The farming on evolved landscapes must not be underrated. The variety of landscapes and buildings that survive reflect the different farming traditions developed to suit regional climates and terrain. The systems may not have been as capital intensive as those on planned landscapes, but they could be highly productive and were well adapted to local environmental conditions. Contemporary commentators were all to ready to dismiss their farmers as backward and unwilling to contemplate change, but the light-land rotational systems promoted by the improvers were not suited to all areas and in fact some of the earliest crops of turnips grown as animal fodder are recorded in the claylands of Suffolk, Hertfordshire and Devon and not in the heartlands of the agricultural revolution. The development of distinctive types of animal accommodation, specifically suited to local conditions, are an indication that there was no lack of initiative amongst the farmers in these regions. After 1870, when corn prices collapsed, it was the highly capitalised 'high' farmers who suffered most and smaller-scale, more traditional mixed farmers were better able to weather the storm.

CHAPTER SIX

The Age of the 'Practical' Farmer: The Farming Community, 1720 to 1820

All agriculture was and still is based on the work of individuals with muddy boots striving to make money from the land.[1]

Of all the members of rural society, the farmer is the one whose role in the 'Age of Improvement' we understand least. Perry wrote in 1981, 'our continual ignorance of the farming community itself is a serious constraint'.[2] Recent work by Turner, Beckett and Afton has revealed much about the business history of the farm, but the farmer himself, whose attitudes and motivation were the driving force behind the enterprise and who was responsible for the implementation of innovative farming practices, is still relatively unknown. This is partly because the word 'farmer' covers a wide social group, from the subsistence smallholder to the large capitalist, and this contrast remained a striking feature of British farming throughout the 150 years after 1720. In 1830 farmers who employed no one outside the family made up nearly half of those recorded.[3] As late as 1880, 71 per cent of agricultural holdings were under 50 acres[4] yet the available evidence is mostly limited to those at the higher end of the scale.

The small farmer kept few records. He sold little and it was not until the farm was over 60 or 70 acres that hired labour was required, so there was little need for accounting. The keeping of diaries and journals became fashionable in the late eighteenth century and are an example of the increasing literacy of at least the upper ranks of the farming community. However it takes a special sort of person to keep the meticulous notes that the best of these journals contain. Most that survive are the work of farmers of over 200 acres. They were also very personal things. Often they were kept for practical reasons which enabled their authors to assess yields over a series of years, comparing them with factors such as the weather conditions and dates of sowing. Rarely are they a complete record of farming life, nor do they contain the sort of statistical information required by economic historians. However, they can provide insights into the motivation of their authors. Men like Cornelius Stovin for instance, writing in the 1860s, had deep religious convictions and saw the hand of God in all his farming activities.[5] They also described the day-to-day organisation of work and the relationship between the farmer and his labourers. Often activities other than farming were included and so show not only social activities, but also local positions held and duties performed. These writings of the farmers themselves help us therefore to get to the heart of farming life.

Contemporaries who wrote about farmers had fixed preconceptions which make interpretation of their writings difficult. Marshall, Young, and later Caird believed that it was the large farmers with capital who were the improvers and that the small farmers were generally 'backward'. Yet large farmers were not necessarily better off, especially if they had to borrow the capital needed to set up their enterprises. In prosperous years farmers might well overstretch themselves and take on farms for which they did not have the capital. In 1781, Thomas de Grey of the Norfolk Breckland estate at Merton wrote to his brother about his farms. 'The distress of our farmers is brought about by a number of causes; by the drought of the last two seasons, insufficient crops, the low prices of several grains and the ambition of hiring great farms which they are unable to stock without borrowing money.[6] In 1804 Rowland Hunt wrote, 'A farm of 50 acres makes many a pauper; a farm of 1,000 acres makes many a bankrupt.' He thought that 150–300 acres was the best size for a farm.[7] The middle years of the nineteenth century saw a rash of farm amalgamations. This suited the landowner as there were fewer buildings to keep up, while allowing the capitalist farmer to make economies of scale. As prices fell after 1870, the situation changed. A reporter on the Gunton estate (Norfolk) echoed the views of many when he complained of the amalgamation of farms which left the buildings on the outfarm to go derelict: 'I cannot understand why these small places have been let to a big farm. I believe the day of the large farm is over.'[8]

Hard divisions between types of farmers are difficult to draw. Many owner-occupiers rented some land and tenant farmers often owned small pieces themselves. At Laxton (Nottinghamshire) there were 38 small freeholders in the eighteenth century but one of them, William Pinder, while owning 86 acres, rented 246. Similarly, but on a smaller scale, William Newstead owned two and rented 27.[9] William Barnard, a farmer in Harlowbury (Essex) in the early 1800s tenanted a large farm, but was also a landowner and maltster.[10] John Carrington always hoped that he might be able to buy his Hertfordshire farm, and was frequently buying and selling property. At his death he owned at least half a dozen cottages as well as an inn in Ware and another near Welwyn.[11] John Peck, who followed his father onto the family farm at Parsons Drove (Cambridgeshire) was also a master brewer at the local brewery.[12] John Leeds of Billingford (Norfolk) came from a landowning family, some of whom, had been tenants of the Holkham estate for several generations. One branch owned 900 acres and ran a successful tanning business, while his father had inherited 270 acres.[13] The tithe apportionments show that as late as the 1840s owners were sometimes letting out their own fields whilst renting from someone else, presumably in an effort to build up a consolidated holding. In spite of the difficulties, however, this chapter will attempt to understand changing lifestyles and social standing of the various types of members of farming community as well as to analyse their role in 'improvement'. The period will be divided into firstly, the phase of agricultural development up to the end of the Napoleonic War boom and the second, the period thereafter.

By the eighteenth century the basic division in responsibility between the landlord and his tenant was recognized. The landlord was responsible for the fixed capital of the farm; the tenant, the working capital. Although the landlord could exercise some influence over farming practice through the terms of the lease, the way the land was worked was primarily up to the farmer. As we have seen, underdraining and marling was often the tenant's responsibility and in times of high prices and high demand for farms, the landlord might well be able to find tenants prepared to take on responsibilty for the internal fencing of newly enclosed land. Sometimes too, they would initially be responsible for new building, with the estate compensating for the cost over a period of years.[14] However, how these new farms and fields were used was up to the farmer, and in these years, dominated by the farming systems of Norfolk and other east-coast grain-growing counties, it was the intensification of cereal production that was being advocated by the publicists. Rotation farming based on the Norfolk four-course was at the heart of improved farming. Crops of turnips and grass were planted in between each year of grain. As fodder crops, they allowed more stock to be kept to provide the manure to keep the land fertile. Its practice depended on a large labour force and was based on hand rather than machine labour. The writers of the *General Views* assessed the standard of farming in individual counties by the degree to which it adhered to this system, and there is no doubt that it allowed for many of its practitioners to become very wealthy during the years of high grain prices. However, it was not the growing of turnips which necessarily resulted in the highest wheat yields. Wheat was suited to heavier soils than barley, where turnips were not an ideal crop. Of the 21 parishes in England as a whole recording the highest grain crops in the tithe files, only a third grew turnips.[15] On the lighter lands of course, cereal growing would not have been possible without marling and the extra manure made available by the increased stock which could be fed off turnips and grasses. Even in Norfolk, the county credited with the introduction of the four-course, it was skilful buying and selling of animals that made the most money. Fortunes were made, not through cereals, but 'though a superior skill in the purchase of stock; seconded by a full supply of money; by which means they were able to time their purchase to the best advantage'.[16] Business acumen as much as skill in farming was important for financial success.

One way of distinguishing the lifestyles of farmers is to look at their houses. Some of the largest farms on the best land were centred on fine old houses, perhaps dating back to the late medieval period (Figure 54). These houses are found particularly in the early enclosed districts, such as the wood-pasture regions of Suffolk, Cambridgeshire and Essex and the midlands where many late-medieval timber framed houses remain. W. A. Copinger wrote disparagingly

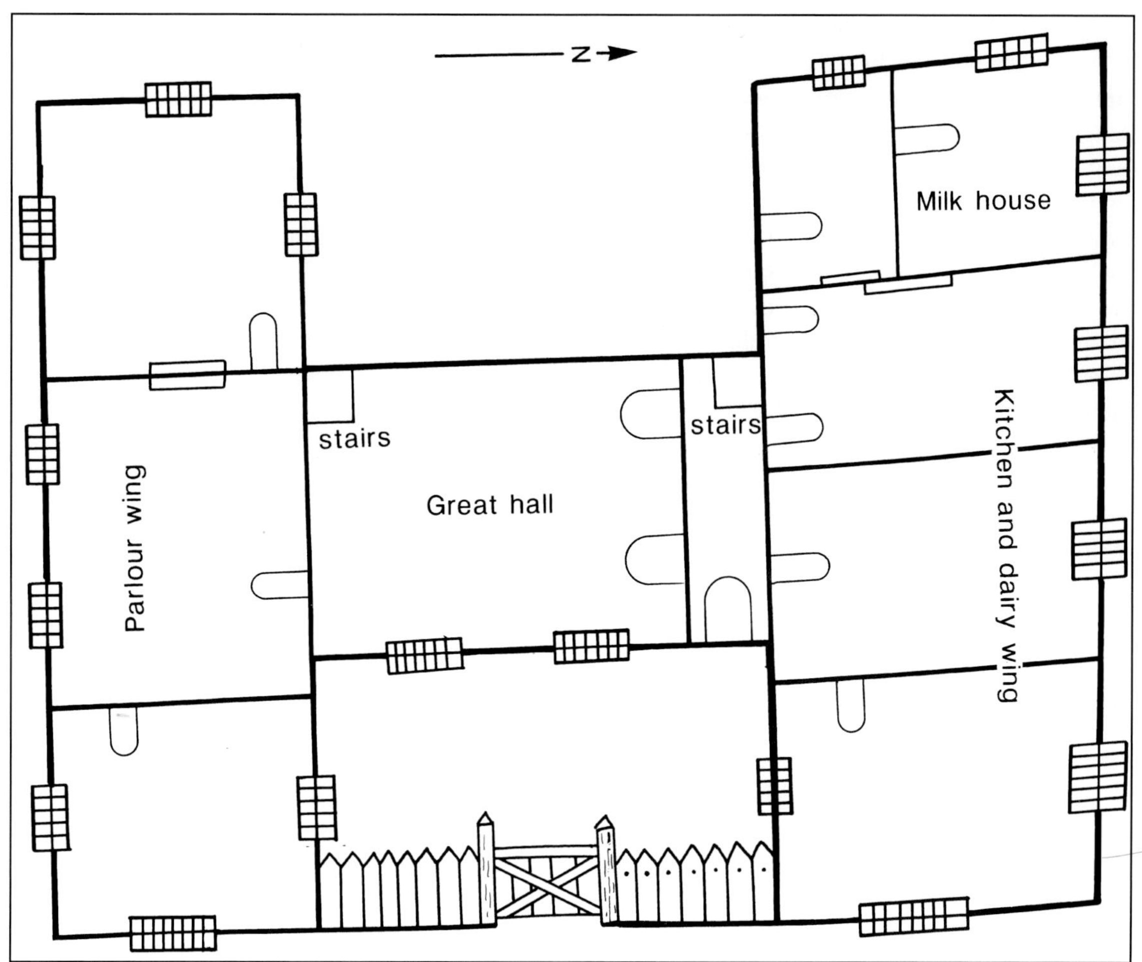

FIGURE 54.
Gervase Markham's plan for a farmhouse and yard published in 1613.
This plan shows a spacious two-storey building with a great hall linking kitchen and entertaining ranges. The dairy and milkhouse were at the rear (west) of the house behind the kitchen range and adjacent to the farmyard, also on the west.
PHILLIP JUDGE

in 1903 of some Suffolk manor houses that had 'deteriorated' into farmhouses.[17] Worcestershire was described as a county of ancient enclosure and the houses 'have consequently been erected at a different – many at a remote – time'.[18] Sometimes they represent the old manor house, and the farm, the original demesne land. By 1813 many 'mansions' in Shropshire had become farmhouses.[19] In Bedfordshire there were farmhouses 'that were formerly the seats of gentlemen who appear to have farmed their own estates'.[20] In Dorset 'many of the houses, particularly in the chalky districts are very ancient buildings and have the appearance of having been the seats of proprietors in former times'.[21] In some areas such as Cheshire, Shropshire, Worcestershire, Middlesex and Northamptonshire, old farmhouses were concentrated in villages, while new ones were being built in the centre of often newly enclosed holdings. In Leicestershire the brick houses of the owner-occupier breeders and graziers contrasted with the older timber-framed homes of the poorer farmers in the villages.[22] Where they were owned by estates with little interest in improvement and where the owner was absent most of the time, houses could well be extremely inadequate. At Laxton the houses were said be in very bad repair as late as 1862. William Cooke's house was 'of mud, brick and thatch ... so old and dilapidated as to be entirely unfit for residence and incapable of repair' and similarly, Benjamin Hill's was 'wretched', 'unfit to live in – possibly dangerous'.[23] Such landlords seldom disturbed tenants who paid their rent and kept to the farming systems usual in the district which might be very low compared with those on the more progressive estates. On Sir Marmaduke Constable's estates in Burton Constable, North Yorkshire, houses in the eighteenth century were said to be 'very ruinous, some of them supported by props, and tenants who fear for their lives gave up their occupation'.[24] On the Adair estate on the Norfolk–Suffolk border the mainly timber-framed houses were described as in 'fair repair' in 1750,[25] but had deteriorated by 1890, when the conditions were said to be 'very trying to the occupier'. The drains were poor and there was a shortage of spring water. Most were damp and the ground around them needed digging away. The privy of Harris's farm at Flixton was described as 'like most of the others, over a ditch and indirectly communicating with the water supply'.[26] The sort of farmer who was prepared to put up with these conditions was a very different sort of person to that found on the improving estates.

In more recently enclosed areas where new farms were created as part of the eighteenth-century restructuring, the farmhouses were square, estate-built structures and a strict hierarchy would delineate the size of house for specific acreages. One of the earliest collection of designs for farmhouses was published by Daniel Garrett in 1747.[27] His simple classical designs included double-fronted houses (Figure 30). On the Duke of Northumberland's Alnwick estates there was much rebuilding in the early nineteenth century. The larger farms were built with double-fronted double-pile houses with a kitchen and parlour at the front and a milk house and kitchen at the back, while the smaller farms were provided with L-plan houses with two front and only one back room.[28] Houses to similar designs were being erected on the Guy's Hospital estates in Herefordshire.[29] By 1800, the farmhouses occupied by tenants of large farms on the Woburn (Bedfordshire), Holkham (Norfolk) and Brockelsby (Lincolnshire) estates were fit for gentlemen. Houses for the Marquis of Stafford's estates in Shropshire and Staffordshire, built between 1815 and 1820 in what James Loch, the agent described as 'a common country style' were equally stratified socially. On the larger farms of between 300 and 500 acres, there was often a servant's wing with a separate staircase. On the 511-acre farm at South Tibberton (Shropshire), there was a common parlour and a best parlour as well as a kitchen and pantry. Attics would have provided sleeping accommodation for farm servants. On the 60-acre Roughclose Farm in Stone (Staffordshire) there was one parlour and kitchen with no servants' stair or sleeping accommodation. Typical of all these planned farmsteads was that the house was on one side of the farmyard; an indication that these tenants were very much working farmers. On the Marquis of Stafford's Sutherland estates, while some farms such as Crakaig included a much older laird's house, others, such as Inverbrora were architect-designed to attract tenants with enough capital to undertake the daunting task of drainage and enclosing which these new east-coast farms needed. Here however, the house was at a slight distance from the buildings with the farm workers' bothies being built into one side of the farmyard.[30]

Cumberland was a county of small farms and although some square, double-pile houses with a kitchen and parlour in the front and back kitchen and milkhouse at the back with four or five bedrooms above had begun to appear by 1750, single-pile houses with services in a lean-to along the back were more usual.[31]

Periods of prosperity and depression can often be isolated by looking at a farmhouse. Even on estate farms where an older house existed, it might be refaced or a new wing in the classical style added during the prosperous years of the Napoleonic Wars. The *General Views* certainly give the impression that everywhere much new building was going on during this period. Later, in the mid-nineteenth century period of 'high farming' extensions in the form of porches and bay windows were typical. The increasing prosperity of the larger tenants is shown by the fine Victorian-gothic houses built at a slight distance from the farmstead on estates such as those of the Dukes of Bedford around Woburn and on the Thorney levels of Cambridgeshire where the architect S. S. Teulon worked (Plate 56, page 146), and the Earl of Pembroke on his large, fertile property around Wilton.

The farming system itself is also reflected in the houses. On the small Cumberland farms 'no great extent of offices are wanted; a barn, a byre for housing their cattle in the winter, and a small stable, are in general, all that is necessary: no regular plan for the form or site seems to have been adopted, every one building to what he thinks most convenient for his stock and situation'.[32] In many of the new farmsteads created during the eighteenth century the farmhouse would be on one side of the farmyard, looking out at the back over the farmyard. As we have seen, this arrangement was evident in the designs of Garrett and applied to large as well as small farms. Sir Christopher Sykes rebuilt the farms on his Sledmere estate in the late eighteenth century. All were built on a yard plan with the house on one side, separated from the livestock by a very narrow passageway. By the turn of the century some farmers, particularly those on larger farms where a bailiff might be employed for the day-to-day running of the farm, began to distance themselves from their business. The farmhouse came to be built at a short distance from the yard. At Leicester Square Farm, South Creake, designed for the Holkham estate (Norfolk) by the country house architect, Samuel Wyatt, the house is at one end of the yard, but set back and divided from it by a wall (Figure 33a, page 82). This trend became particularly apparent in the mid-nineteenth century by which time new farmhouses were built at a distance from the farmyard.

The employment system in practice is also illustrated through house design. Living-in was a feature of many farms, particularly in the pastoral and dairying districts. Whilst this was dying out across the south by the mid-eighteenth century, it persisted further north far longer and meant houses were designed with servants' lofts and separate staircases. As far south as Northumberland the bothy system dominated. Here labourers were housed in small, single-storey cottages, or bothies, but were usually fed in the farmhouse. These might be built as a row at a short distance from the farmstead, or they might take up one side of a large courtyard farm. Living-in farm servants were becoming less usual by the end of the eighteenth century, especially in the arable districts. Allowances were paid in lieu of board or the provision of a cottage, but even here they were still to be found on some farms. Randall Burroughes of Wymondham (Norfolk) mentions John Smith, who left his household after twelve years in October 1795 in order to get married. This left Hudson as his 'only hired servant in the family'. Other labourers were let cottages.[33] In the north, whether they were living in the house or in bothies, the labourers typically moved farms every year and this too spread new farming ideas.[34]

Living within their houses, old and new, were the farmers themselves, often with families, relations and both domestic and farm servants. Once the farm was over about 70 acres hired labour was usually required and the farmer would increasingly become a manager rather than a worker. On very large farms even the organisation of the day's work was left to a bailiff, but most employers would like to ride round the farm nearly every day to see how the work was going. However, there was also time for leisure. Surviving diaries show that amongst larger farmers at least, visiting was a typical pastime, particularly in the shooting season and friends would be entertained for weeks at a time.[35] Visiting was an important way in which new ideas were passed on. The Culley brothers, famous as livestock breeders in Northumberland, travelled to improve their agricultural knowledge and George Culley's journals survive from his agricultural tour of the midlands and the south made in 1765, of eastern England and Scotland in 1771, of Ireland in 1775 and the midlands in 1784–1785. Indeed he may well have been responsible for making the idea of the agricultural tour popular.[36] John Grey of Dilston took on the management of Milfield Plain in Glendale (Northumberland) at the age of 28 in 1803 and transformed it from a race-course into a profitable farm. He was said to have learnt much from Culley on their many rides back from Wooler market.[37] Lincolnshire farmers were said to 'live comfortably and hospitably as good farmers ought to live' and to travel regularly to see other farms.[38] John Carrington of Bacon's Farm, Tewin (Hertfordshire) was equally hospitable. His relatives and friends from London were frequent visitors and he also seems to have entertained several long-term lodgers during the Napoleonic Wars.[39] John Leeds of Billingford (Norfolk) went for short visits to Cambridge and London as well as a six-week tour of Scotland and the north of England where, with two farming friends he visited leading farmers.[40] The Northumberland farmer, George Hughes of Glendale, kept a journal from 1789 to 1800 and this shows that he rarely strayed beyond the nearest market towns, but he did travel to Scotland for a tour of several weeks, visiting farms.[41] In 1868 Cornelius Stovin went with farming companions on a tour in Ireland, also with the aim of learning from observation.[42] What the European Grand Tour did for the education of the nobility, a British tour of progressive farms did for the wealthier class of farmers.

Other members of a farming household might include farm students. Farmers often sent their sons on a more or less formal basis to friends, relations or well-known farmers to gain experience elsewhere before coming back to the family farm, or being set up on their own. This was a practice that increased considerably in the early nineteenth century. Arthur Young took students on his farm at Bradfield Combust (Suffolk). The farmers of Northumberland were so well-known for the superiority of their farming that they were 'seldom without pupils from various and distant parts of the kingdom' to whom they were able to charge as much as £100 a year.[43] Culley's correspondence shows that by the Napoleonic Wars the Glendale area had become a 'mecca for pilgrimage' and both he and his neighbours took in students.[44] Joan Butler wrote in 1869 'The tenant farmers of Northumberland are very often in education and in all that essentially constitutes a gentleman not a whit inferior to the aristocratic landowners from whom they rent their land ... This "middle class" will only exist where farms are large and leases long.'[45] We know for instance that the agricultural journalist, James Caird was sent from his native Scotland to Northumberland for several years before taking on a farm at Baldoon (Wigtownshire) in 1841.[46] A farm diary for 1842 which was kept by a farm student survives in Northumberland Record Office. In it the student, who was serious enough to be reading Sir Humphrey Davey's *Agricultural Chemistry*, recorded details of the farming methods and livestock husbandry on the 700-acre farm.[47]

Many farming households therefore consisted of more than the immediate family and even where servants were not living in there might well be guests or students staying. This could only be beneficial as it kept farmers in touch with the wider world and provided scope for discussion of the state on farming nationally and locally and allowed the comparison of experiences. The success of men such as Culley would be scrutinized and his methods might be copied, simply because they made money. The example of a good farmer was therefore more likely to be followed than that of a landlord who did not rely on his farming for his income.

A great variety of phrases are used by contemporary writers to describe the farmers of the Napoleonic War period. There is no doubt that in all regions there were some men to whom the adjectives, 'well-educated', 'liberal', 'intelligent', 'enterprising', 'enlightened' and 'industrious' could be applied. Some such men, as in Lincolnshire, were 'free from foolish expensive show or pretence to emulate the gentry',[48] whilst in Northumberland, 'the character of a farmer is so respectable that gentlemen who possess landed property from £500–£1,500 per annum think it no debasement to follow the profession'.[49] However all the commentators noted that the characters and abilities of farmers varied as much as the farms they held. Some were less inclined to rush into a change of farming practice. In the pastoral regions of Herefordshire which were not suited to the new ideas of the arable east, the old-fashioned farmer received 'any new experiment in agriculture with great hesitation, if not reluctance. When its utility is confirmed by repeated trials, he slowly and gradually falls into the practice.'[50] In such regions of early enclosure, where expenditure on land reclamation was not as important as on the new arable lands, the need for capital was not as important. Here it was the cost of good livestock which would have figured most prominently.

In the years of high prices and farming optimism, the improvement of newly-reclaimed land was not undertaken so much by the landlords as by the large capitalist tenant farmers who took on the freshly delineated farms, often with the fields within the ring fence still to be enclosed and it was these men whom the agents would be looking for. The leases for the newly enclosed Sutherland farms are typical of many for similar holdings in the boom years of the Napoleonic Wars when it was a landlord's market. The tenant was encouraged to build, but only on a plan approved by the estate. He should enclose along the lines laid down in the lease with double stone dykes to be built within a strictly controlled time scale. Drains also had to be dug and this might involve straightening existing burns. It might be several years before the tenant could expect a crop and rents were often very low for the first few years. He would also be paid 'ameliorations' in the form of allowances against rent for capital work undertaken, but these did not always cover more than two-thirds of the cost.[51] At Holkham, the way regular payments are recorded over several years in the audit books, suggests that during the war years, the estate was able to leave the initial expenditure to the tenant who would then receive re-imbursement over a period of time.[52] Thomas de Grey referring to a dry Breckland estate in Norfolk wrote that the tenants reckoned it cost the equivalent of three years' rent to stock a farm, 'but although they pretend, they are seldom worth so much'.[53] The three most important questions to be asked of a prospective tenant were likely to be his ability to raise capital, his politics and his religion. It was generally reckoned at the end of the eighteenth century that it cost £5–£7 an acre to stock a farm, so an applicant for a 300-acre farm needed between £1,500 and £2,000, and because this was a large sum of money, it is likely that this ideal was rarely met. Arthur Young complained that many farmers took on more land than they could stock. 'The great ambition of many farmers is not to farm *well* but to farm *much*. Nine out of ten had rather cultivate 500 acres in a slovenly manner, though constantly cramped for money, than 250 completely, though they would always have money in their pockets.'[54] Mid-nineteenth century census returns show that most tenants could be found from within a short distance and so inquiries amongst neighbours and at local gatherings such as those on market days were usually sufficient to establish a potential tenant's suitability. However, sometimes inquiries were made further afield. A reference sought by Thomas de Grey in the 1770s brought the answer, 'He may bring £1,500 or upwards as his mother and his wife's father are people of decent property, he is a working man and a good tenant on my land. In regard to his principle, I have never heard anything that was dishonest.'[55] Undoubtedly the first direction a prospective tenant would look to raise money would be to his family, but he might also go to well-established local farmers. The diary of James Warne of Wool, near Dorchester covers the year 1758 and shows him both borrowing and lending money. It is clear from inventories that an informal network of credit existed with farmers often having both loans outstanding and debts which they owed.[56]

In times of farming prosperity there would be no problem in letting a farm as agriculture was seen as a good investment. The agent might well have several tenants to choose from. However, in less good times, it would not be so easy and tenants or prospective tenants could well have the upper hand in any negotiations. De Grey wrote in the poor years of the early 1780s, 'I hear of farms to be let in every part of the country.' He went on to say, 'The Norfolk farmers have long ceased to be humble dependents; we must therefore bear with their language which is to be treated on equal terms.'[57] Certainly as early as 1770 Norfolk farming society was led by a few farmers, each working often as much as 1,000 acres of light land. Arthur Young believed that it was only large-scale farmers who could command the capital to undertake the enclosing, marling and keep the large flocks of sheep that were needed to fold on and therefore manure the land. None of this could be effected by small ones – 'or such as are called middling ones in other counties'. He lists five men, all in the dry north-west, at least one of whom (Mr Carr of Massingham) was a tenant of the Holkham estate.[58] He was writing five years before Thomas William Coke inherited the estate and so it is clear that dramatic changes in the farming practices of the region were being made by these men. Landlords such as Coke were merely carrying on what their tenants had begun in the hope of sharing in the profits to be made on the newly enclosed land through the increase in land values and therefore, rent. In his *General View of the Agriculture of Norfolk*, published in 1804, Young lists 57 farmers whom he believed were at the forefront of agriculture. Although well spread across the county they would have been a socially cohesive class who would have met regularly at Norwich market on a Saturday, as well as at the annual sheep shearings at Holkham. Such men were typical of those to be found through the eastern arable regions of Britain where as we have seen, light lands were being enclosed, marled and drained from the 1750s onwards. In these areas the large farmers on the publicity-conscious estates dominate.

What is less clear is the role of the farmer in the pastoral regions and on smaller farms. While Young was adamant that it was only on the large farms that improvement was to be found William Marshall took a different view. It was on the comparatively small farms of East Norfolk which had been 'enclosed marled and ploughed, since time immemorial' that the best examples of 'Norfolk husbandry were to be found'.[59] There is frustratingly little documentary evidence to support Marshall's view, although south and east Norfolk, both areas of small farms, were the first to adopt turnips as a fodder crop.[60] The authors of the *General Views* for other counties expressed differing opinions. In Dorset, where five or six farms had been put together to make sheep farms of up to 2,000 acres, there were those who argued that if that land was divided into ten to twelve farms, the farmers would be able to bring up their families 'in comfort'. The labour would all be done by the family and therefore 'carefully attended to'. While the large farmers tended to sell to the national market and leave the local ones unstocked, the smaller ones would 'fill (local) markets with provisions of all kinds'.[61] The reporter for Middlesex thought there should be farms of all sizes to 'suit every extent of capital'.[62] Another view of the problem is given by the reporter for Herefordshire who wrote, 'Without large farms, improvements in agriculture and breeding would be cramped, if not suppressed, and without small ones, no persons but those of property could embark in agricultural pursuits; and the lusty peasantry which forms so material a part of our national strength, would lose the stimulus and reward of industry'. The occupiers of 40, 80 or 100 acres 'live hard, labour hard and bring little to market'.[63] A different problem arose in areas adjacent to industrial districts. In Lancashire, for example, many of the small farmers had 'other employment of a mechanical nature' and so did not focus solely on their farming. However even here, it was admitted there were exceptions.[64] Around London there were those for whom farming was a secondary occupation, their 'primary occupation being in London' and so did not give the farm the attention necessary to make it profitable. In this area there were those who 'having acquired a great fortune in other pursuits, retire to farming with the idea of uniting profit and amusement in their agricultural labours'. Middleton was scathing of these people who knew very little about farming, 'having hastily imbibed a notion that it is a very pleasant pursuit', and usually gave up after a few years. Some of this group however took to serious farming as a profession. These were some of the most innovative in the county as they came to the business fresh with no preconceived ideas.[65]

How far it is fair to say that it was only the large farmers who were innovators is a question almost impossible to answer as the records simply do not exist but certainly there are descriptions which would support the idea that small farmers could be innovative and manage their land well. Arthur Young was critical of those who did not rely on their farms for their income, yet automatically criticised small tenant farmers, calling them 'stupid fellows' because they refused to take up new ideas. 'The track in which they are, they know will produce something: should they leave it for uncertainties which may produce nothing … Let the landlord try experiments, and I warrant, if a few years show them to answer, the tenant will adopt them.'[66] The incumbent of Stansfield in Suffolk described several of his parishioners on farms of under 50 acres as good industrious farmers. John Raye, farmer of 40 acres, had 'the best fields of any man'. Where comparisons can be made between yields and farming practices on large and small farms within a single parish, there was no obvious difference.[67] Conversely there were farmers on the large farms of the Holkham estate who came in for criticism from the agent, Francis Blaikie in 1816 as 'old fashioned and backward'. Of one farm he wrote with exasperation, 'no hope of the present occupier and his son seems to have weak intellect'.[68]

However, the small farmer could not have had the financial freedom and flexibility of his larger neighbours. He did not have the capital to 'mix with the world. He can not travel and reads little.' For this reason he gave a bad name to small farms. In Devon on the poor heavy soils of the Culm Measures in the north of the county, the farms were small and isolated. The farmers 'continue much at home unless necessarily called from thence by attendance at fairs and markets'.[69] In such areas change was likely to be very slow indeed.

The 'problem' of the small farmer was seen at its most intense in Wales. Much of the principality was seen as characterised by a class of peasant farmers stubbornly attached to old ways and semi-subsistence farming. Most of the small family-run farms in Wales were occupied by men with little capital. A Herefordshire estate owner wrote to his steward in 1733, 'I am sorry that nothing but Welsh tenants offer for Upcot – they are the worst of tenants, generally poor and without stock.'[70] The strong feeling of local community and isolation fostered by chapels and the Welsh language meant that farmers' sons were unwilling to move away, resulting in land hunger and poverty. The divide between the anglicised landlords and their Welsh tenantry lead to ill-feeling resulting in tithe wars and much publicised evictions at election time in 1859 and 1868. This antipathy could be exploited by the Welsh Land League, which, although not as strong as in Ireland or Scotland succeeded in widening the gap between many farmers and their landlords.[71] The importance of livestock rather than cereals in the farming system meant that Welsh farmers were at an advantage when grain prices fell in the 1870s, but there were still 'scores of estates in Wales that require the entire rental expended upon them for many years merely to bring them back into full cultivation'.[72] However the poverty of the region should not be over-emphasised. There were large, highly capitalised farms in the Vale of Glamorgan and Clwyd as well as the Castlemartin area of Pembrokeshire where farmers lived and farmed in the style of their English counterparts.

In other regions the small farmer remained important, particularly in the upland pastoral areas where cattle rearing and sheep grazing were the principal occupations, and also in the dairying districts such as the grasslands of Lancashire and Cheshire, Devon, Gloucestershire and North Wiltshire as well as parts of Leicestershire, Rutland and Suffolk.[73] In Cumbria the independent 'statesman' farmers took advantage of the area's position on the major north-south droving route which allowed them to enter the commercial field and prosper. However, the area was not suited to the arable-based mixed farming of the eastern 'agricultural revolution' and, with the notable exception of J. C. Curwen, owners of the few large estates were more interested in consolidating their holdings in the coal-rich areas and developing the ports of Whitehaven and Workington than in agricultural improvement. The statesmen held on to the old ways of their fathers. Many were subsistence farmers who sold and bought little. They 'lived poorly and laboured hard'.[74] The rather romantic view of observers was that they were of 'high character for sincerity and honesty, and probably few people enjoy more ease and humble happiness'. Yet even here there was a move towards amalgamations and an increase in the size of farms between 1750 and 1820. 'The simplicity of ancient times' was being lost with the statesman selling and being 'reduced to the necessity of working as labourers in those fields which perhaps he and his ancestors had for many generations cultivated as their own'.[75] However, the statesman class remained influential with 37 per cent of farmers in the lakeland counties described as 'yeoman' in 1829,[76] often combining farming with a craft or industrial activity.[77] In such circumstances, there were few opportunities for change, but in an area best suited to pastoral farming and hill grazing, there was little scope for 'improvement' as the commentators of the time perceived it.

Much of pastoral Devon was also dominated by small farmers, often owner-occupiers of ancient origin who took their names from their dwellings. Their farming had changed little since the time the enclosure of their farms was completed in the sixteenth century. Typical of this group were the Sokepitches of Clyst St George, who had 'vegetated' on their small freehold since the time of Henry II. A contemptuous neighbour wrote of them in 1768, 'with supine indolence they have slumbered over their little farm that is blessed with fertility and every natural advantage of land and water'. They preferred their hunting to the cares of an efficient farm and there were 'scores of such ancient, contented, obstinate families all over Devon to whom the words, "change" and "improvement" were wholly foreign'.[78]

There is no doubt that by the end of the eighteenth century farmers as a whole were more literate and open to new ideas than a century before and the growth in the number of farming books is proof of this. The first major phase for the establishment of new agricultural periodicals and newspapers was during the period of prosperity, 1780–1815. However, there was considerable scepticism over how much farmers actually read. Lord Somerville, president of the Board of Agriculture complained that farmers were 'not a reading class'.[79] In 1784, Arthur Young produced his first edition of *Annals of Agriculture* which ran to 34 volumes and the *Farmers' Magazine* was launched from Edinburgh in 1800. However, Arthur Young too was always dubious about how much farmers read. 'I would not be understood to expect too much from the common farmers reading this, or indeed any book; I am sensible that not one farmer in 5,000 reads at all. But the country abounds in gentlemen farmers whose ideas are much enlarged and whose practice is founded less on prejudice.'[80] He was disappointed by *Annals'* limited circulation, but an analysis of the readership has suggested that it could have been as high as 3,000: a not inconsiderable figure.[81] It was not only national publications that would have been influential. Local papers were widely available in inns, libraries and assembly rooms and reported on agricultural matters as well as quoting London corn prices from the *Mark Lane Express.*

Probably more influential than the written word was personal contact. Farmers, unlike some of their landlords did not farm for publicity, but to make money. They did not buy new implements or invest in expensive stock to be part of a fashionable movement for 'improvement', but because they hoped for higher profits. For this reason they might well distrust the ambitious schemes of their landlords, or ideas written up by them in the journals of the time. 'The example of one who is a good farmer, must have a much more beneficial effect in his neighbourhood, than that of a great landowner, however successful his practice may be.'[82] Land agents sometimes saw the best way of improving the farming of a neighbourhoud as being to encouraging tenants from more progressive regions to take on farms and set a good example. The valuer of the Wynnsay (Montgomeryshire) property suggested in 1763 the settling on the estate of a few 'improving' English tenants as 'the most likely expedient to bring the Welsh farmers out of that dull, slovenly method thay have been for ages pursuing'.[83] In his report on the farming of the Uists in 1800, Blackadder, having described in glowing and rather optimistic terms the potential for improvement, recommended the placing of an 'overseer' on one of the farms, 'who shall manage it in an industrious and farmer-like stile, so that it may be in the power of any of the inhabitants to follow the example of good husbandry'.[84] Advertisements in northern papers for farmers who would introduce the 'Scotch or Northumberland mode of farming' were not uncommon.

As we have seen, farmers often went visiting. John Carrington went to visit neighbours to see a new threshing machine at work or an alteration being made to a river 'by the wheat barn through the farmyard for a thrashing machine by water'. In Hertford market place he had seen a chaff cutting machine that would grind malt, beans and barley. 'Saw it work, the whole for grinding and cutting together, twelve guineas'.[85] For more formal contacts the 1790s saw the first hesitant beginnings of farmers' clubs and associations. National societies such as the Royal Society of Arts, founded in 1756 with an early concern for farming matters drew members from the land-owning class. The oldest of the local societies, the Bath and West, founded in 1777, held its meetings in the fashionable spa resort. The hope was that ideas discussed at the meetings would then be passed down from landowner to tenant, and by 1800, 35 counties had some sort of agricultural society.[86] Many of these were small and based on county or market towns and their aims were to act as a forum for discussion and the spreading of information.[87] While many counties, such as the agriculturally famous Northumberland had no society, Lancashire, not a county renowned for agricultural 'improvement', had four, based in Manchester, West Derby, Whalley and Lancaster respectively.[88] Possibly it was population density and ease of communication which were important factors determining whether societies were successful. All the societies were dominated by the principal proprietors and occupiers and indeed Stevenson wrote of Dorset 'for an agricultural society to prove an effectual means of improvement, it is indispensably necessary that its more opulent members should be liberal in their subscriptions'.[89] Their main functions seem to have been to hold discussions on such topics as the best way to grow turnips, to encourage experiments, to award premiums for the improvement of waste, good crops, ploughing, implements and different classes of stock as well as to encourage a spirit of industry amongst labourers. A typical aim was 'to reward the labour and industry of those poor labourers and cottagers who have brought up the greatest number of legitimate children either without any, or with the smallest relief from their respective parishes'.[90] How far down the social scale the influence of these early societies, with a membership of perhaps 200, went, is difficult to know, but they provided the basis from which the much more influential mid-century societies grew. They also indicate that there was already in many counties, a core of articulate farmers and landowners leading agricultural thinking.

Well-represented as members of these clubs and societies and an important group not to be overlooked were the farming clergy, many of whom farmed their glebe land themselves. Some of these men, such as the Revd Thomas Howes of Morningthorpe (Norfolk) kept journals.[91] Several corresponded with Arthur Young and wrote to the *Annals* on subjects as varied as carrots, liming, planting wheat, the culture of hemp and 'the night rolling of turnips'. The Revd Cooke was responsible for the invention of a popular seed drill and the Revd Chevallier for the development of an improved strain of barley. His description of how this was achieved is typical of the academic interest this class of educated farmer took in experiment:

> An extraordinary fine ear was observed and selected by a labourer of mine in the parish of Debenham (Suffolk) in 1819. In the spring of 1820 I planted 27 grains in my garden. In 1825 I planted half an acre of this species and half an acre of the common species – the land under precisely similar conditions of cultivation. The produce of the first amounted to 8 and a half coombs; of the second 6 and a half coombs. The ears of the first averaging 34 grains and of the second 30.[92]

The clergy continued their interest in agriculture as active members of county and national societies. The Revd Mr Huxtable (1808–1887), Rector of Sutton Walden in Dorset, was well known for his enthusiasm for progressive farming methods.[93] The most famous, the Revd W. L. Rham was the author of *The Dictionary of the Farm* (1844) and an early member of the Royal Agricultural Society's Journal Committee.

The picture that emerges is of an increasingly educated and innovative farming community aware of new ideas and ready to experiment, no doubt motivated by the very high prices of the Napoleonic Wars. It was likely that the greater output of the soil went to swell the profits of the tenants rather than the landlords. Rents rose at a slower pace and farms were amalgamated, thus squeezing out the old fashioned tenants with little capital. Allen's figures shows a decline from 328 to 145 farms over the 100 years after 1700 on a Buckinghamshire estate of about 20,000 acres.[94] However, it is likely that large progressive farmers were still the minority, with the majority of the farming community still working small farms using tried and tested methods. In this there was undoubtedly an east/west divide, with the mainly pastoral farmers of the west working smaller holdings and under less pressure to change than the increasingly extensive mixed arable farms of the east.

CHAPTER SEVEN

Practice with Science: The Farming Community, 1820 to 1870

> I tell you that to introduce scientific farming into England, in the face of tradition, custom, and prejudice, is a far harder task than overcoming the desert sand.
> Richard Jefferies *'A Man of Progress' Hodge and his Masters (1880)*

As farming emerged from the post-Napoleonic War depression, its community continued to be made up of a wide variety of farmers of varying social standing, wealth, education and lifestyle from the large scale 'gentlemen farmers' who would both ride to hounds and spend a day sorting their sheep for clipping,[1] to those who were little better off than the farm labourers around them. Some of the most innovative farmers came to grief. The stock of Mr Purdy, of Castle Acre (Norfolk) one of Thomas William Coke's more famous tenants, was sold to pay off creditors in October 1822.[2] John Leeds of Billingford (Norfolk) described the particularly bad years of 1825–1826 in his journal. Banks failed and brought down farmers with them. It was difficult to sell corn and 'the confidence of the county appears to be almost done away with ... a great many speculative men as well as steady men of business failing every day for want of sufficient confidence'.[3] The early 1830s were years of rural unrest best remembered for the Swing riots, which reduced farming confidence and made farms difficult to let. As late as 1835 some farmers were still experiencing problems with the agent to a south Norfolk estate writing that the tenants were 'an industrious frugal set of men ... and if they do not get on it is from the times and seasons working against them'.[4]

Throughout the early 1840s there were concerns in advance of the repeal of the Corn Laws. In November 1842 the Suffolk farmer, Richard Girling wrote, 'all trade very dull, a great many failures and many likely to follow, bankers will not allow their accounts to be overdrawn and the country in a very unsettled state'.[5] By 1850, the situation had improved and the census of 1851 enables some idea of numbers of farmers in each category of farm size to be analysed. 249,431 farmers are recorded in England of whom 97,656 farmed under 50 acres. Although it would have been possible to support a family on such a farm, it is likely that many of these farmers were combining farming with a craft or trade. In 1901 Walker believed that 75 per cent of these farmers were worse off than day labourers. Their only hope was to join cooperative alliances but they valued their independence and would 'sooner fight or fail on their own'.[6] Westmorland and Cumberland stand out as having the highest percentage of farms between 50 and 100 acres (23 per cent). While in most counties at least 50 per cent of farms were under 50 acres this figure rose to 80 per cent in the industrial areas of Lancashire and West Yorkshire. Farms of between 100–299 acres made up 51.2 per cent of all farms over 50 acres and took up about 50 per cent of the land and therefore could be regarded as 'typical' farms.[7] About 5,000 farms were over 300 acres (roughly equivalent to the number of members of the Royal Agricultural Society at the time) and very few over 1,000 acres. However there were considerable regional variations within this national pattern.[8] Only on the wide moors of Northumberland and the wolds of East Yorkshire were a quarter of farms over 300 acres. Elsewhere in the counties dominated by the great corn and sheep farms of the southern chalklands more than 20 per cent of farms were over 300 acres. In the counties dominated by the pasturelands of the south-west, the mixed farms of the midland clays and the market gardens around London fewer than 10 per cent were this large. It is these larger farmers who were the 'high' farmers of the period. It was generally agreed that at least 250 acres was needed before high farming was worthwhile and it was the farmers of such holdings who dominated the membership lists of the Royal Agricultural Society (Table 1, page 141).

As we have seen, although the main period of land reclamation and transformation was over by the 1830s, there was no let up in the amount of capital needed by farmers. Not only was the cost of under-drainage often passed on to tenants, but the increased use of fertilisers and bought-in animal feed associated with high farming made farming a much more capital-intensive operation, with estimates of the amount of investment needed by the tenant varying from £38 to £20 an acre.[9] The financial stability of a prospective tenant was still the most important quality sought. The scarcity of tenants with enough capital was a continual concern to land agents. In 1842, the agent to Lord Walsingham on his sandy Breckland estate estimated that 'to farm Sturston with spirit and to improve it as now offered will require, I think, nearly £5,000. Mr Farrer has £8,000, is not a Dissenter and does not care about politics'. In the same year a tenant had been found at Swaffham fair for Meade Farm who 'has capital, is a churchman and a conservative'.[10] Lord Napier however doubted the business acumen of one candidate for one of his farms in the Borders. 'I confess his having offered such a high rent makes me doubt his prudence.'.[11] Indeed, when letting a farm, landowners often preferred to take a man who offered less rent, but commanded greater experience.[12] Lord Napier's agent, when looking for tenants for these huge sheep farms, looked for practical men. Mr Todd applied for a farm in Ettrick in 1837. He was not only a 'good pastoral farmer'; he was said to be a 'superior' man, 'useful to the parish in many respects' with 'literary attainments' and 'medical knowledge' with an interest in education, but these were undoubtedly unusual qualities in a farmer.[13]

Smaller-scale owners would be just as anxious to ensure that their land was not reduced in value by their tenants, but the relationship between tenant and landlord was likely to have been very different as the social divide was not so great. The correspondence between a lesser Suffolk landlord and his tenant found in the records of a Woodbridge solicitor shows that they were almost social equals, happy to visit each others' houses, but still the landlord was not prepared to see his land ruined by poor farming. 'I shall have the farm looked over by a proper person and if you have not the proper crops next year I shall give you regular notice at Lady Day and make you quit the farm next Michaelmas.'[14]

It is the large estates that dominate the written record and their tenants are the ones about whom we know most. Here as elsewhere, the majority of farmers were farmers' sons and many farms on Lord Yarborough's north Lincolnshire estates passed down the generations.[15] The Holkham records show about 80 different names for the period 1790 to 1840 but five of these families dominated, different branches of each family holding several of the 70 estate farms. In 1850 18 farms were held by different members of these families. A member of one, John Leeds, kept a journal for five years from 1825 which gives some insight into a typical well-to-do farmer on a large, well-run estate.[16] Other branches of the family farmed two other Holkham-owned farms. John appears to have been to the local grammar school and then may well have gone away as a farm student before returning to the family farm at the age of 19, when he took on much of the responsibility for running it. The first part of the journal is taken up by extracts from a textbook on English history, Johnson and Boswell's *Tour of the Hebrides* as well as snippets of poetry and theology. The diary is well written and contains quotations from Sinclair's statistical writings as well as various veterinary and agricultural textbooks. He went to the theatre, concerts, lectures and dances at the local assembly rooms. He was interested in field sports and friends frequently came to stay. Perhaps the most interesting point to be revealed is the very little impact the Holkham estate made on his farming. The crop rotations practiced were not as laid down in his lease, and the farm, admittedly an outlying one, was not visited by the agent. He did go to the audit dinner and to the sheep shearings every year, and Coke's birthday was celebrated by a dinner at a neighbouring town, but that was all. The farm at this stage was mostly well run according to the Norfolk system, but later in his life, the Holkham letter books show that John Leeds fell on hard times. By 1851, the farm was said to be out of condition and not enough stock were kept; 'It is feared that the want of capital is the root of the evil.'[17]

The journals of men such as John Leeds make it clear that on these larger farms much of the day-to-day management was left to a foreman. The farmer might well set their tasks for the day and ride across the farm as often as he could, but more of his time was spent in the buying and selling of his produce. Contemporary journals list prices to be used in comparison in following years. Randall Burroughes of Wymondham (Norfolk) records a day-long haggling

FIGURE 55. Tenant farmers. Portraits of tenant farmers are difficult to come by. John Hudson and the Reverend Rham were two unusually progressive farmers who were members of the founding council of the Royal Agricultural Society. Henry Overman (*below*) was a well-known 'high' farmer. The Overman family were prominent Norfolk farmers and tenants of the Holkham estate in the nineteenth century and into the 1950s.

ROYAL AGRICULTURAL SOCIETY AND THE FARMERS' CLUB

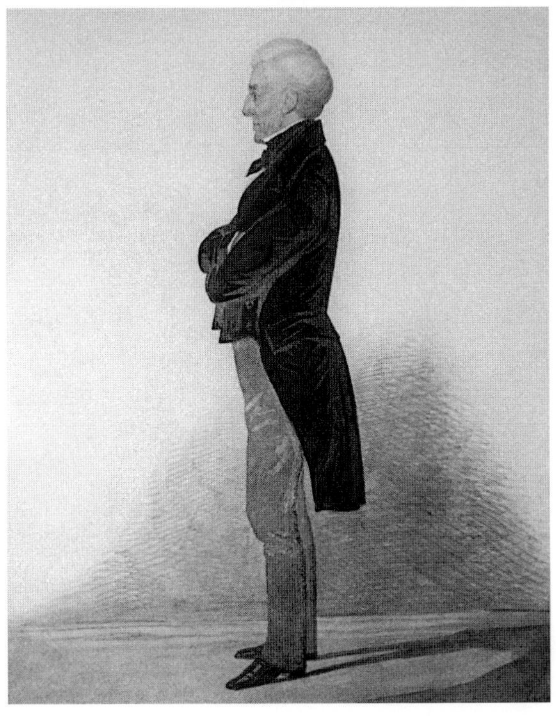

with a local butcher over the price of some cattle.[18] Stovin spent a good deal of time at the local markets and fairs assessing prices and comparing yields.[19] The diary of an un-named farmer from Witham in Essex in the 1840s shows him making regular visits to Chelmsford and Braintree markets as well as negotiating at Witham and in the public houses in various villages. Buying and selling seems to have taken up most of his time with prices and deals all meticulously recorded.[20] John Leeds or his father went to Norwich market every Saturday[21] and the weekly climax at Bacon's Farm was Saturday market at Hertford. Carrington's diary records faithfully the corn price throughout the Napoleonic Wars.[22]

More famous, was the Holkham tenant, John Hudson (Figure 55) who was described in the *JRASE* shortly after his death in 1869 as 'one of the first exponents and chief illustrators of the principles and practice of high farming'. He had become a member of the society by 1842 and a council member in 1843 and his portrait survives at the headquarters of the Society. He was always active in promoting his ideas. We know little about his origins except that he was born near Kings Lynn in 1795. Local legend had it that he came from a humble background, starting adult life as postilion to one of the local gentry. He was said to have obtained the necessary capital for farming by marrying a wealthy widow of Lynn.[23] (If this was true, he had remarried a wife three years younger than himself by 1851). He took on two neighbouring farms on the Holkham estate in 1822, controlling altogether over 1,400 acres. The farms were said to be in poor condition, the tenant of one of the farms had had to sell up for creditors and the farms had been refused by three previous prospective tenants. By increasing the number of cattle kept and feeding with oil cake and by artificial manures all costing him over £4,000 a year, he was able to double his barley crop. He owned one of the few stationary steam engines in the county and experimented with steam ploughing.[24] In 1843 he told the author of *The Agriculture of Norfolk*, published that year, that 'with more capital and more skill, this country might be an exporting rather than importing country'.[25] Like other high-profile farmers he visited London and the Royal shows, but still had time for country pursuits such as shooting parties. By 1856 he was rumoured to be worth £100,000![26]

No doubt rags-to-riches stories are unusual and some farmers lost by such intensive methods. One of the most controversial who aroused in his contemporaries the conflicting emotions of admiration and scorn was J. J. Mechi. An Italian immigrant who made a fortune in London, he bought in 1841 130 acres of poor land at Tiptree (Essex) which he intended, by heavy investment, to turn into a productive and efficient unit. His experiments resulted in a highly successful book *How to Farm Profitably*. His farm was regularly visited and his visitors' book containing many famous names, survives in the British Library. Sceptics pointed out that his expenditure of £6,000 per annum could hardly make sense on such a small farm. This view seemed to be justified when Mechi was in serious financial difficulties by the 1860s and finally was declared bankrupt shortly before his death in 1880. How far this was the result of his farming or London business interests is unclear.[27] However successful Mechi's farming activities were in the long run, they were for thirty years from the mid-1840s a shop-window for innovation and the publicity given by people like Mechi and Hudson to the new methods stimulated discussion and progress amongst many more typical farmers. John Hastings of Longham (Norfolk) could write in 1842 'Progress increases as knowledge itself increases'[28] and Cornelius Stovin who by the 1870s was taking advantage of the new labour-saving machinery, and using the new fertilisers on his Lincolnshire farm appreciated that 'farming [had] become a scientific as well as an industrial occupation.'[29]

It was only on the large arable farms that such things were possible. The new farms established on the old royal forest of Exmoor were most suited to livestock farming and their first tenants who were 'strangers' to the area failed to make a success of their farms and were replaced by local men. Unusually for the period, many of these new tenants had begun life as farm workers. William Carter of Litton Farm had begun life as an ox-boy and risen to become one of the best breeders of North Devon cattle and 'many other examples may be named on Exmoor alone of labourers who have grown into farmers ... good land let at low rentals ... has been turned to good account by the hard working and intelligent labouring class of North Devon and west Somerset.'[30]

As for the earlier period, it is very difficult to know what sort of profits farmers were making mid-century. 'The leathern purse or canvas bag being full or otherwise [was] ... the only indication of money gaining or loosing for many.'[31] Others relied on their bank books to tell them whether they were solvent or not, and the situation is complicated because when they did try and estimate their profits they tended to include household expenses as part of their outlay. Income could also vary greatly from year to year, but where large farmers did not over-extend themselves and managed to keep clear of bank failures, their profits, though erratic, could be considerable and as high as 20 per cent in good years, compared with the industrialist's 10 per cent.[32] Even in not spectacularly prosperous years some farmers made very large profits. A tenant of an 865-acre farm in Leicestershire retired in the 1840s with savings of £80,000.[33] Most felt they were doing well enough so long as they were able to meet their bills and their rent, and keep a satisfactory balance in the bank. All they wished for was to live pretty well off the farm, take a day to go to market, set aside occasional days for shooting, keep horses and ponies for the children and get out a trap to go and visit friends and relations.[34] However, there were many less risky investments than high farming in mid-Victorian Britain. To quote a novelist of the period, 'Funds pay punctual and gates never want repairin'.'[35]

By the 1840s fora for discussion were becoming firmly established in the form of farmers' clubs and agricultural associations. As we have seen, these had their beginnings in the eighteenth century, and about 100 are recorded as existing in England and Wales by 1835. This number had risen to 700 by 1855. Many of these were somewhat ephemeral. Once the initial enthusiasm was passed, many disappeared and numbers declined from the 1870s. The Bath and West, the largest and best known of the local societies, was revived by Thomas Dyke Acland in the 1850s. It ran a show with a particular emphasis on dairying, and also published a journal.

Below the county associations, which tended to be dominated by the landowners and largest tenant farmers, were the farmers' clubs. These had a far more general membership and sponsored an impressive range of activities. They ran libraries which not only provided access for farmers to technical and topical farming literature, but the information on which discussions could be based. They also encouraged the demand for agricultural literature. As well as the spreading of information through discussion and programmes of lectures, made possible after the spread of railways to rural districts, were provided by many clubs. Most clubs continued to run shows and award prizes as well as encourage experimentation. There is no doubt that they provided a formal and informal point of contact for the scattered farming community and allowed for the dissemination of knowledge which would not have been easy in any other way.[36] Visits to such places as Mechi's farm were certainly part of many an East Anglian club's programme and would have stimulated discussion. There would have been few farmers who would not have tried in a small way to emulate at least one of the new ideas with which they were presented.

On a national scale the two most important societies were The Highland and Agricultural Society of Scotland, founded in 1783 which provided much of the inspiration for the founding of the Royal Agricultural Society of England, in 1838. By 1821, the Highland had a membership of over 1000 and the following year began its own *Transactions* and established an annual show. Annual shows and a published journal were the two main tools at the disposal of the major societies whose members were too scattered to make regular meetings practical for most of them. In 1842, Philip Pusey wrote of the Royal's achievements over the previous four years. The *Journal*, he felt had not only publicised experiments and new developments but, more importantly, the good traditional practices that were to be found in the different regions. 'I am certain that four years ago no one knew how much good farming there was. Now that these things have come to light, we may hope that they will not only be spoken of, but be practiced more generally.'[37] By 1854 the membership of the Royal was over 5,000, scattered across all the country (Table 1). 286 members gave a London address, suggesting that there was a considerable non-farming element within the Society and 274 members were Welsh and 76 Scottish. Not surprisingly perhaps, the largest English county (Yorkshire) also provided the largest county membership (296), with Devon, another large county providing 197. There were 256 members from Norfolk, long famous for its improved farming. Counties near London such as Kent, Essex and Surrey all provided over 150 members, whilst Middlesex could only muster 50. However, the influence of the Society went far beyond its members. Attendance at its shows, which were held at a different venue every year could be as high as the 18,900 who went to Manchester in 1869.[38]

Another important function performed by the Society was the interest which it took in agricultural education. We know little of the elementary education of farmers' children. John Carrington hired a tutor for his children, while at about the same date John Leeds attended Hingham Grammar School. Stovin, although a great reader to the extent that he could identify particular fields with his favourite authors whose books he had read while leaning against a tree, always regretted his own lack of formal education. He sent his son to Louth Grammar School where he was disappointed at the narrowness of the classical curriculum. His daughter, on the other hand, at her small private school, studied geography, modern history and poetry.[39]

Table 1: The distribution of members of the Royal Agricultural Society of England, 1854

Yorkshire	296	Suffolk	134	Cambridgeshire	69
London	286	Oxfordshire	119	Cheshire	67
Norfolk	256	Staffordshire	118	Cornwall	63
Devon	197	Northamptonshire	115	Buckinghamshire	57
Kent	193	Berkshire	113	Worcestershire	53
Sussex	175	Nottinghamshire	115	Middlesex	50
Shropshire	168	Hertfordshire	110	Cumberland	47
Hampshire	163	Warwickshire	99	Durham	46
Essex	159	Herefordshire	87	Huntingdon	31
Lancashire	150	Wiltshire	83	Rutland	21
Northumberland	150	Derbyshire	80	Westmoreland	15
Somerset	150	Leicestershire	72	Isle of Wight	11
Surrey	140				
		Members outside England			
Wales	274	Ireland	55	Others	30
Scotland	76	Isle of Man, Channel Islands	7		
		TOTAL	5260		

It was in the vocational education of future farmers that the Society was most concerned and from 1866 there was a standing committee for education which offered prizes to the sons of tenant farmers, or owner-occupiers of less than 500 acres. To qualify, the candidates had to spend a year with a 'practical agriculturalist' or at an approved school or college. The prizes were then awarded according to how well the candidates performed in Oxford or Cambridge local examinations in such subjects as mathematics and chemistry as applied to agriculture. From 1870, the Society was setting its own examinations in agriculture, chemistry, mechanics and natural philosophy, land surveying, book keeping and anatomy. How many students availed themselves of this system is unclear, but it shows a demand to spread the availability of recognised qualifications beyond the formal, and expensive colleges to the wider farming community.

Farming literature, too, was increasing through the middle years of the century and was a reflection of the wave of interest in scientific farming. Not only was this in the form of the many encyclopaedias of the period, but periodicals and newspapers gave considerable attention to the technical and scientific aspects of agriculture, the more popular press abstracting information from the less widely read journals. However, readership probably remained low and J. C. Morton, editor of his own paper entitled *The Gazette*, thought that only those occupying more than 100 acres could be regarded as potential purchasers. Yet it is likely that either by direct purchase, or through the libraries and reading rooms of farmers clubs, pubs and assembly rooms, a substantial proportion of larger farmers was kept informed of agricultural progress.[40] The mid-century saw levels of expertise amongst farmers which had been confined to a small group of improvers, become more general. Henry Evershed, writing of Surrey in 1852, stated that the greatest improvement in the county was 'the spread of intelligence amongst the generality'.[41]

The years up to 1870 saw the farmer as the lynchpin of rural society when the rural middle class was almost entirely made up of farmers, but gradually during the nineteenth century their social position *vis-a-vis* the tradesman and merchant declined. Very few tenants became magistrates as this was a sphere dominated by the gentry, some of whom, such as Randall Burroughes[42] and Rider Haggard,[43] were also working farmers. However many, such as Cornelius Stovin were Poor Law Guardians.[44] Seventy years earlier John Carrington had been a surveyor of the highways, overseer of the poor, a tax assessor and a chief constable.[45] John Peck of Parsons Drove (Cambridgeshire) was also a constable, tax assessor and valuer, frequently employed as an arbiter in disputes. In the 1830s and 1840s he was a vigorous campaigner for better drainage and served as a commissioner on local drainage boards.[46] William Barnard was a trustee of the local turnpike.[47] In many parishes without a resident landlord such as Stovin's Binbrook (Lincolnshire) and Hastings' Longham (part of the Holkham estate, Norfolk) the local large farmers had to take on the role of squire within their community. In 1859 John Hastings was instrumental in the building of Longham school and in 1867 he took the initiative for the restoration of Longham church, although in both cases much of the funding came from the Holkham estate. He also built a double cottage for two married couples or four widows not under the age of 60 years and endowed them with six acres which he hoped would provide coal for the poor as well as for the upkeep of the cottages.[48]

As times became more difficult, the reactions to depression were as different as the farmers themselves. The agricultural essayist Richard Jefferies described a great variety in his vignettes of country life based on his knowledge of the Wiltshire countryside. He had much to say about those who gave themselves airs and graces, buying coaches, hiring gardeners, sending their daughters away to finishing schools where they learnt to play the piano, entertaining in the drawing room with glasses of sherry and refurnishing their houses. These people, rather than putting money away against the hard times, were borrowing from banks that were prepared to fund those with what looked like a safe income made from farming. It was they who were the first to suffer when the depression came and the banks began to call in their loans. Others who had taken to high farming did so with their own capital. Jefferies' 'Man of Progress' bought his estate which he then drained, enlarged the fields so that they could be worked using steam power, bought the best pedigree stock and aimed for nothing less than excellence. He could make profits, even on his high capital expenditure, in the good years, but by the late 1870s he too was regretting his high capital investment. Alongside these farmers were those who simply took on farms to enjoy the countryside. Running their farms with the help of a bailiff the farms paid their way and contributed to the household expenses whilst the tenant hunted and enjoyed the life of a country squire.

In contrast were the old-fashioned farmers who continued much as their fathers had before them. Some were muddlers and thus came to grief, whilst the more canny ones survived. None were impressed by the lecturers who came down to the local farmers' clubs with new ideas. They had seen the 'scientific farmers' come and go and believed that the greatest virtue was in paying their way rather than borrowing in order to capitalise their farming.[49]

In conclusion it is clear that throughout the period 1720–1870 the terms 'farm' and 'farmer' covered a huge variety of men and types of operation. However, some very general points can be made. Gradually, standards of living were rising. Housing was improving and the farmer had more purchasing power. Railways meant he could travel more and thus some aspects of rural isolation were breaking down. 'The farmer of 1871 spends more income than his father did in 1821, but while money has in one sense less purchasing power, mechanical and manufacturing skill have placed numberless things within his reach that even rich farmers in former times could not acquire.'[50]

Secondly we see the gradual decline of the small farmer and the continued professionalisation of the business. Throughout the period the new ideas were spreading further through the farming community. Thirsk wrote of the seventeenth century that it was 'through the efforts of country gentlemen first and foremost that initiatives were taken to spread innovations across the realm'[51] and the Fussells believed that it 'would be easy to exaggerate the number of farmers who adopted new methods' in the period before 1730.[52] Mingay also thought that well into the eighteenth century 'The progressive, market orientated and scientifically minded farmer was surrounded on all sides by ignorance and prejudice.'[53] Young however was not so condemning, writing in 1764, 'Let the landlords experiment, and if a few years prove them to answer, the tenant will adopt them.'[54] Goaded on by the high prices of the Napoleonic Wars, new ideas which would increase yields were likely to be taken up by an ever widening circle of farmers and certainly there is plenty of evidence that the number of such people was rising by the 1790s. Increasingly, the successful farmer had to be a good entrepreneur. He needed to spend as much time around the markets as on his farm. At the same time he needed to keep abreast of developments in farming practice. During our period the means for the dissemination of information were increasing and new ideas were likely to filter through to a much greater proportion of the farming community, with the role of education becoming more appreciated. The accolade of being a 'practical' farmer was being modified to take account of scientific knowledge. This was particularly true in the 1850s as the new fertilisers

FIGURE 56.
Farmhouse on the Thorney Level (Cambridgeshire). The Thorney Level was finally drained and Thorney village, designed by S. S. Teulon, built in the 1850s. The large fenland farms were provided with farmsteads and houses suited to the social standing of tenants of large-scale cereal enterprises.

were coming on the market. 'Our practical ignorance cannot be bliss unless it is pleasant to buy things at double their value and loose good crops into the bargain.'[55] The fact that British farming remained at the forefront of progressive agriculture throughout the nineteenth century is an indication that the farming community was well able to rise to the challenge – more so perhaps than British industry.

Variations in house style continued to distinguish the different classes of farmer throughout the nineteenth century. The highest class of farmer might live in a Jacobean manor house or a sizable gothic-Victorian establishment with 'a cool and lofty drawing room; elegantly framed looking glasses; chairs in good taste, and … a number of handsomely bound books' (Figures 56 and 57). Below this, the smaller farmhouse might be old fashioned with an open hearth, 'some quite good prints on the walls and a fair number of books in addition to the family Bible'.[56] Jefferies describes the typical middling type of Wiltshire farmhouse as one built as 'two distinct houses under one roof'. The rear would be taken up by the dairy, brewhouse and farm servant's quarters while the front was the residence of the farmer's family. Below this were the low thatched houses, 'little better than large cottages', found on small farms. In the pastoral districts, the dairy would take up a large part of the house. It would open onto the kitchen which was also the main living room (Figure 58). Jefferies describes the huge open fireplace with its seats in the

FIGURE 57. Three designs for farmhouses published by W. Stephens in his *Book of the Farm* in 1866.

inglenook, the stone floor, the beamed ceiling with the floor boards of the upper room laid directly upon it, and the lack of furniture, except for the locally made eight-day clock. Writing in 1892, he concludes by saying, 'let the artist who wishes to secure such a scene from oblivion set to work speedily, for these scenes are fast fading away.[57]

FIGURE 58.
A farmhouse interior, 1846. This painting by Thomas Webster shows a traditional farmhouse kitchen of a type disappearing by the 1870s.
BRISTOL MUSEUMS AND ART GALLERY

CHAPTER EIGHT

Fields, Farmsteads and Farmers

> Raw land is only a chance to prosecute the struggle for existence, and those who try to earn a living by the subugation of raw land, find that they make the attempt under most unfavourable conditions, for land can be 'made' or brought into use only by great hardship or exertion.[1]

This book has set out to investigate the role of the farmer, his landlord and the land itself in the agricultural changes of the period when the growing of grain was at the centre of much of British agriculture, between about 1720 and 1870. The evidence for this interrelationship which the landscape itself can provide is a crucial element in this attempt to integrate social agricultural and landscape history.

The landscape, buildings and written evidence show, as Tom Williamson has recently demonstrated, that different 'agricultural revolutions' were significant in the various British regions.[2] Kerridge's seventeenth-century revolution[3] was in the southern chalklands where water meadows allowed for more sheep to be kept and the development of 'up and down husbandry'. That of Allen[4] was concentrated on the fertile claylands where the small yeoman farmers were active in the eighteenth century, while at the end of the eighteenth century the landowners of the large light-land estates of the east saw the advantages of careful farming methods based on large quantities of manure allowing for the growing of cereals on no more than half of the arable. It was not until the mid-nineteenth century that these ideas spread into the most difficult terrain where strong, often steam-powered ploughs were used to break up land that previous generations could not cope with and where cultivation was only worthwhile if agricultural prices were high. The work of the drainage of the fens which began in the seventeenth century could not be completed until the introduction of ever-more powerful pumps in the nineteenth. 'The arablisation of the fens arguably made the single greatest contribution to [meeting] Britain's escalating demand for wheat in the eighteenth and nineteenth centuries.'[5]

It is also clear that the history of farms and farmers cannot, even in the cereal dominated period covered by this book, be solely considered from the point of view of arable production. Some regions were always predominantly livestock producers and as such were certainly not backward. The number of sheep in England increased by 2.5 million between 1854 and 1870 and cattle by 600,000.[6] Much of the increased grain yield went to feed this livestock.[7]

The nineteenth century saw the establishment of the finest British breeds, such as the Suffolk sheep and Aberdeen Angus beef cattle, that were exported world-wide. As we have seen, even in the mainly arable east, William Marshall recognised in the 1780s that the greatest fortunes were made in livestock and all farmers needed to be good judges of cattle. Our story is therefore not a simple one and not surprisingly when we consider a topic so closely linked to the varying topography of Britain, there is great local diversity. Evidence for all these phases and their regional distinctiveness can be seen in the landscapes of the regions.

It follows that the dividing of the countryside into 'ancient' and 'planned' landscapes is too simplistic for the purposes of this analysis. The term 'ancient' suggests that there has been little change, but all farmed land has undergone continuous change and so the word, 'evolved' would seem more accurate in this context. Here the major developments were for livestock when small enclosures were created from the open fields by individual farmers, often little controlled by manorial systems. Similar farms developed along the edges of forests and highlands as farmers nibbled away out from the edges of medieval cultivation. These individual reclamations continued through to the nineteenth century in some areas and in total may represent as important an assault on the 'wastes' as any of the more publicised large-scale landlord enterprises.[8]

'Planned landscapes', as has been shown here, cover a wide variety of periods and agricultural systems. The earliest regular enclosures were created by agreement and on the initiative of farmers with or without the support of their landlords, again mainly for pastoral farming. The later larger and more regular fields were the work of the landlords and for arable farms. They often covered old fens, uplands, common and waste as well as open fields, and in the more remote and inhospitable areas many such landscapes have since reverted to semi-natural and rough pasture. Agricultural development was certainly not confined to the planned regions. Arthur Young commented on the progressive methods of the rich yeoman farmers of the long-enclosed Suffolk claylands. Some of the earliest records of turnip growing are as fodder for animals in the wood-pasture regions of East Anglia.[9]

This diversity is also seen in buildings. The scattered vernacular houses of the evolved farms are frequently on ancient sites. Beside them are the farmsteads and barns, which may well have been built as multi-purpose buildings dating from the seventeenth century or earlier and which show signs of continuous development. In the eighteenth century separate stables were built and by the nineteenth century barn accommodation was being increased and cattle accommodation added. Later in the century cattle provision was extended. The quality of many of the houses indicates the early prosperity of these yeoman farmers while the continuous expansion of the farmsteads shows their adaptation to changing circumstances on the limited capital available for investment.

On the planned landscapes resulting from the agreement of local farmers, older houses and buildings also remain within ordered fields. Again they demonstrate the social standing of their occupiers. Where these farms were tenanted, the interest of the owner is shown in the types of building provided. Frequently where the enclosure was carried out at the initiative of the tenant, the lack of landlord concern is shown in the poor quality of the early buildings. This apathy was only broken in the late nineteenth century, when, faced with declining rents, the owner was jolted into action and erected often rather shoddy livestock sheds in an attempt to keep farms occupied.

Fine planned and model farms with their gentry-style houses are mainly confined to the large and wealthy estates where new landscapes were created. Even here however the first generation of buildings, erected during the prosperous years of the Napoleonic Wars were often initially paid for by tenants rather than their landlords.

The landscape and its buildings demonstrate the changing relationship between the landlord and the farmer. Most of the British countryside was farmed by tenants, but it is the methods of the larger farmers occupying land on the most extensive estates about which we know most. While from the human perspective the small farmers made up an important component of rural society, they produced only a small proportion of the nation's food. The balance between large and small farmer is one that can also be demonstrated in the landscape and settlement patterns, resulting in further regional differences.

The relationship between landlord and tenant was governed very much by the shifting fortunes of agriculture. Whig landowners were quick to stress the unity of interest with the toast, 'A good understanding between landlord and tenant' being drunk at many an audit dinner; but the truth was very different. While the landlord wanted the highest rent he could get, alongside the keeping of his lands in good heart, the tenant wanted to keep rents low and take as many crops off the farm as possible. The late seventeenth century was a period of sluggish prices and tenants could be hard to find. The last thing landlords wanted was a vacant farm and surveys of the work of land stewards in the late Stuart period show that tenants knew the strength of their position and often exploited it to the full.[10] This situation changed in the eighteenth century with prices gradually rising and farms being in greater demand. Landlords were able to pass on much of the expense of drainage and building to their tenants and to enforce strict husbandry clauses. While there were years of depression when agents complained of the assertiveness of tenants, as the century moved on landlords were in a strong enough position to make their views known when their tenants were breaking their leases and over-cropping. In fact, they themselves were probably doing more long-term damage by some of their more ambitious reclamation schemes than were their tenants' husbandry methods. This all changed with the slump after the Napoleonic Wars when tenants again had the upper hand. Rents rose during the years of 'high farming' and as we have seen the more extravagent of buildings and reclamation schemes were the work of the wealthiest landowners. With hindsight many of these gave little long-term benefit to either the landlords or their tenants.

Rather it was a case of too much money being a dangerous thing and many of the much trumpeted 'achievements' of the landlords were not really as great as they were made out to be. As Pell wrote, in his typical Victorian style in 1887, 'While the field laughs with grain, it is more than possible that the owner groans at the cost of its artificial fertility.'[11] The same criticism of the landlords' misguided investment has been levelled at their expensive planned and model farms, but they should certainly not be dismissed simply as expensive follies. If nothing else these farms demonstrate the 'spirit of the age' and certainly provided a pool of ideas, and, on occasion, examples of best practice, some of which were practical for others to follow.[12]

As in so many areas of agricultural history, the regional diversity of Britain has resulted in a wide variety, this time in the roles and significance of the landord and their tenants. Tenants and owner-occupiers on the fertile lands were certainly initiators of change which resulted not only in increased arable production but an improvement in the quality and quantity of livestock. However, over much of the light land of the east there can be no doubt of the importance of the landowner in providing the infrastructure for the new farming, particularly in the years of low prices. But everywhere, it was the farmer who actually farmed and landlords themselves were very well aware of the importance of successful farming to the maintaining of healthy rent rolls. Between them, farmers, landlords and labourers ensured that an increasingly urbanised and growing population was fed during the initial stages of industrialisation, when there was little food available from overseas. The landscape of Britain had to be made to serve this end.

It is clear though that some landlord investment was ill-conceived, the product of an over-optimistic belief in the power of science and the possibilities of the market. The misguided direction which such reclamation had taken was already recognised by Pell in 1887. Writing of the grubbing up of Wychwood Forest (Oxfordshire) and the preparing of it for arable farming, he describes processes which in the past would 'have been slowly worked out during centuries' as 'undertaken and completed in almost as many years'. 'The English flora and fauna in all their natural fitness and beauty were violently and ruthlessly destroyed to make way for artificial grasses and cereals'. In a similar vein he describes a moor where 'the snipe, the dotterel and the woodcock were common' which had been enclosed, ploughed and reseeded for improved pasture. Unlike Pusey, who, scarcely forty years previously had stated as the duty of the landlord to improve 'needless deserts', Pell was questioning the wisdom of such activity. The ecological cost was beginning to creep into the equation. The reasons for this change of heart are many. Firstly, as it was becoming clear that reclamation at any cost was not financially viable, it was easy to criticise past activity. Second, as the spectre of famine declined with an apparently endless supply of cheap food being available from America, the moral duty to provide more food was less valid. Most of Britain was naturally better suited to pastoral farming than grain and corn was king for little more that the period covered by this book. The opening up of global markets over the last 130 years has made this ever more obvious. Pell attempted to produce figures showing the financial viability or otherwise of various projects, but all are suspect, as there are so many imponderable variables. What is certain, as he states, is that the value of such schemes could not be quantified in financial terms only. He quotes Arthur Young as suggesting that the satisfaction taken by the owner in his morning stroll across some of his works counted for much and of such 'no very accurate accounts can be found'.[13] Pell concluded:

> The most a prudent improver can do is to humbly provide for contingiencies, to remember that at present there are no exact rules of science under which he can conquer this dour earth of ours; and costly though it be, he must be content to do what, with no assurance of great reward, his ancestors have done before him – adopt those measures which many failures and much painful experience have shown to be of most service in the particular spot on which he applies his energies and resources.[14]

If the 'philosophy of improvement' with which we began this book had not gone full circle, it had in the face of declining agricultural prices, at least matured into an understanding that the varied regions of Britain could not be forced into a single agricultural pattern. The optimism that science could conquer all had gone and an understanding that the climatic, topographical and soil characteristics must be allowed to dictate the system most suited to the region had taken its place. The thinking of Pell and many of his contemporaries was very different to that of the previous generation, but is one with which we can empathise today.

Notes

Abbreviations used in notes

ESO Essex Record Office
NRO Norfolk Record Office
SRO Suffolk Record Office
PP Parliamentary Papers

Notes to Chapter One: 'The Age of Improvement' 1720–1870: The Philosophies Driving Farming Change

1. Turner, Beckett and Afton (2001).
2. English (1990), 150.
3. Lord Belhaven (1699), preface.
4. Kerridge (1967), 181–221.
5. Griffiths (2002), 11.
6. Bettey (1999), 180–1.
7. Bettey (1999), 185.
8. Kerridge (1967), 266.
9. Fussell (1955), 43.
10. NRO, Lestrange MS.
11. Beckett (1989), 590.
12. Allen (1992), 310.
13. Overton (1985), 205–21.
14. Kerridge (1967), 326, quoting T. Fuller *Holy State and Profane State* 1841 ed. 107.
15. Griffiths (2002), 17.
16. Chartres (1985), 406–501.
17. Young (1772), p. viii.
18. Turner, Beckett and Afton (1997), 34.
19. Wade-Martins and Williamson (1998), 229, quoting ESO D/DL/C4/1.
20. Wade-Martins (1995), 63–4.
21. Wordie (1983), 483–505.
22. Chartres (1985), 444.
23. Daniels and Seymour (1990).
24. Curwen (1809), 238.
25. Cobbett (1930), 181.
26. Thomas *Man and the Natural World* (1983), 254–6.
27. RA Add 32/2020, quoted in J. Roberts (1997).
28. Young (1784), 61.
29. Ruggles (1786), 21.
30. Ruggles (1787), 90.
31. Wade Martins and Williamson (1994), 20–37, 24.
32. Laurence (1727).
33. Adam (1972), II, 267.
34. Hull University Library DDBM/27/3 The Blackadder report on the Uists 1800.
35. NRO WLS XXIX/6/15/ 416x4.
36. Davies (1810), 121–2.
37. Harvey (1988), 49–54.
38. Read (1858), 265–303, 278.
39. Wade Martins *A Great Estate at Work* (1980), 121.
40. Pusey (1850), 381–438, 381.
41. Pusey (1845), 521.
42. Clarke (1900), 15.
43. Goddard (1988), 80–1.
44. Pusey (1842), 169–215, 170.
45. Pusey (1842), 169–215, 208.
46. Pusey (1842), 169–215, 215.
47. Caird (1852), 503.
48. Caird (1890), 1–36, 29.
49. Caird (1888), 125.

Notes to Chapter Two: Landscapes of 'Improvement' to 1830

1. Pusey (1849), 462–79, 479.
2. Allen (1992), 68–87.
3. Howell (1985), 278.
4. Hall (2001), 25.
5. Butlin (1979), 64–82.
6. Turner (1980), 42.
7. Wade Martins and Williamson (1999), 42.
8. Hollowell (2000), 1; Chapman and Seeliger (2001).
9. Wade Martins and Williamson (1999), 41.
10. Chapman and Seeliger (1997), xviii.
11. Wade Martins and Williamson (1999), 139–40; Cambridge (1845), 333–42; Turner (1845), 479–88.
12. Williamson (2000), 56–79.
13. Hollowell (2000), 5 and 24.
14. Broad (1980), 77–89.
15. Turner (1980), 146.
16. Havinden (1961), 73–83.
17. Turner (1980), 37.
18. Williamson 1 (2000), 56–79, 67, quoting Lincoln Record Office, Misc Dep 77/16.
19. Wolterton estate archives, MS leases 4/1–4.
20. Beckett (1990), 39.
21. Butlin (1979), 64–82, 78–9.
22. Mingay (1997), 28.
23. Darby (1973), 334–5.
24. Darby (1973), 337.
25. Hainsworth (1992).
26. Thompson (1966), 505–17, 508.
27. Darby (1973), 302.
28. Vancouver (1813).
29. Bettey (2000), 27–61, 94.
30. Hall (2001), 13.
31. Williamson (2000), 66.
32. Pitt (1813), 64, 69.
33. Mingay (1989), 974–5 and 998–9.
34. North Yorkshire Record Office ZNK M1/3.
35. North Yorkshire Record Office ZNK M1/17.
36. Young (1771), 3, 98–9, 106 and 81.
37. Hall (2001).
38. Pitt (1813), *Leicestershire* 69.
39. Pitt (1813), *Leicestershire* 80.
40. Williamson (2002), 46.
41. Parker (1975), 45.
42. Parker (1975), 43.
43. Turner (1980), 33,52.
44. Beckett (1990), 42.
45. NRO Le Strange BH8.
46. Mingay (1997), 28.
47. Turner (1975), 489–510.
48. NRO WLSXVII/20 415x5.
49. NRO c/scel/16.
50. Parker (1975), 84.
51. Williamson (2002), 72 and 74.
52. Gleave (1973), 98–115.
53. Batchelor (1813), 475.
54. Becket, Turner and Cowell (1998), 141–55.
55. NRO WLSXXVII/20/15 415x5.
56. Holderness (1971), 159–83, 165–7.
57. Williamson (1999), 41–52, 43.
58. Young (1771), 1, 271.
59. Phillips (1999), 53–72, 57.
60. Wogan (1815), 109.
61. Holland (1813), 210.
62. Duncomb (1813), 98.
63. Williamson (2002), 101–2.
64. Glyde (1856), 338.
65. Smout (2000), 98.
66. Spring (1955), 73–81.
67. Dickson and Stevenson (1815), 488.
68. Vancouver (1813), 333.
69. North Yorkshire Record Office ZNCX/2/1/1695.
70. North Yorkshire Record Office ZNCX/2/1/1998.
71. Young *Hertfordshire* (1813), 157, 160.
72. Bacon (1844), 291–2.
73. Darby (1973), 339.
74. NRO Petre box 9/1–4.
75. NRO Petre box 17/1).
76. Thompson (1966), 505–17, 516.
77. Williamson (2000), 56–79, 57.
78. NRO WLS XXL VII/19 415x5.
79. Young (1773), 39.
80. Young (1795), 10–12.
81. Young (1799), 12–59.
82. Quoted by Turner (1980), 88.
83. Williams (1970), 51, 55–69.
84. Turner (1980), 146.
85. Birtles (1999).

86. Mingay (1997), 58.
87. Young (1804), 185, and for instance 107, 'As to cottage cow keepers they are all over ...'
88. Wade Martins (1980), 120.
89. Davis (1794), 20.
90. Wade Martins and Williamson (1999), 40.
91. NRO WLSXXIX/2/10 416 x 4 1400 dozen rabbits continued to be kept after enclosure on one 1800-acre farm.
92. Chapman 24 (1976), 1–17.
93. Cocks (1970), 245–56.
94. Hey (2000), 203.
95. Smout (2000), 95–6.
96. Sheppard (1966), 11.
97. Brown (1967), 34–52.
98. Williams (1970), 172–3.
99. Williams (1970), 125–6.
100. Sheppard (1958), 11–12.
101. Young (1798), 113–36.
102. Taylor (1999), 141–56.
103. Loch (1820), 220–6.
104. Spring (1955), 73–81.
105. Spring (1955), 80.
106. Pitt *Leicestershire* (1813), 68.
107. Silvester (1999), 122–40, 128–9.
108. Howell (1985), 272–5.
109. Wiliam (1986), 7.
110. Dodd (1927), 210.
111. Bowen (1914), Appendix 1.
112. Creegan (1996), 5–23.
113. Smith (1798), 30 and 33.
114. Banks (1977), 75.
115. *Statistical Account of Scotland* 7 (1793), 440.
116. Roxburghe MS uncatalogued papers.
117. Douglas (1798), 91.
118. RCAHMS (2001).
119. Wade Martins (1996–97).
120. *Statistical Account of Scotland* **21** (1799), Appendix 151–81.
121. Ross (1972).
122. Cadell (1913).
123. Devine (1994), 126.
124. Smith (1813), 33, 57 and 80.
125. Devine (1999), 136.
126. Graham (1818), xx.
127. Kerr (1803), xx.
128. Mackenzie (1813), 330.
129. Argyll and Bute Archives DC2.
130. Taylor (1790), 265–6.
131. Beckett (1990), 55.

Notes to Chapter Three: Landscapes of 'Improvement' after 1830

1. Wade Martins and Williamson (1999), 131.
2. Pusey (1842), 169–215, 205.
3. Low (1834).
4. Tuckett (1860), 258–66.
5. Wade Martins (1980), 76.
6. Quoted in Williamson (2002), 148 and 82.
7. Pusey (1845), 521.
8. Phillips (1999), 53–72, 64.
9. Goddard (1991), 165–90.
10. Pusey (1842), 170.
11. Jones (1968), 23.
12. Phillips (1999), 53–72.
13. Bacon *Norfolk* (1844), 379–85.
14. Select Committee on agricultural customs BPP 1847/8 VII Q. 3290.
15. Loch (1829), 196.
16. Wade Martins (1995), 103 and 129.
17. Stevenson (1853), 275–324.
18. Roxburghe estate archives payment books.
19. Sheppard (1966), 11; C. Taylor (1999), 155.
20. Clarke (1848), 101.
21. Wade Martins (1995), 128–9.
22. Clarke (1848), 104.
23. Duke of Bedford (1897), 34–54.
24. Clarke (1848), 113.
25. Williams (1970), 209–15.
26. Clarke (1848), 133.
27. Watson (1845), 79–102.
28. Perry (1981), 164.
29. This description is based on Thompson 'Report on the improvement of waste land' *THASS* 1853–55, 90–8; Forbes 'Report on the improvement of waste land' *THASS* 1853–55, 99–109; Macpherson Grant 'Report on the improvement of the farm of Marypark' *THASS* 1849–51, 79–94.

30. Mills *et al.* (1997), 31–2.
31. Maclelland (1875), 9–11.
32. Macdonald (1875), 168.
33. Macdonald (1886), 85.
34. Thompson (1987), 224.
35. Macdonald (1884), 1–123.
36. Carter (1979), 55–60.
37. Thompson (1853–55), 90–8.
38. Caird (1994), 136–58.
39. Wade Martins (1996–97), 33–54.
40. Wade Martins (1996–97), 33–54.
41. Howell (1977), 40–1.
42. Wade Martins (1991), 67–70.
43. Orwin (1929), 36–7.
44. Orwin (1929), 59.
45. Pusey (1843), 288.
46. Pusey (1849), 462.
47. Wade Martins and Williamson (1999), 196–209; Caird (1852), 205.
48. Roals (1845), 518–21 – Roals claimed a 50 per cent interest on his investment!
49. Bettey (1999), 193.
50. Copland (1866), 762.
51. Pusey (1849), 478.
52. Perry (1973), 366.
53. Pusey (1849), 477.
54. Caird (1888), 124–5.
55. Read (1888), 139.

Notes to Chapter Four: The New Farms

1. Newman 'The Anti-Corn Law League and the Wiltshire Labourer' in Holderness and Turner, *Land, Labour and Agriculture, 1700–1920* (1991), 96.
2. Williamson (2002), 47.
3. RCHME *Houses of the North York Moors* (1987), 154; Everett (1968), 54–60.
4. Witts (1777).
5. Markham (1635), 24–6.
6. Lord Belhaven (1699), 32.
7. Alnwick MS 4/41.
8. Appleby (1995), 25–34.
9. Holkham MS letter books 1827, 86.
10. Adam (1972), 1, 38.
11. Wade Martins (1996–97), 33–54, 42.
12. Cited by Daniels and Seymour (1990), 497.
13. Royal Archives Nathaniel Kent's *Journal* 1.
14. Wade Martins (2002), 105.
15. Loch (1820), 56.
16. Young (1771), 2, 98–9.
17. Young (1771), 2, 428–40 and pl 6–7.
18. Robinson (1981), 42–3.
19. Smith (1798), 14–15.
20. Marshall (1804), 160.
21. Lake (1989), 114.
22. Argyll and Bute Archives DC2/6.
23. Harvey (1988), 49–54.
24. National Archive of Scotland RHP 47870/1.
25. Roxburghe MS uncatalogued letter book.
26. Smith (1810), 57–9.
27. Singer (1812), 86.
28. Somerville (1805), 34–48.
29. Henderson (1812), Appendix 43–48.
30. National Library of Scotland dep. 313/3587/1.
31. Kent (1775), 146.
32. Wade Martins (2002).
33. Denton (1864), 2.
34. Wade Martins (2002), 96.
35. Pusey (1851), 35.
36. Thompson (1850), 186.
37. Spooner and Elliot (1850), 278.
38. Hall (1913), 129.
39. Buist (1840), 298–319.
40. Macdonald (1884), 50 and 100.
41. Ralston (1885), 95–6.
42. Roberts (1879), 409.
43. Wade Martins 1996–97, 51.
44. Bedfordshire Record Office R5/869/1.
45. Bedfordshire Record Office R5/869/1.
46. Wade Martins (2002), 147–8.
47. Browick (1862), 247.
48. Andrews (1852), 7.
49. PRO CRES 16–1 1851 241.
50. Wade Martins (2002), 162–4.
51. Brigden (1986), 33–5.
52. Harvey (1998), 49–54.

Notes to Chapter Five: Evolved Landscapes

1. Rackham (1986), 4.
2. Nankervis (1991).
3. Rackham (1986), 183.
4. Marshall (1796), 2, 6.
5. Herring (1999), 23.
6. Fox (1999), 273–9, 274.
7. Hoskins (1943), 80–92.
8. Staines (1969), 45.
9. Tanner (1848), 483.
10. Wilmot (1999), 294.
11. Harrison (1984), 365.
12. Vancouver (1809), 80.
13. Wilmot (1999), 299–300.
14. Beckett (1982), 107.
15. Beckett (1982), 100.
16. Denyer (1991), 16–17.
17. Wade Martins (1995), 49.
18. Marshall (1980), 512–13.
19. Dickenson (1852), 289.
20. Beckett (1982), 102.
21. Brunskill (1974), 25.
22. Wade Martins and Williamson (1999), 20–3.
23. Young *Suffolk* (1813), 8.
24. Wade Martins and Williamson (1999), 108.
25. Wade Martins and Williamson (1999), 50.
26. Young (1786), 193–224.
27. Biddell (1874), 26.
28. Wade Martins and Williamson (1999), 65–6.
29. For example, Williamson (1986), 419–31.
30. Marshall (1796), 1, 106.
31. Wade Martins and Williamson (1999), 137–40.
32. Jessop (1878), 6.
33. David (1971), 152.
34. Minutes of evidence on the charging of entailed estates for drainage PP XII (1845), qu 417 and 418.
35. Rackham (1986), 93.
36. Barnwell and Giles (1997), 156.
37. Barnwell and Giles (1997), 45–6.
38. Tanner (1848), 488.
39. Alcock (1966), 128–9.
40. Suffolk Record Office HA1 HB4/2.
41. Wade Martins (1991), 199.
42. RCHME (1987), 156.
43. Wiliam (1986), 68.
44. Suffolk Record Office HA1/HB4/2.
45. Bailey and Culley (1794), 208.
46. Messenger (1975), 327–51.
47. Young (1786), 204.
48. Theobald (2000).
49. Morgan (1963), 117–31.
50. Evans and Jarrett (1987), 199–209; Evans and Jarrett (1988), 139–93; Austin (1985), 71–9.
51. Brunskill (1982), 116.
52. Alcock (1969), 97–8.
53. Alcock, Child and Laithwaite (1972), 227–33.
54. Cox and Thorp (1994).
55. Messenger (1973), 49.
56. Denyer (1991), 67.
57. RCHME (1987), 154.
58. Wade Martins and Williamson (1999), 90–1.

Notes to Chapter Six: The Age of the 'Practical' Farmer: The Farming Community, 1720 to 1820

1. Macdonald (1979), 5.
2. Perry (1981), 162.
3. Porter (1996), 854.
4. Howkins (1994), 53.
5. Stovin (1982) – for instance 'The more labour man puts into his work, the more proportionate energy does God impart. Man receives aid from heaven in proportion to his own exertions. In looking round my farm I am gazing on part of God's dominions'.
6. NRO WLSXXIX/2/9.
7. Hunt (1804), 59.
8. NRO T Rose 'Report on the Gunton estate' (1894), Gunton MS.

9. Mingay (1963), 22–3.
10. Jones (1992), 7.
11. Branch-Johnson (1956), 38.
12. Dairy of John Peck, 1814–51, Wisbech Museum and Library.
13. NRO MS34018.
14. For the Holkham estate, Wade Martins (1980), 143; for Sutherland, Wade Martins (1996–97), 42; for North Yorkshire RCHME (1987), 154; for the Lancashire Pennines, Pearson (1985), 122.
15. Williamson (2002), 19–20.
16. Marshall (1787), 1, 345.
17. Sandon (1977), 245.
18. Pitt (1813), 19.
19. Plymley (1813), 95.
20. Batchelor (1813), 19.
21. Stevenson (1815), 83.
22. Pitt (1813), 22.
23. Beckett (2000), 736.
24. Roebuck (1976), 15.
25. SRO/3/1.
26. SRO/4/26.
27. Garrett (1747).
28. Stevenson 'Northumberland farm buildings' n.d. Alnwick Castle MS.
29. Duncomb (1813), 29.
30. Loch (1820), plate 17.
31. Bailey and Culley *Cumberland* (1794), 208.
32. Bailey and Culley *Cumberland* (1794), 208.
33. Wade Martins and Williamson (1995), 33.
34. Macdonald (1979), 17.
35. For example the farming journal of the Norfolk farmer, J. P. Leeds (NRO MS34018), shows the degree of visiting with friends from as far away as London and Cambridge staying.
36. Macdonald (1979), 9.
37. Butler (1869), 259.
38. Young *Lincolnshire* (1813), 45.
39. Branch-Johnson (1956), 38.
40. NRO MS34018.
41. Macdonald (1979), 34.
42. Stovin (1982), 1.
43. Baley and Culley (1813), 30.
44. Macdonald (1979), 17.
45. Butler (1869), 259.
46. DNB supplement (1917), 365–8.
47. Macdonald 1976–77, 139–45.
48. Young *Lincolnshire* (1813), 45.
49. Baley and Culley (1813), 30.
50. Duncomb (1813), 35.
51. Wade Martins (1996–97), 41–2.
52. Wade Martins (1980), 185.
53. NRO WLSXXIX/2/35 416x4.
54. Mingay (1989), 39.
55. NRO WLSXXVI/17 415x4.
56. Mingay (1990), 74–5.
57. NRO WLSXXIX /2/22.
58. Young (1771), II, 160–1.
59. Marshall (1787), I, 2.
60. Overton (1985), 205–21.
61. Stevenson (1815), 90.
62. Middleton (1813), 54.
63. Duncomb (1813), 32–3.
64. Dickson and Stevenson (1815), 117.
65. Middleton (1813), 58–9.
66. Young (1764), 189.
67. Wade Martins and Williamson (1999), 194–6.
68. Holkham MSS F. Blaikie 'Report on the estates of Thomas William Coke, Esq in the county of Norfolk' 1816.
69. Vancouver (1808), 107.
70. Howell (1985), 277.
71. Howell (1981), 1, 71–80.
72. Gibson (1879), 47.
73. Mingay (1989), 36.
74. Baley and Culley *Westmorland* (1794), 302.
75. Baley and Culley *Cumberland* (1794), 209.
76. Brunskill (1974), 25.
77. Pringle (1794), 299–301.
78. Hoskins (1943), 84–5.
79. Goddard (1983), 117.
80. Young (1772), viii.
81. Goddard (1983), 117.
82. *Farmer's Magazine* XXI (1820), 480.
83. Howell (1985), 294.
84. University of Hull Library DDBM/27/3.
85. Branch-Johnson (1956), 26.
86. Hudson (1972), x–xi.
87. Fox (1979), 47.
88. Dickson and Stevenson (1815), 649.
89. Stevenson (1815), 465.
90. Boys (1813), 211.

91. NRO MC150/52.
92. Quoted in Raynbird (1849), 185.
93. Mingay (2000), 766.
94. Allen (1992), 83.

Notes to Chapter Seven: Practice with Science: The Farming Community, 1820 to 1870

1. NRO MC40/163 486x3 dairies of H. W. Coldham, 1834.
2. Wade Martins (1993), 38.
3. NRO MS34018.
4. NRO MEA3/205.
5. SRO JA1/59.
6. Walker (1901–2), 88.
7. Mingay (2000), 759–60.
8. Overton (1996), Table 4. 13.
9. Perry (1973), 372.
10. NRO WLSXVIII/12/2 and WLSXXII/9 413x9.
11. Lord Napier and Ettrick MS private collection.
12. Mingay (2000), 771.
13. Lord Napier and Ettrick MS private collection.
14. SRO HB10/427/347.
15. Mingay (2000), 773.
16. NRO MS34018.
17. Holkham MS EG/12 H. W. Keary *Report on the Holkham Estate* (1851).
18. Wade Martins and Williamson (1995), 20.
19. Stovin (1982), 11.
20. ESO D/DBsF38.
21. NRO MS34018.
22. Branch-Johnson (1956), 28.
23. Armstrong (1963), 63.
24. Wade Martins (1980), 114–19; Jenkins (1869), 460–74.
25. NRO Bacon MS 4363.
26. Armstrong (1963), 63.
27. Brigden (1986), 190–3.
28. NRO Bacon MS 4363.
29. Stovin (1982), iii.
30. Sidney (1878), 85–6.
31. Dickenson (1852), 224.
32. Mingay (1976), 49.
33. Perry (1973), 377.
34. Mingay (2000), 803.
35. Surtees, *Hillingdon Hall* quoted in Perry (1973), 378.
36. Fox (1979), 43–64.
37. Pusey (1842), 215.
38. Goddard (1981), 248.
39. Stovin (1982), 4 and 8.
40. Goddard (1983), 116–30.
41. Evershed, 422.
42. Wade Martins and Williamson (1995).
43. Rider Haggard (1899).
44. Stovin (1982), 14 'I am appointed guardian in his place, so you will perceive I am not without honour in my own country'.
45. Branch-Johnson (1956), 116–51.
46. Dairy of John Peck of Parson Drove, 1814–51, Wisbech Museum and Library.
47. Jones (1992), 9.
48. Wade Martins (1980), 122.
49. Jeffries (1981).
50. Scot Skirving (1873), 48.
51. Thirsk (1985), 190.
52. Fussell (1955), 68.
53. Mingay (1989), 41.
54. Young (1764), 190.
55. Read (1858), 278.
56. Mingay (1976), 52 quoting Hippolyte Taine's tour of England in 1862.
57. Jefferies (1981), 21.

Notes to Chapter Eight: Fields, Farmsteads and Farmers

1. Pell (1887), 355.
2. Williamson (2002), 158.
3. Kerridge (1967).
4. Allen (1992).
5. Williamson (2002), 163.
6. Turner (1998), 159.
7. Walton (1999), 29.
8. For instance the work of Aberdeenshire crofters as distinct from the landlord reclamations; I. Carter (1979).

Notes

9. Overton (1985); Young *Suffolk* (1813).
10. Hainsworth (1992), 74.
11. Pell (1887), 365.
12. Wade Martins (2002).
13. Pell (1887), 367.
14. Pell (1887), 374

Bibliography

R. J. Adam (1972) *Sutherland Estate Management* 2 vols.

N. W. Alcock (1963) 'Devonshire linhays' *Transactions of the Devonshire Association* **95** 117–131.

N. W. Alcock (1966) 'A Devon farm, Bury Barton, Lapford' *Transactions of the Devonshire Association* **98** 105–129.

N. W. Alcock (1969) 'Devonshire farmhouses, Part II Some Dartmoor Houses' *Transactions of the Devonshire Association* **101** 83–97.

N. W. Alcock, P. Child and M. Laithwaite (1972) 'Sanders, Lettaford: a Devon Long-house' *Proceedings of the Devon Archaeological Society* **30** 227–233.

R. C. Allen (1992) *Enclosure and the Yeoman: Agricultural Development in the South Midlands 1450–1850.*

G. Andrews (1852) *Agricultural Engineeering.*

J. Appleby (1995) 'Farm building designs for Lord Scarsdale at Kedleston Hall, Derbyshire' *Journal of the Historic Farm Buildings Group* **9** 25–34.

H. Armstrong (ed.) (1963) *Armstrong's Norfolk Diary.*

D. Austin (1985) 'Dartmoor and the upland village of south-west England' in D. Hooke (ed.) *Medieval Villages* 71–79.

R. N. Bacon (1844) *Agriculture of Norfolk.*

J. Bailey and G. Culley (1794) *General View of the Agriculture of Cumberland.*

J. Bailey and G. Culley (1794) *General View of the Agriculture of Westmorland.*

J. Bailey and G. Culley (1813) *General View of the Agriculture of Northumberland.*

N. Banks (1977) *Six Inner Hebrides.*

P. S. Barnwell and C. Giles (1997) *English Farmsteads 1750–1914.*

T. Batchelor (1813) *A General View of the Agriculture of Bedfordshire.*

J. V. Beckett (1982) 'The decline of the small landowner in eighteenth- and nineteenth-century England: some regional considerations' *Agricultural History Review* **30** 97–111.

J. V. Beckett (1989) 'Land ownership and the land market' in G. E. Mingay (ed.) *Agrarian History of England and Wales* **6** 1750–1850.

J. V. Beckett (1990) *The Agricultural Revolution.*

J. V. Beckett (2000) 'Agricultural Landownership and Management' in E. J. T. Collins (ed.) *Agrarian History of England and Wales 1850–1914* **7 i** 693–756.

J. V. Beckett, M. Turner and E. Cowell (1998) 'Farming through enclosure' *Rural History* **9.2** 141–155.

Bedford, Duke of (1897) *The Story of a Great Estate.*

Lord Belhaven (1699) *The Country-man's Rudiment, or An Advice to the farmers of East Lothian on how to Labour and Improve their Ground.*

J. Bettey (1999) 'The development of water meadows in the southern counties' in H. Cook and T. Williamson (eds) *Water Management in the English Landscape.*

J. Betty (2000) 'Downland' in J. Thirsk (ed.) *The English Rural Landscape* 27–61.

H. Biddell (1874) 'Agriculture' in *White's Suffolk Directory* 24–30.

S. Birtles (1999) 'Common land, poor relief and enclosure' *Past and Present* **165**, 74–106.

I. Bowen (1914) *Enclosure of Common Land in Wales.*

J. Boys (1813) *A General View of the Agriculture of Kent.*

W. Branch-Johnson (1956) *The Carrington Diary.*

R. Brigden (1986) *Victorian Farms.*

Bibliography

J. Broad (1980) 'Alternate Husbandry and Permanent Pasture in the Midlands 1650–1800' *Agricultural History Review* **28** 77–89.

T. Browick (1862) 'On the management of a home farm' (1862) *Journal of the Royal Agricultural Society of England* **23** 247–269.

A. V. Brown (1967) 'The last phase of enclosure on Otmoor' *Oxoniensia* **32** 34–52.

R. W. Brunskill (1974) *The Vernacular Architecture of the Lake Counties.*

R. W. Brunskill (1982) *Traditional Farm Buildings of Britain.*

G. Buist (1840) 'On the Agriculture of Fifeshire' *Quarterly Journal of Agriculture* **60** 298–319.

J. E. Butler (1869) *Memoir of John Grey of Dilston.*

R. A. Butlin (1979) 'Enclosure in England 1600–1750' in H. S. A. Fox and R. A. Butlin (eds) *Change in the Countryside* 64–82.

H. M. Cadell (1913) *The Story of the Forth.*

J. Caird (1852) *English Agriculture in 1850–51.*

J. Caird (1888) 'Recent experiences in laying down land to grass' *Journal of the Royal Agricultural Society of England* 2nd series **24**.

J. Caird (1890) 'Fifty years, progress of British agriculture' *Journal of the Royal Agricultural Society of England* 3rd series **1** 1–36.

J. B. Caird (1994) 'The making of the Gairloch crofting landscape' in J. R. Baldwin (ed.) *Peoples and Settlement in North-west Ross-shire* 136–158.

W. Cambridge (1845) 'On the advantage of reducing the size and number of hedges' *Journal of the Royal Agricultural Society of England* **6** 333–342.

I. Carter (1979) *Farm Life in north-east Scotland.*

J. Chapman (1976) 'Parliamentary enclosure in the uplands: the case of the North York Moors' *Agricultural History Review* **24** 1–17.

J. Chapman and S. Seeliger (1997) *A Guide to Enclosure in Hampshire.*

J. Chapman and S. Seeliger (2001) *Enclosure, Environment and Landscape in southern England.*

J. A. Chartres (1985) 'The marketing of agricultural produce' in J. Thirsk (ed.) *The Agrarian History of England and Wales* **5 ii** 1640–1750 406–501.

E. Clarke (1900) 'Philip Pusey' *Journal of the Royal Agricultural Society of England* 2nd series **11** 1–18.

J. A. Clarke (1848) 'On the Great Level of the Fens' *Journal of the Royal Agricultural Society of England* **8** 80–133.

C. Clay 'Landlords and estate management in England' in Thirsk (ed.) *The Agrarian History of England and Wales* **5 ii** 1640–1750 119–250.

W. Cobbett (1930) *Rural Rides* (ed. Cole).

E. Creegan (1996) 'The changing role of the House of Argyll in the Scottish Highlands' in N. T. Phillipson and R. Mitcheson (eds) *Scotland in the Age of Improvement* 5–23.

J. S. Cocks (1970) 'Exploitation' in C. Gill (ed.) *Dartmoor a New Study* 245–256.

J. Cox and J. Thorp (1994) 'Beetor Farm, North Bovey, Devon' 2 vols, unpub. MS.

S. Copland (1866) *Agriculture, Ancient and Modern.*

J. C. Curwen (1809) *General Hints on Agricultural Subjects.*

S. Daniels and S. Seymour (1990) 'Landscape design and the idea of improvement, 1730–1814' in R. A. Dodgshon and R. A. Butlin (eds) *An Historical Geography of England and Wales.*

P. A. David (1971) 'The landscape and the machine' in D. N. McCloskey (ed.) *Essays on a Mature Economy* 145–205.

T. Davies (1794) *General View of the Agriculture of the County of Wiltshire.*

W. Davies (1810) *General View of the Agriculture of North Wales.*

H. C. Darby (1973) 'The age of the improver' in H. C. Darby (ed.) *New Historical Geography of England.*

J. B. Denton (1864) *Farm Homesteads of England.*

S. Denyer (1991) *Traditional Buildings and Life in the Lake District.*

T. M. Devine (1994) *The Transformation of Rural Scotland.*

T. M. Devine (1999) *The Scottish Nation 1700–2000.*

W. Dickenson (1852) 'The farming of Cumberland' *Journal of the Royal Agricultural Society of England* **13** 202–300.

R. W. Dickson and W. Stevenson (1815) *A General View of the Agriculture of Lancashire.*

A. H. Dodd (1927) 'The enclosure movement in North Wales' *Bulletin Board of Celtic Studies* **3** 210–238.

R. Douglas (1798) *General View of the Agriculture of Roxburghshire and Selkirkshire.*

J. Duncomb (1813) *A General View of the Agriculture of Hereford.*

B. English (1990) *The Great Landowners of East Yorkshire 1530–1910.*

D. H. Evans and M. G. Jarrett (1987) 'The deserted village of West Whelpington, Northumberland, Third Report, Part One' *Archaelogia Aeliana* 5th series **15** 139–93.

S. Everett (1968) 'The Domesday Geography of three Exmoor Parishes' *Proceedings of the Somerset Archaeological and Natural History Society* **112** 54–60.

H. Evershed (1853) 'On the farming of Surrey' *Journal of the Royal Agricultural Society of England* **14** 395–424.

D. Forbes (1853–55) 'Report on the Improvement of waste land' *Transactions of the Highland and Agricultural Society of Scotland* 99–109.

H. S. A. Fox (1979) 'Local Farmers' Associations' in Fox and Butlins (eds) *Change in the Countryside* 43–63.

H. S. A. Fox (1999) 'Medieval farming and rural settlement' in R. Kain and W. Ravenshill (eds) *Historical Atlas of South-west England.*

G. E. and K. R. Fussell (1955) *The English Countryman.*

D. Garrett (1747) *Designs for Farmhouses, etc. for the Counties of Yorkshire, Northumberland, Westmorland and the Bishoprick of Durham.*

J. Gibson (1879) *Agriculture in Wales.*

M. B. Gleave (1973) 'Settlement in the Yorkshire Wolds, 1770–1850' in D. R. Mills (ed.) *English Rural Communities.*

J. Glyde (1856) *Suffolk in the Nineteenth Century.*

N. Goddard (1981) 'Agricultural societies' in G. E. Mingay (ed.) *The Victorian Countryside* **1** 245–257.

N. Goddard (1983) The Development and influence of agricultural newspapers, 1780–1880' *Agricultural History Review* **31** 116–130.

N. Goddard (1988) *Harvests of Change.*

N. Goddard (1991) 'Information and innovation in early Victorian farming systems' in B. A. Holderness and M. Turner (eds) *Land, Labour and Agriculture 1700–1920* 165–190.

P. Graham (1818) *General View of the Agriculture of the County of Perthshire.*

E. Griffiths (ed.) (2002) *William Wyndham's Green Book, 1673–1688.*

D. R. Hainsworth (1992) *Stewards, Lords and People: The Estate Steward and his World in Later Stuart England.*

A. D. Hall (1913) *A Pilgrimage of British Farming.*

D. Hall (2001) *Turning the Plough. Midland Open Fields: Landscape Character and Proposals for Management.*

G. V. Harrison (1984) 'The south-west: Dorset, Somerset, Devon and Cornwall' in J. Thirsk (ed.) *Agrarian History of England and Wales Regional Farming Systems 1640–1750* **V ii** 358–389.

N. Harvey (1988) 'The engine house of the oldest agricultural steam engine in the world' *Journal of the Historic Farm Buildings Group* **2** 49–54.

M. Havinden (1961) Agricultural progress in open-field Oxfordshire' *Agricultural History Review* **9** 73–83.

J. Henderson (1812) *General View of the Agriculture of Caithness.*

P. Herring (1999) 'Cornwall' in G. Fairclough (ed.) *Historic Landscape Characterisation, the State of the Art.*

D. Hey (2000) 'Moorlands' in J. Thirsk (ed.) *The English Rural Landscape* 188–207.

B. A. Holderness (1971) 'Capital formation in agriculture' in J. P. Higgins and S. Pollard (eds) *Aspects of Capital Formation in Britain* 159–183.

H. Holland (1813) *A General View of the Agriculture of Cheshire.*

S. Hollowell (2000) *Enclosure Records for Historians.*

W. G. Hoskins (1943) 'The reclamation of the waste in Devon 1550–1800' *Economic History Review* **13** 80–92.

D. W. Howell (1977) *Land and People in Nineteenth-Century Wales.*

D. W. Howell (1981) 'The regions and their issues: Wales' in G. E. Mingay (ed.) *The Victorian Countryside* 2 vols I 71–80.

D. W. Howell (1985) 'Landlords and estate management in Wales' in J. Thirsk (ed.) *Agrarian History of England and Wales Regional Farming Systems 1640–1750* **5 ii** 252–297.

A. Howkins (1994) 'Peasants, servants and labourers: the marginal workforce in English agriculture' *Agricultural History Review* **42** 49–62.

K. Hudson (1972) *Patriotism with Profit.*

R. Hunt (1804) 'Memoir on the distribution of farms, farm buildings, etc.' *Communications to the Board of Agriculture* **1**.

R. Jefferies (Futura ed. 1981) 'The farmer at home' in *Toilers in the Field* 15–49.

H. M. Jenkins (1869) 'Lodge Farm, Castle Acre' *Journal of the Royal Agricultural Society of England* 2nd series **5** 460–474.

A. Jessop (1878) *Arcady: for Better, for Worse.*

E. L. Jones (1968) *The Development of English Agriculture 1815–1873.*

J. Jones (1992) *Seedtime and Harvest.*

N. Kent (1775) *Hints to Gentlemen of Landed Property.*

W. Kerr (1809) *General View of the Agriculture of Berwickshire.*

E. Kerridge (1967) *The Agricultural Revolution.*

J. Lake (1989) *Historic Farm Buildings.*

E. Laurence (1727) *The Duty of a Steward to his Lord.*

J. Loch (1820) *An Account of the Improvements on the estates of the Marquis of Stafford.*

D. Lowe (1834) *Practical Agriculture* 1st edn.

A. Macdonald (1884) 'Agriculture of the counties of Elgin and Nairn' *Transactions of the Highland and Agricultural Society of Scotland* 4th series **16** 1–123.

A. Macdonald (1886) 'Agriculture of the county of Selkirk' *Transactions of the Highland and Agricultural Society of Scotland* 4th series **18** 69–123.

J. Macdonald (1875) 'On the Agriculture of the county of Caithness' *Transactions of the Highland and Agricultural Society of Scotland* 4th series 7 166–257.

S. Macdonald (1976–77) 'The diary of an agricultural apprentice in Northumberland, 1842' *Local Historian* **12** 139–145.

S. Macdonald (1979) 'The role of the individual in agricultural change: the example of George Culley of Fenton, Northumberland' in H. S. A. Fox and R. A. Butlin (eds) *Change in the Countryside* 5–21.

S. Macdonald (1979) 'The diffusion of knowledge among Northumberland Farmers 1780–1815' *Agricultural History Review* **27** 30–39.

G. S. Mackenzie (1813) *General View of the County of Ross and Cromarty.*

T. Maclelland (1875) 'The agriculture of the stewarty of Kirkcudbrightshire and Wigtonshire' *Transactions of the Highland and Agricultural Society of Scotland* 4th series 7 1–68.

J. Macphearson (1853–55) 'Report on the improvement of the farm of Marypark' *Transactions of the Highland and Agricultural Society of Scotland* 79–84.

G. Markham (1635) *The First Book of the English Husbandman.*

J. D. Marshall (1980) 'Agrarian wealth and social structure in pre-industrial Cumbria' *Economic History Review* New Series **33** 503–521.

W. Marshall (1787) *Rural Economy of Norfolk* 2 vols.

W. Marshall (1796) *Rural Economy of the West of England* 2 vols.

W. Marshall (1804) *The Landed Property of England.*

P. Messenger (1973) 'Farm buildings of West Cumbria' unpub. MA dissertation, School of Architecture, Manchester University.

P. Messenger (1975) 'Lowther farmstead plans: A preliminary survey' *Transactions of the Cumberland and Westmorland Antiquarian and Archaeological Society* **75** 327–351.

J. Middleton (1813) *General View of the Agriculture of Middlesex.*

J. Mills *et al.* (1997) *Rosehaugh: A House of its Time.*

G. E. Mingay (1963) *English Landed Society in the Eighteenth Century.*

G. E. Mingay (1976) *Rural Life in Victorian England.*

G. E. Mingay (ed.) (1989) *Agrarian History of England and Wales 1750–1850* **VI**.

G. E. Mingay (1989) 'Agricultural productivity and agricultural society in eighteenth-century England' *Research in Economic History* **Supplement** 5 31–47.

G. E. Mingay (1990) 'The diary of James Warne, 1758' *Agricultural History Review* **38** 72–78.

G. E. Mingay (1997) *Parliamentary Enclosure in England.*

G. E. Mingay (2000) 'The farmer' in E. J. T. Collins *Agrarian History of England and Wales 1850–1914* 7 759–809.

D. Morgan (1996) 'The Devonshire linhay: an historic building type' unpublished MA thesis.

J. Nankervis (1991) *Wicca, A Farm in West Cornwall.*

E. Newman (1991) 'The Anti-Corn-Law League and the Wiltshire Labourer' in B. A. Holderness and M. Turner (eds) *Land, Labour and Agriculture 1700–1920* 91–107.

C. S. Orwin (1929) *The Reclamation of Exmoor Forest.*

M. Overton (1985) 'The diffusion of agricultural innovation in early modern England: turnips and clover in Norfolk and Suffolk' *Transactions of the Institute of British Geographers* new series **10**.

M. Overton (1996) *Agricultural Revolution in England 1550–1850.*

R. A. C. Parker (1975) *Coke of Norfolk.*

S. Pearson (1985) *Rural Houses of the Lancashire Pennines.*

A. Pell (1887) 'The making of the land of England: a retrospect' *Journal of the Royal Agricultural Society of England* 2nd series **23** 355–374.

P. J. Perry (1973) 'High Farming in Victorian Britain: the financial foundation' *Agricultural History* **52** 364–379.

P. J. Perry (1981) 'High farming in Victorian Britain, prospect and retrospect, *Agricultural History* **55** 156–166.

W. Pitt (1813) *General View of the Agriculture of Leicestershire.*

W. Pitt (1813) *General View of the Agriculture of Northamptonshire.*

W. Pitt (1813) *General View of the Agriculture of Worcestershire.*

A. D. M. Phillips (1999) 'Arable land drainage in the nineteenth century' in H. Cook and T. Williamson (eds) *Water Management in the English Landscape* 53–72.

J. Plymley (1813) *General View of the Agriculture of Shropshire.*

J. H. Porter (1966) 'The development of rural society' in G. E. Mingay (ed.) *Agrarian History of England and Wales 1750–1850* **6** 836–934.

A. Pringle (1794) *General View of the Agriculture of Westmorland.*

P. Pusey (1842) 'On the progress of agricultural knowledge during the last four years' *Journal of the Royal Agricultural Society of England* **3** 169–215.

P. Pusey (1843) 'On the agricultural improvements in Lincolnshire' *Journal of the Royal Agricultural Society of England* **4** 287–316.

P. Pusey (1845) 'Notes' *Journal of the Royal Agricultural Society of England* **6** 521.

P. Pusey (1849) 'On the theory and practice of water meadows' *Journal of the Royal Agricultural Society of England* **10** 462–479.

P. Pusey (1850) 'On the progress of agricultural knowledge in the last eight years' *Journal of the Royal Agricultural Society of England* **11** 381–438.

P. Pusey (1851) *What Ought Landowners and Farmers to Do?*

O. Rackham (1986) *The History of the Countryside.*

W. H. Ralston (1885) 'The agriculture of Wigtonshire' *Transactions of the Highland and Agricultural Society of Scotland* 4th series **17** 92–133.

W. and H. Raynbird (1849) *Agriculture of Suffolk.*

C. S. Read (1858) 'Recent improvements in Norfolk farming' *Journal of the Royal Agricultural Society of England* **19** 265–303.

C.S. Read (1888) 'Recent experience in laying down the land to grass' *Journal of the Royal Agricultural Society of England* 2nd series **24** 138–9.

Bibliography

H. Rider Haggard (1899) *A Farmer's Year.*

J. Roals (1845) 'On converting a moory hillside into catch meadow' *Journal of the Royal Agricultural Society of England* **6** 518–521.

C. Roberts (1879) 'Sutherland reclamations' *Journal of the Royal Agricultural Society of England* **15** 397–487.

J. Roberts (1997) *Royal Landscape: The Gardens and Parks at Windsor.*

J. M. Robinson (1981) *Georgian Model Farms.*

P. Roebuck (ed.) (1976) *Constable of Everingham Estate Correspondence 1726–1743.*

I. S. Ross (1972) *Lord Kames and the Scotland of his Day.*

RCAHMS (2001) *'Well shelterd and Watereds, Menstrie Glen, a Farming Landscape near Stirling.*

RCHME (1987) *Houses of the North York Moors.*

Thomas Ruggles (1786) 'Picturesque farming' *Annals of Agriculture* 7.

Thomas Ruggles (1787) 'Picturesque farming' *Annals of Agriculture* **8**.

Eric Sandon (1977) *Suffolk Houses: a Study in Domestic Architecture.*

R. Scot Skirving (1873) 'On the agriculture of East Lothian' *Transactions of the Highland and Agricultural Society of Scotland* 4th series **5** 1–48.

J. A. Sheppard (1958) 'The draining of the Hull Valley' *East Yorkshire Local History Society* **8**.

J. A. Sheppard (1966) 'The drainage of the marshland of Holderness' *East Yorkshire Local History Society.*

S. Sidney (1878) 'Exmoor reclamation' *Journal of the Royal Agricultural Society of England* 2nd series **14** 72–97.

R. Silvester (1999) 'Medieval reclamation of marsh and fen' in H. Cook and T. Williamson (eds) *Water Management in the English Landscape* 122–140.

Dr Singer (1812) *General View of the Agriculture of Dumfries.*

J. Smith (1798) *General View of the County of Argyll.*

S. Smith (1813) *General View of the County of Galloway.*

T. C. Smout (2000) *Nature Contested.*

R. Somerville (1805) *General View of the Agriculture of East Lothian.*

D. Spring (1955) 'A great agricultural estate – Netherby under Sir James Graham' *Agricultural History* **29** 73–81.

W. C. Spooner and J. Elliot (1850) 'On the construction of farm buildings' *Journal of the Royal Agricultural Society of England* **11** 270–272.

R. Staines (1969) 'Devon agriculture in the mid-eighteenth century' *Exeter Papers in Economic History* **2** 28–45.

C. Stephenson (1853) 'The farming of East Lothian' *Transactions of the Highland and Agricultural Society of Scotland* **14** 275–324.

W. Stevenson (1815) *General View of the Agriculture of Dorset.*

J. Stovin (ed.) (1982) *Journals of a Methodist Farmer.*

H. Tanner (1848) 'The farming of Devonshire' *Journal of the Royal Agricultural Society of England* **9** 454–495.

C. Taylor (1999) 'Post-medieval drainage of marsh and Fen' in H. Cook and T. Williamson *Water Management in the English Landscape* 141–156.

J. Taylor (1790) *Statistical Account* **11**.

John Theobald (2000) 'Changing landscapes, changing economies: holdings in Woodland High Suffolk' PhD thesis UEA (unpub).

J. Thirsk (1985) 'Agricultural innovations and their diffusion' in J. Thirsk (ed) *Agrarian History of England and Wales* **5** ii 533–89.

K. Thomas (1983) *Man and the Natural World.*

A. Thompson (1853–55) 'Report on the improvement of wasteland' *Transactions of the Highland and Agricultural Society of Scotland* 90–98.

H. S. Thompson (1850) 'Farm buildings' *Journal of the Royal Agricultural Society of England* **11** 185–7.

F. M. L. Thompson (1966) 'The social distribution of landed property in England since the sixteenth century' *The Economic History Review* 2nd series **19** 505–517.

W. P. L. Thompson (1987) *History of Orkney.*

P. D. Tuckett (1860) 'On the modification of the four-course system' *Journal of the Royal Agricultural Society of England* **21** 258–266.

M. Turner, J. Beckett and B. Afton (1997) *Agricultural rent in England 1690–1914.*

M. Turner, J. Beckett and B. Afton (2001) *Farm Production in England 1700–1914.*

J. H. Turner (1845) 'On the necessity for the reduction or abolition of hedges' *Journal of the Royal Agricultural Society of England* **6** 479–488.

M. E. Turner (1980) *English Parliamentary Enclosure.*

M. E. Turner (1975) 'Parliamentary enclosure and landownership change in Buckinghamshire' *Economic History Review* **35** 489–510.

M. E. Turner (1998) 'Counting sheep: waking up to new estimates of livestock numbers in England c. 1800' *Agricultural History Review* **46** 142–161.

C. Vancouver (1809) *General View of the Agriculture of Devon.*

C. Vancouver (1813) *General View of the Agriculture of Hampshire and the Isle of Wight.*

S. Wade-Martins (1980) *A Great Estate at Work.*

S. Wade-Martins (1993) 'Evidence from farm sales' in P. Wade-Martins *Black Faces* 36–55.

S. Wade-Martins (1995) *Farms and Fields.*

S. Wade-Martins (1996–97) 'A century of farms and farming on the Sutherland Estate 1790–1890' *Review of Scottish Culture* **10** 33–54.

S. Wade-Martins (2002) *The English Model Farm, Building the Agricultural Ideal 1700–1914.*

S. Wade-Martins and T. Williamson (1994) 'Floated water-meadows in Norfolk – a misplaced innovation' *Agricultural History Review* **42** 20–37.

S. Wade-Martins and T. Williamson (1995) *The Farming Journal of Randall Burroughes.*

S. Wade-Martins and Tom Williamson (1998) 'The development of the lease and its role in agricultural improvement in East Anglia, 1660–1870' *Agricultural History Review* **46** 127–141.

S. Wade-Martins and T. Williamson (1999) *Roots of Change.*

S. Wade-Martins and T. Williamson (1999)b 'Inappropriate technology? The history of "floating" in the North and East of England' in H. Cook and T. Williamson (eds) *Water Management in the English Landscape* 196–209.

E. G. F. Walker (1901–2) 'Small farming at the beginning of the twentieth century' *Journal of the Bath and West of England Society* 4th series **12** 78–89.

J. R. Walton (1999) 'Varietal innovation and competitiveness of the British cereals sector, 1760–1930' *Agricultural History Review* **47** 29–57.

J. Watson (1845) 'On reclaiming heathland' *Journal of the Royal Agricultural Society of England* **6** 79–102.

E. Wiliam (1986) *The Historic Farm Buildings of Wales.*

M. Williams (1970) 'Waste land in England and Wales' *Transactions of the Institute of British Geographers* **51** 55–69.

M. Williams (1970) *The draining of the Somerset Levels.*

T. Williamson (1986) 'Early co-axial fieldsystems on the East Anglian boulder clays' *Proceedings of the Prehistoric Society* **53** 419–431.

T. Williamson (1999) 'Post-medieval drainage' in H. Cook and T. Williamson (eds) *Water Management in the English Landscape* 41–52.

T. Williamson (2000) 'Understanding enclosure' LANDSCAPES **1** 56–79.

T. Williamson (2002) *The Transformation of Rural England, Farming and the Landscape 1700–1870.*

S. Wilmot (1999) 'Farming in the nineteenth century' in R. Kain and W. Ravenshill (eds) *Historical Atlas of South-west England.*

E. Witts (1777) *Journal of a Tour.*

G. B. Wogan (1815) *A General View of the Agriculture of Cornwall.*

J. R. Wordie (1983) 'Chronology of English enclosure 1500–1914 *Economic History Review* **36** 483–505.

A. Young (1764) 'Common farmers vindicated from the charge of being universally ignorant' *Museum Rusticum* 3.

A. Young (1771) *A Six Months' Tour through the North of England* 4 vols.

A. Young (1771) *Farmers' Tour of the East of England* 4 vols.

Bibliography

A. Young (1772) *A Six-Week Tour in the Southern Counties.*

A. Young (1773) *Observations of the Present State of Waste Lands in Great Britain.*

A. Young (1784) 'Enquiry into the state of the kingdom' *Annals of Agriculture* **1** 9–87.

A. Young (1786) 'Minutes relating to the dairy farms of high Suffolk' *Annals of Agriculture* **5** 193–224.

A. Young (1795) 'Waste lands' *Annals of Agriculture* **24** 10–13.

A. Young (1798) 'Notes on a tour though Holderness, Beverley and Hull in 1797' *Annals of Agriculture* **31** 113–136.

A. Young (1799) 'Waste lands' *Annals of Agriculture* **33** 12–59.

A. Young (1804) *General View of the Agriculture of Norfolk.*

A. Young (1813) *General View of the Agriculture of Hertfordshire.*

A. Young (1813) *General View of the Agriculture of Lincolnshire.*

A. Young (1813) *General View of the Agriculture of Suffolk.*

Index

Also available from Windgather Press ...

The English Model Farm: Building the Agricultural Ideal, 1700–1914

Susanna Wade Martins

> 'an excellent work which must surely be the last word on the subject ...' *Post-Medieval Archaeology*
>
> 'an important and timely reassessment ...' *The Agricultural History Review*

In this exploration of the 'model farm' phenomenon, Susanna Wade Martins tells the fascinating story of a significant yet largely undiscovered aspect of England's countryside.

In the eighteenth and nineteenth centuries landowners – inspired by the fashion for 'improvement' and the Enlightenment ideals of beauty, utility and profit – built an enormous range of picturesque and classical buildings on their farms. This richly illustrated book reveals for the first time the glory of this architecture, and how model farms – which were usually built as part of a wholesale restructuring of an estate – fitted into the wider landscape. The book includes a county-by-county summary of England's most important model farmsteads.

Published in association with English Heritage with the support of the Countryside Agency.

Pb 0-9538630-5-0; 242 pp; illus: 21 colour, 103 b/w; £18.99. Published 2002.

Landscapes for the World: Conserving a Global Heritage

Peter Fowler

The best of the world's cultural landscapes – the results of humanity's interaction with the environment over millennia – are a legacy of enormous importance. Since 1992 the international community has begun to protect these special places, through UNESCO's World Heritage Programme. This book asks why these places matter to all of us. It also takes us on a tour of the landscapes so far inscribed on the World Heritage List.

The book explores some extraordinary places, which anyone interested in landscape would wish to visit: places such as the Tongariro volcanic landscape in New Zealand; the Portuguese port wine region of Alto Douro; and the rice-growing terraces of the Cordilleras in the Philippines. The author, who has been actively involved in the inscription process, asks how we can recognise a World Heritage landscape and discusses the politics of designation and conservation. Britain has many World Heritage sites – Avebury and Stonehenge for instance – but only two World Heritage landscapes: Blaenavon and Kew Gardens. The book helps place Britain's landscape heritage in its global context.

Pb 0-9545575-9-x; 240 pp; illus: 15 colour; 66 b/w; £18.99. Publication July 2004.

Landscape Encyclopaedia: A Reference Guide to the Historic Landscape

Richard Muir

This book is an essential reference tool for anyone with a serious interest in Britain and Ireland's historic landscapes.

The countryside of the British Isles provides amateur and professional landscape researchers with an enormously rich resource. Excited by a discovery in the field, you turn to books, journals or the internet to find out more. You quickly find, however, that landscape history is a complex subject, an inter-disciplinary mix of archaeology, geography and history with its own terminology and literature. What, for instance, is a clachan? What exactly is a hillfort? How did the open-field farming system work? And how can you find out more about these terms? This book provides the answers.

Nearly 1,000 entries provide explanations of the major terms, features and ideas discussed in landscape history and archaeology. Cross-referenced entries and up-to-date guides to further reading point towards routes for exploring a subject in more detail. The book takes a balanced and even approach to geographical coverage, with landscape terminology from Ireland, Scotland, and Wales covered in as much detail as from England.

304 pp; illus: 106 b/w;
Hb 0–9545575–0–6 £50.00.
Pb 0–9545575–1–4 £19.99.
Publication April 2004.

Landscapes of Britain

Britain has an extraordinarily rich mix of historic landscapes. This major series explores this diversity, through accessible and attractive books that draw on the latest archaeological and historical research. Places in Britain have a great depth of historical connections. These books show how much there is to be discovered.

Discovering a Welsh Landscape: Archaeology in the Clwydian Range

Ian Brown, with photography by Mick Sharp and Jean Williamson

In the far north-east corner of Wales, a line of hills looks east across the plain into England, guarding the way towards Snowdonia. Designated an Area of Outstanding Natural Beauty, the Clwydian Range has a very rich archaeology. This beautifully illustrated book tells the story of this landscape: a history of Wales in microcosm.

The Clwydian Range is a crossroads, a place where outside influences have always been profound. We learn of the mammoth bones left in the area's caves by Paleaeolithic hunters; of the great chain of Iron Age hillforts that crown the Range; of the bronze brooches in Romano-British burials; and from the medieval period, of motte and bailey castles and Gothic churches. The Industrial Revolution left its mark, and Gerard Manley Hopkins found inspiration here. Throughout, the photographs capture the spirit of his original 'landscape plotted and pieced'.

Published with the support of Denbighshire County Council.

Landscapes of Britain. Pb 0-9545575-7-3; 160 pp; illus: 32 colour, 75 b/w; £16.99. Publication June 2004.

The Peak District: Landscapes Through Time

John Barnatt and Ken Smith

The Peak District – Britain's first National Park – has some of Britain's richest archaeological landscapes.

This new edition of the indispensable introduction and guide to the area's landscape draws on the extensive archaeological research that has taken place in the Peak since 1997. With new maps and interpretations, it tells the story of a famous landscape's evolution.

Prehistoric barrows, stone circles, Romano-British settlements, medieval fields, ancient drove-ways, nineteenth-century lead mines: all are prominent in this extraordinary area. The authors in particular explore the Peak's prehistoric sacred landscapes, such as the great henge at Arbor Low; the dramatic impact of farmers on the land in medieval and post-medieval times; and the industrial archaeology– the lead rakes, quarries and coal mine shafts that pock-mark the landscape. The book also features an updated gazetteer of sites and a comprehensive bibliography.

Landscapes of Britain. Pb 0-9545575-5-7 160 pp; illus: 14 colour, 74 b/w; £16.99. Publication June 2004.

A Frontier Landscape: The North West in the Middle Ages

N. J. Higham

The historic counties of Lancashire and Cheshire – at the periphery of the kingdom, both politically and economically – have been comparatively neglected in the history of the English landscape. This book redresses the balance. N. J. Higham portrays North West England as a frontier landscape which, between c. 1050 and 1550, went through successive changes which have left a deep impression on the region today.

The book starts by painting a picture of the North West at the time of Domesday: a sparsely settled land of little hamlets, fells, woods and marshes. It then tells the story of the region's dynamic economic growth between 1100 and 1350: the development of open fields, the new exploitation of wastes and woodland, and an expanding population. Manchester, Liverpool and above all Chester grew as potent urban centres, and Tudor enclosure also had a major impact on the countryside.

Landscapes of Britain. Pb 0-9545575-6-5 240 pp; illus: 12 colour, 75 b/w; £19.99. Publication 25 June 2004.

The Humber Wetlands: The Archaeology of a Dynamic Landscape

Robert Van de Noort

The lowlands of the Humber Basin form one of Britain's most extensive wetland areas. This book reveals for the first time the buried ancient landscapes which lie under the peat. It is the result of a ten-year English Heritage funded project, which aimed to identify and explore this archaeology before it was damaged by peat extraction, development and drainage.

Robert Van de Noort explores people's experience of the Humber Wetlands over the last 10,000 years. He reveals how prehistoric peoples settled the wetlands at places such as Holderness, and how they used natural resources, for spiritual as well as economic reasons. The discovery of unparalleled prehistoric boats in the area has transformed our understanding of prehistoric maritime history. Roman, Vikings, and climate change have also left their mark on today's landscape.

Published in association with English Heritage

Also available from Windgather Press

Landscapes of Britain. Pb 0–954–5575–4–9; 208 pp; illus: 6 colour, 75 b/w; £18.99. Publication June 2004.

Also available from Windgather Press

Other titles

The Ancient Yew: A History of **Taxus baccata**
Second Revised Edition

Robert Bevan-Jones

> 'A detailed, highly readable and fascinating history of this remarkable tree.' *Tree News*

The gnarled, immutable yew tree is one of the most evocative sights in the British and Irish landscape, an evergreen impression of immortality. This book – revised since first publication in 2002 with the latest research findings – brings together all the evidence about the dating, history, archaeology and cultural connections of the yew. It tells the extraordinary story of the yew's role in the landscape through the millennia, and makes a convincing case for the origins of many of the oldest trees, as the markers of the holy places founded by Celtic saints in the early medieval 'Dark Ages'. The book includes a gazetteer (with locations) of the oldest yew trees in Britain.

Pb 0-9545575-3-0; 205 pp; illus: 14 colour, 53 b/w; £18.99. Published January 2004.

Oak: A British History

Esmond Harris, Jeanette Harris and N. D. G. James

The oak tree has long provided people in Britain with a wonderful natural resource. This book explores how people have managed and exploited oak-woods since the Neolithic and how they have used its timber: in ships, furniture and buildings. It also reclaims the disappearing forestry and carpentry skills of our ancestors and discusses the myths and symbols that have connected people in Britain with oak over hundreds of years. The book includes an appendix giving details of over 700 particularly significant oak trees, with notes on their location and historical connections.

Pb 0-9538630-8-5; 242 pp; illus: 10 colour, 51 b/w; £16.99. Published 2003.

Shaping Medieval Landscapes: Settlement, Society, Environment

Tom Williamson

> '... if what you really want is to get right down in the dirt

Also available from Windgather Press

> with medieval farmers, to see the land as they saw it, to understand how it worked and how they drew life from it, this is the book for you.' *Current Archaeology*
>
> 'A wonderful piece of work, Williamson's best yet.' *Christopher Taylor*
>
> '... an extremely interesting and original argument ... Research on the history of the medieval landscape has neglected the influence of environment and geography in recent years and this book firmly places them back on the agenda.' *British Archaeology*

This book from 2003 has already become a classic text in English landscape history. Tom Williamson shows how subtle differences in soils and climate shaped not only the diverse landscapes of medieval England, but the very structure of the societies that occupied them.

Pb 0-9545575-8-1; 214 pp; illus: 59 b/w; £18.99. Published February 2004.

Village Hamlet and Field: Changing Medieval Settlements in Central England

Carenza Lewis, Patrick Mitchell-Fox and Christopher Dyer

> '... lays the basis for a fundamental change of approach to settlement studies.' *Medieval Archaeology*

Pb 0-9538630-03-4; 227 pp; illus: 44 b/w; £17.99. Published 2001.

Markets in Early Medieval Europe: Trading and 'Productive' Sites, 650–850

Edited by Tim Pestell and Katharina Ulmschneider

This groundbreaking book reveals how new discoveries by archaeologists and metal-detectorists are transforming our understanding of early medieval Europe's economy. It surveys the evidence for inland markets and trading sites, in Anglo-Saxon England and across Scandinavian and Frankish Europe.

Hb 0-9538630-7-7; 304 pp; illus: 77 b/w; £25. Published 2003.

Also available from Windgather Press

Landscape Detective: Discovering a Countryside

Richard Muir

> 'Anyone with an interest in piecing together the past will enjoy following the twists and turns of the investigations.'
> *Yorkshire Journal*

Pb 0-9538630-2-6; 146 pp; illus: 17 colour, 67 b/w; £16.99. Published 2001.

Suffolk's Gardens and Parks: Designed Landscapes from the Tudors to the Victorians

Tom Williamson

> 'Considerably more than just an introduction to Suffolk's designed landscapes … a formidable achievement.' *Landscape History*

Pb 0-9538630-0-x; 205 pp; illus: 19 colour, 57 b/w; £17.99. Published 2000.

Bloody Marsh: A Seventeenth-Century Village in Crisis

Peter Warner

> '… A book which uses a single intense beam to light up a whole age. It is a gem.' *BBC History Magazine*

Pb 0-9538630-1-8; 146 pp; illus: 44 b/w; £16.99. Published 2000.